It's three, maybe four o'clock in the morning. I'm in our house on Todt Hill in Staten Island, lying in bed like I'm paralyzed. Can't move, can't lift my arms, can't open my mouth. I'm too scared to think straight. Louie didn't call and he didn't come home yet. For all I know, he's out someplace in Jersey shooting a guy in the back of the head—killing somebody he never met in his life before to pay off a favor for somebody else he never met . . .

MY STORY OF LOVE, MURDER, AND MADNESS

MAFIA WIFE

LYNDA MILITO WITH **REG POTTERTON**

AVON BOOKS

An Imprint of HarperCollinsPublishers

In telling my story, I have chosen to change the names of many of the people who have been involved in my life and in Louie Milito's life. In a few instances, such as the case with Sammy Gravano and John Gotti and other prominent figures, I have used their real names, as it would be obvious to readers that I am writing about these people.

AVON BOOKS
An Imprint of HarperCollins*Publishers*
10 East 53rd Street
New York, New York 10022-5299

Copyright © 2003 by Lynda Milito and Reg Potterton
All photographs courtesy of the author.
ISBN: 0-06-103216-6
www.avonbooks.com

First Avon Books paperback printing: April 2004
First HarperCollins hardcover printing: May 2003

Avon Trademark Reg. U.S. Pat. Off. and in Other Countries,
Marca Registrada, Hecho en U.S.A.
HarperCollins® is a registered trademark of HarperCollins Publishers Inc.

Printed in the U.S.A.

10 9 8 7 6 5 4 3 2 1

Contents

Prologue   1

Part I   1947–1964

CHAPTER 1   Growing Up Is Hard To Do   13
CHAPTER 2   Keeping Secrets   25
CHAPTER 3   Guilt and Fantasy   32
CHAPTER 4   Peppermint Twist   38
CHAPTER 5   Sex Ed   42
CHAPTER 6   Meeting Louie   48

Part II   1964–1979

CHAPTER 7   Leader of the Pack   57
CHAPTER 8   Take a Favor, Give a Favor   77
CHAPTER 9   What Do You Know,
             You're Jewish   93
CHAPTER 10   All in the Family   118
CHAPTER 11   Straightened Out   128
CHAPTER 12   A Person Would Have
             to Be in a Coma   147
CHAPTER 13   The Charge Is Murder   152
CHAPTER 14   Cash Makes People Smile   172
CHAPTER 15   Fat Farm, with Bars   180
CHAPTER 16   Sammy Gravano,
             Animal Lover   185

Part III
1980–1988

CHAPTER 17	Tough Guys Fall	195
CHAPTER 18	Moving Up to Todt Hill	218
CHAPTER 19	Burying the Needle	226
CHAPTER 20	No Longer Bulletproof	236
CHAPTER 21	I Know About Frankie	246
CHAPTER 22	Maybe We'll Get a Miracle	255
CHAPTER 23	No Happy Hour at Tali's	267
CHAPTER 24	The Disappearance	272

Epilogue
282

Acknowledgments
309

MAFIA WIFE

Prologue

It's three, maybe four o'clock in the morning. I'm in our house on Todt Hill in Staten Island, lying in bed like I'm paralyzed. Can't move, can't lift my arms, can't open my mouth. I'm too scared to think straight. Louie didn't call and he didn't come home yet. For all I know, he's out someplace in Jersey shooting a guy in the back of the head—killing somebody he never met in his life before to pay off a favor for somebody else he never met.

It's part of what Louie does, only I don't know it when he's doing it, and by the time I know for sure, it's too late to get out. It's not like he comes in the house and says he's had a big day and he had to stop off on the way home and kill somebody for some people who don't like the guy. Mostly what Louie tells me in the twenty-four years we are together is what comes out between the lines, and mostly I don't want to see it and I don't want to think about it.

If I could have read between the lines before we got married, things might have been different. Or maybe they would have stayed the same. I don't know. A sixteen-year-old high school dropout like me when I met Louie, you see what you want to see, you don't pay attention to the things you don't want to know about. And what I saw in him from the start was an escape from a life under my mother's thumb in a house I couldn't stand living in. Too late now for shoulda woulda coulda.

This particular night when I'm lying in bed with my brain boiling like it can't stop, I'm thinking a million things at once. Did he get pinched again? Will it be prison again? If he goes, what about our two kids? What about me? How will we get by with no money coming in? Mostly I'm thinking what I always think when he's out late like this: maybe this time it's Louie who gets the bullet in the back of his head.

And that's how it turns out—not that night but a few years later. They gave him one in the head and one under the chin, and my husband Louie Milito disappeared from our life forever. Sammy Gravano told the FBI that some other guys killed Louie. He knows this, he says, because he was in the room, watching.

Some other guys. Sure. Like he had nothing to do with it.

After they both got made with the Gambino crime family in the seventies, first Louie, then Sammy, when someone needed a piece of work done in Brooklyn, in New York, or Jersey, or Philly, it was often Louie and Sammy who got the call. Be there, do this, don't screw up. For years they were partners; they robbed and killed together, they were known as good earners—stand-up men who pulled in a lot of money and passed it up the Gambino line through the underbosses, who took their cuts, to Paul Castellano. And Paul, being the boss, took his.

When Louie and Sammy were younger, before they got on the Gambino books, they did what they had to do to get noticed by certain people in Bensonhurst and Bay Ridge, the neighborhoods in Brooklyn where we all came from. That's where we went to school, it's where we hung out. We knew everybody and we knew who didn't belong there when we saw them on the streets.

Getting noticed is where it all starts in that life. People

with connections hear that so-and-so over in Bensonhurst knows how to take care of himself, he doesn't mind taking risks, he's tough enough to do whatever has to be done. He has already killed somebody or he's got what it takes to kill somebody if that's what he's told to do. Louie and Sammy, both from straight, hardworking Italian families, made natural recruits.

In Bensonhurst, like in places all over New York and New Jersey and in big cities everywhere, when it comes to organized crime and how it works, there's not much to choose between one place and another except that the bigger the city, the bigger the business.

From the bottom up there are first the wannabes—the gofers and hangers-on, guys who may be too dumb or too crazy to be trusted with serious responsibility, who are friends of friends and so on and so forth. Above them are the associates, who usually belong to a crew of maybe ten guys but have not taken the oath that marks them as "made" men. There is another term for getting made—the people we knew called it getting "straightened out."

A made man is a full member. Being made means that he has killed somebody, will kill again when told, and because of that has taken the oath that binds him for life to the Mafia. But first, last, and always is the money, because that's what it's all about. Honor, respect, loyalty? That's for the movies.

Louie and Sammy got rich from stealing—manipulating people out of money, Louie called it. But Louie had different methods from Sammy, who was first and foremost a taker, especially from people who thought they could trust him. Louie, by contrast, was born with a softness and a gentle nature that he couldn't get away from, and if that sounds hard to believe about a man who did his share of killing and who left me with mental and physical scars from twenty-four years of abuse, I'm sorry, but that was as much a part of his character as the parts that made him one of the most dangerous men in the Gambino family.

Old man Carlo Gambino died in bed in 1975, and his

brother-in-law Paul Castellano took over as boss. Sammy claims he was the one who got Louie made with the Gambinos, but that's a typical Sammy invention. When Sammy was a brokester with holes in his sweaters Louie was wearing custom suits and driving a new Cadillac. He was already with Paul while Sammy was scratching for dollars with the Colombo people, who are doing next to nothing for him because their boss, Joe Colombo, was little better than a living vegetable after getting shot in the head in the summer of 1970.

Sammy Gravano was what you call a street dog, a thug. His idea of a big score was selling swag tires. Louie told me he had to beg his higher-ups to get Paul Castellano to take Sammy in. For years Paul told Louie that Sammy was a rat weasel and to stay away from him because he didn't smell right, but Louie always spoke up for Sammy, eventually getting him in with the Gambinos.

If Paul Castellano had listened to his own advice, he might still be breathing, him and his number-one, Tommy Bilotti. But Paul was never big on listening, and the end result is that Paul and Tommy both got killed by Sammy's people in Manhattan the week before Christmas, 1985.

The first time I told Louie he should watch out for Sammy Gravano he gave me a backhand across the face for disrespecting somebody he called his business partner, his brother, his most loyal friend. But that was one of Louie's problems—being big on things like loyalty and respect. He was old-fashioned enough to take his oath seriously, and he figured it was the same with Sammy.

If they would let me, I would love to be alone with Sammy. It's a scene I've played over in my mind many times. I would just sit there and stare at him. I would ask him how he could have done this to Louie. He did to Louie what Louie would never do to him. That's the question I would like Sammy Gravano to answer—that and others.

You can say it is not good to hate, or that hatred does more harm to the person who feels it than to the one who is hated, but this is the man who destroyed my family and my life, just as he destroyed other families and their lives. All the hatred in my heart—and I know it is filled with hatred—is concentrated on this man who Louie trusted and for years put ahead of his own wife and children.

I hate him for being set free as a reward for turning on John Gotti, the boss who replaced Paul Castellano after he was murdered. I hate him because the government set him free after he admitted he killed and was involved with the deaths of nineteen people. And I hate him because my two children, Deena and Louis, who knew him as Uncle Sammy from the moment they were born, have found no peace inside themselves since Sammy killed their father.

The only good news I have heard since Louie's murder was that Sammy Gravano got pinched for selling Ecstasy pills to kids in Arizona. The drugs came from a connection in New York, and last I heard he will be on trial at the U.S. District Court in Brooklyn, facing twenty years. It's funny, because Louie, who loved children, would never sanction what Sammy did. Never. They should turn Sammy loose in the general population in the worst prison in the country with a sign around his neck saying RAT. Although I do feel sorry for Debra, his wife, and his children, Gerard and Karen. Debra was our friend, and Gerard and Karen I watched grow up.

I read these words and I know how much damage these thoughts have done; I know it and I can't seem to do anything about it. You think I don't understand what hatred does to the mind and the heart? You think I haven't felt it eating at my insides, like a poison you can't get out of your brain, day in and day out, year in and year out, even before that night when Louie didn't come home? You can say, Well, what Lynda Milito needs to do for herself is put the past behind her and focus on the here and now, because if she can't bring herself to do that, she and her kids can kiss their future good-bye.

Wouldn't that be nice.

I don't want sympathy from anyone, I'm not asking people to read this book and say, Look at this poor woman, what a terrible life she's had, aren't we lucky we didn't have to go through what she went through. I could have made other choices, there were plenty of times when I could have walked away from Louie and his life, when I *should* have walked away, but I couldn't do it, and even if I'd left, he would have found me and put me in that box under the ground he was always threatening me with. Did I believe him? Yes, I did. And most of the time I didn't want to leave him. The good side would show and I would "forget." No matter. Louie was so far involved, there was no way out for him.

I can't say if writing this book will make things any better for me or the children. God knows, we can't talk to each other about the past without it ending in a shouting match. It gets to the point where every word between us is like a smash in the face, and for this we're all to blame.

Sometimes I feel like I have lost my children. My daughter refuses to believe that her father did one bad thing in his life and my son can't even admit that he was ever in jail more than once. All three of us are hiding from the truth, we can't face it, I know that, and because we can't deal with the truth, we twist it and beat each other with our own versions of it. Sometimes I think we have turned into monsters. Where did our closeness go? It's like it was just squashed. Or was it ever really there?

I hoped when I started this book that in some way it would help turn us back into normal people. We could find a way to love each other again, be good to each other, and share our lives like we used to. I don't know if that's possible anymore, I don't even know if any of us deep down even want it. I'm not the only one poisoned here—it's in Louis and Deena too, like some virus of hatred and distrust we can't seem to get out of our systems no matter how much we try to live normal lives. They blame me for the choices I made like I blame them for their choices, and the worst part is, there are times when nobody blames me more than I blame myself.

I don't have friends, I don't trust anyone, not the men I've met since Louie died, not their families—not my own three brothers, especially not them and their families. We don't talk. I see no end to this in my lifetime, which is why I sometimes think it would be best just to end it, end the torture, and not have to think about it anymore. I feel at times that no one cares, that I'm all alone. But I have two children and two grandchildren who still need me. If there's anything I can take solace in and maybe find just a little bit of joy, it would be because of them.

The only reason I don't end it is because I *refuse* to believe that there's no hope for me or for Deena and Louis. I can't accept that, I won't accept it. If they can read the truth about what happened to us and how it happened, there's a chance they will understand that none of it was their fault, and maybe that will help them see that things happened to the three of us because of who Louie was and because of the type of life he led and the life he made for us. I'm sure Louie wouldn't want us to struggle to survive this way.

How he got into that life is something that comes later in this story, although now, as I look back, I realize that among all the many things we had in common, at least Louie and me made choices. He was a thief from the time he was a teenager, and for years after we met I went along with it. The day he got straightened out with the Gambinos, Deena would have been around nine and Louis was maybe three years old. So what choice did they have—or me? It wasn't like he came to me and said, Lynda, the boss of the Gambino family wants me to join with them as a made man. What do you think I should do?

The first clue I ever had that he made that move was the way we got treated when we went out afterwards—men crowding around to kiss him on both cheeks, headwaiters in clubs and restaurants fussing over us like we were royalty, guys coming by with gifts for the house. When Louis was confirmed at ten years old he got envelopes stuffed with money. You'd have to be a moron not to notice the clues. But that's not the point—the point is, when Louie Milito got made with the Gambino family, he knew what it meant: From now on and for the rest of his life there would be no getting out of it until he was dead. Their secrets would be his secrets and he would do what they told him to do or suffer the consequences. He knew that and he accepted it. The problem was that when he took that oath with Paul, it was like the kids and me took it too, only we didn't get to say the words. We didn't even know he was saying them for us.

What do I think of him now? I don't know. It changes. Yeah, I felt the force of him in every way, physically and mentally, because when he got mad and started laying down the law about one thing or another he made it plain that my job was to listen until he stopped talking. Those eyes, so black and cold when he was angry. It was impossible to look at him and not be scared. There were times I was frightened, but couldn't help speaking my piece. I took the knocks, I didn't care.

So what I think about him now depends on how I feel from day to day. So much about him was good—his silly clowning around for the kids, his patience and kindness, his old-fashioned attitude as a husband and father. Here was a man who killed other men when he was told and did everything he could to help friends in need, who for most of his life enjoyed nothing more than hunting in the woods and skinning the animals he killed and at the same time adored every pet we ever had—who turned every family birthday into a celebration, who was a soft touch for his children, a hero to them and to his wife . . . oh, yes, he was all of that and, besides, we loved him.

What would he say if he knew I was writing this book?

I'm sure he would accept my decision considering how his children were treated when he disappeared.

Louie used to answer a very important question of mine. I would say, If anything happened to you, what would happen to the kids? He would answer very sharply, "Louie Milito's children will be taken care of. They will not want for anything. It has already been discussed." What respect did anyone have for Louie when they treated his children the way they did? There is no doubt in my mind that Louie would agree. It's fourteen years; and I waited long enough. It's not just for my own peace of mind or for our kids, but I want people to know that Louie was both good and bad, and I want to leave a legacy behind. I want people to know and remember Louie. I'd like to think that my story could help other women who find themselves locked into marriages where they don't have a say, where they get beaten or shouted down and are too frightened to leave because they lack the confidence or cannot stand to leave their children.

You take away the Mafia element from Louie and me and what you have left is just another marriage, not much different from most people's except that the foundation, walls, and roof of our marriage were all tied together by Louie's life in crime. My life, too, because I took part in it, I helped him make the money. I used to think if I wanted to stay alive, I didn't have any choice. There really was no way out. But now in the end, I know I made the choice and I will not blame it on anyone.

I feel like I have much useful advice for women in bad marriages. This I know. You can't make something good when it's bad all the way through. If it's so bad it can't be fixed, you have to get out. If your husband scares you, it's time to leave. Anyone who lives in fear of the man in her life will never, ever know any happiness as long as that fear exists. And if she's anything like me, she won't find peace inside herself even when the fear goes. The fear disappears when you can find peace inside yourself.

When I think back, the best part of my life was when

Louis and Deena were at Staten Island Academy. I used to go to their school with a grin on my face. It was a small school, the teachers knew me, about twenty kids per class, not all crowded like it is today. Deena was the captain of her basketball team; that made me *so* happy. To know that my daughter was the captain. Then Louis tried out for soccer and came home yelling that he made the team. I loved to help them with their projects for the science fair. I used to draw for them; that was a reprieve from homework for them. And also a reprieve for me. It was happiness. That's what made me look away from Louie's bad side. There's gotta be some good side to all this, I would say. And in these small ways, through my children, I found it.

For fourteen years after Louie was killed, the memories come back at me, pushing everything else out of my brain, and sometimes I feel like I'm trapped in a movie theater where the doors are locked and all I can do is watch the screen, seeing the scenes in my life flashing by over and over again.

I

1947–1964

CHAPTER 1

Growing Up Is Hard To Do

My mother, Sophie Dostis, was a Sephardic Jew born in Greece. She came to America with her parents when she was two months old. My father, Louie Lustig, was a Russian Jew born in this country. Sophie, who changed her name to Sally, had four sisters and a brother; my dad had three brothers. Grandpa Dostis died before I was born, leaving his wife, Dinah, to raise their six children. Both families, Dostises and Lustigs, worked mostly in the garment and textiles industries around New York City.

For a while it looked as though I wouldn't see my third birthday. Polio hit me in 1949, when I was about two years old. They said it came from the drinking water where we lived on West 27th Street in Coney Island. People say that two-year-olds don't remember anything, but they're wrong. What I remember when I was still in the hospital in Brooklyn is Grandma Dostis yelling at my mother to make sure I stayed awake to keep from dying.

I don't recall falling on the floor when a nurse forgot to put up the side of the crib, or my mother raising hell and threatening to sue the hospital, but that's what the family always told me. According to them, when the doctors heard the lawsuit word they asked if there was some way around this and my mother says, Sure, you can pay for my daughter to go to that special rehab hospital they have upstate in West Haverstraw. This is where the rich people sent their kids during the polio epidemic we had in those years.

Years later my uncle Nat told me that he had to carry me into the hospital because Dad was too scared to hold me in case I died in his arms, he was crying so hard he could hardly walk himself.

I wore steel leg braces and the shoes that go with them, I remember that, but what I remember most is the terrible, empty loneliness I felt when my family went back home from Haverstraw after the weekend visits. Lying in that crib in a ward with all the other sick kids wailing and screaming, I felt as if I would never get out and would die without ever seeing my family again. I probably didn't even realize I was sick and maybe at this point my mother didn't yet figure out she didn't like me, because she came when she could, so I guess she hadn't written me off as a disappointment—the heartache in her life, as I later found out she thought of me. All I know is I didn't want to be in that place, I wanted to be home with people around me I knew, and because I wasn't, maybe it made me feel I wasn't wanted.

What I know is this: People need to make children feel special, even if it's just in small ways, like a smile or a hug for doing something right instead of messing up. Children want to feel that grown-ups appreciate them and are proud of them. I didn't get this from my mother, and I didn't get it from my two brothers. We were too far apart in years. By the time I started kindergarten, my brother Harvey was seventeen and Arthur was fifteen, so it's not like the three of us had much in common except that we lived under the same roof with the same parents.

Louie Lustig, my father, was what we called a knockaround Jew. He did a lot of things before I was born, including being a pool hustler who nobody ever beat, but when I was a kid, he was a peddler or a traveling salesman in the garment business. He picked up the overage, which is like the extras left over, from factories in the city, and drove around the Catskill hotels and bungalow colonies, selling clothes from the back of his old Rambler wagon. In the summers he worked as a ticket taker at the Monticello racetrack upstate, and for a couple of years in the fifties he had a full-time job at a Brooklyn sweatshop on 86th Street that made camel-hair and cashmere topcoats.

Before he got into the garment business, Dad did a one-man dance act, soft shoe and tap, at a club in the Catskills where he sometimes worked as a volunteer emcee. He was also a carney man on Coney Island with a Guess Your Weight booth and a Pig Slide, which is where you throw a ball at the target and a live pig falls down a chute into a tank of water.

I tell people this and they say it's a terrible thing to do to pigs, but in those days before television it was okay, and to my way of thinking it's a whole lot kinder than something like the *Jerry Springer Show* and the rest of that cruel stuff you see on TV.

Dad loved all living things, he was famous for being gentle. He couldn't hurt anything. If a fly or any kind of bug got in the house he'd catch it in a jar or something and take it outside and let it go. One of my uncles told me that after Dad closed down his Pig Slide he went all over New York State until he found a farmer who took the pigs from him on the condition they wouldn't allow them to be butchered.

Uncle Sam Dostis, my mother's brother, was the rich one in our two families. He made a fortune in textiles. As a kid, my brother Arthur started working at Uncle Sam's factory on Canal Street in New York, and later on Arthur also became a multimillionaire, thanks to Sam Dostis. For as long as she lived my mother never let my father or the rest of the family forget what the Lustigs owed to her genius brother, Mister Success, who to me was a schmuck and a skinflint on account of the way he was always putting down my father.

Except for Grandpa and Grandma Lustig, who had a New Jersey sewing factory that made housecoats, the Dostis and Lustig families lived close to each other in Brooklyn, first in Coney Island, then in Bensonhurst. So I grew up with uncles, aunts, and cousins all over the neighborhood, but with the exception of my Aunt Sandra, who called me "Lindoola" and went out of her way to make me feel special, I never felt close to the Dostis side of the family. To me, they were not what you call giving people. It's like my aunt Regina, who is married to my uncle Nat Lustig, says: "They are not from the spenders."

We didn't have a lot to spend in our house, that's for sure. Maybe that's why my older brother Harvey joined the Navy when he was a kid. Arthur, my second brother, had it pretty good, because when the Army drafted him he was already working for my uncle, Sam Dostis. In fact my uncle Sam tried to get him out of the service through some political connection but it didn't work. Arthur was back at work with him as soon as he got out of the Army, and he never looked back.

After my brothers left home and up until my brother Gary was born, I was the only child in the house. I remember being upset because I didn't have any toys to play with, and one of the neighbors must have found out, because when I was about four she gave me my first doll. I kept it with me for thirty-some years, until she got lost, when Louie and me moved into our first house.

I called the doll Toni because she came from the Toni Home Perm people in some kind of promotion they had in the early fifties. She had a shoulder-length blonde pageboy style with bangs, a red gingham dress with a white blouse under a bolero vest, and yellow zigzag piping on the hem of the skirt, and Mary Jane white shoes with white bobby socks. Mostly I played with her on the floor in my room and sometimes I'd take her into the kitchen and hold a napkin under her chin while I gave her water. Some days I would be her mother and tell her how much I loved her, how beautiful she was and how happy she made me, and some days I was her big sister or we were best friends dressing up for a party.

The truth is, being with her made *me* happy, it makes me happy today, fifty years later, thinking about the two of us. Maybe this is why I never stopped buying dolls and now have a collection that fills a couple of rooms in my house. No matter how bad things got with my mother, knowing that Toni was waiting for me in my room gave me something to look forward to. It may sound ridiculous but without her I don't know if I would have got through those early years of my life.

My father was the exact opposite to the Dostis family temperament, and maybe that was because he came from a two-parent home. He was a born full-time giver, and what he gave me was love and affection I never got from anyone else when I was little. If my mother made me feel like I was some kind of mistake in her life and it was my fault for being born, which she did, over and over again, almost as far back as I remember, it was always Dad who let me know that to him I was special. When Mom shouted at me over something, it was Dad who did what he could to make me feel better—but he didn't dare say anything when she was there, it was always after she was out of the room. My poor father was even more frightened of her than I was.

If Mom thought he was taking my side in a fight with her, she punished him by picking on him, humiliating him in front of me, and I've never been able to forgive her for this. I figured she did it to show the both of us who was boss in that house, because with her it was her way or the highway. If he tried to defend me she turned on him right away. I remember, when I must have been about five or six years old, I was in the bath, and my dad came home with a big stuffed toy for me. She yelled at him for wasting money and threw it out the bathroom door. He gave me a doll not long afterwards and she got mad at him all over again. That was the last time he brought any toys home for me.

I wasn't what you would call a moody kid, not when I was real young, anyway, which was long before I started adding up the twos and getting fours. I wasn't noisy and I didn't talk a whole lot, but I was real inquisitive and I wanted to learn. By the time I was seven or eight I wanted to go to the synagogue on 20th Avenue and learn about being Jewish, but Mom didn't want me anywhere near the place.

I have always been proud to be Jewish. It made me different, and I liked that. Being in a minority makes you try harder, not to be accepted by non-Jews, because who cares about being accepted by them if they don't want you—what I wanted was to *understand* the meaning of my religion. Mom just wasn't interested. Our two families, the Dostises and the Lustigs, were Jewish, her friends were Jewish, and we didn't have a single religious object in the house. The day the whole family went to a seder at my Aunt Ray Nachman's house in Coney Island was my first and for a long time my only experience of any kind of religious service, and I loved every minute of it. What I liked was the fact that the whole family got together, my own special comfort zone. It was also like being part of something older and bigger and more important than myself and our life as a family—it was a part of me and I was a part of it.

Dad prayed sometimes at the synagogue on 20th Avenue, but I wasn't allowed to go. "You have to ask your mother about that," he said. At Purim I used to watch other Jewish kids coming out of the synagogue with apples on sticks and wish I could be with them.

Most times the fights Mom picked with my father had nothing to do with me or anything connected to whatever *our* fight was about. If she was upset, he would take it to heart and it wound up in his stomach. She knew how soft he was and how he hated arguments, and she knew how much he depended on her and would never, no matter what, walk out on her.

Their fights were usually about money. Why didn't he bring more home? How much longer did he expect her to ride around in our old station wagon? Usually her rich brother, Sam Dostis, came into the conversation. "Look at Sam—he started with nothing! Look at what Sam did! You Lustigs never got anywhere!" And then she would bring up my brother Arthur and how he would have ended up in some dead-end job but instead he was making a success out of his life, and we had her brother, Sam, to thank for it.

She would just nag at Dad until he got a migraine, and he would take a shot of scotch and go sit in the living room, waiting for the headache to go away. Or she would give him the silent treatment, like he wasn't worth talking to. On days like this he would sometimes take me and a bunch of kids in the station wagon to Coney Island, and he'd go and play pinochle at the Knights of Pythias Cresco Club while we played Skeeball on the boardwalk. Back then it was safe to play there. This must have been around 1953, when I was about six going on seven, and if I was too young to understand much about my parents' marriage, I was sure of one thing: I loved my father with all my heart but I understood early on that I couldn't count on him to stand up to her. And I know he loved me, he couldn't help it and I never doubted it. I guess I must have figured out that he wanted to show it, but just didn't know how to do it without her tearing him down. My father let me know he loved me, but only when it was safe.

With his dog, Butch, though, things were different. The first time I ever saw Dad get mad with my mother was when she and my brother Harvey took Butch up to the Bronx ASPCA to have him destroyed. It wasn't because the dog made a mess in the house or chewed up the furniture, it was because my mother couldn't stand the idea of my father having something in his life that she didn't control or that didn't take orders from her, and Butch didn't have time for anybody except Dad. They loved each other. That's one of my happiest memories, Dad playing his harmonica while Butch howled and wagged his tail.

We called Butch the thirty-eight-dollar mutt because that's how much he ate in bills once when nobody was home. Dad waited out in the yard with Butch for three days until the money came back. Then he washed the bits and mailed them off to the United States Treasury and got a full refund.

Mom didn't tell Dad that she and my brother Harvey took the dog to the pound to have him put to sleep. My father came home from work one night and Butch wasn't at the door waiting for him. Right away it's, "Where's the dog? What happened to Butch?" I knew he was gone but I didn't say anything. My father was running all over the house, calling for him. He went out into the backyard and onto the street. I was sitting on the kitchen table, too frightened of my mother to open my mouth, and Dad was getting more and more frantic.

He was also starting to get angry, and he kept on at Mom, asking her when she last saw the dog and demanding to know if someone had let him out of the house by accident. My mother got very quiet, and I think this must have made my father suspicious, because this wasn't like her—and it wasn't like him, either, which may have frightened her, because in the end she told him that they had taken the dog to the pound.

For a minute I thought my father was going to hit her, but instead he got me and my kid brother, Gary, to drive up to the Bronx with him, because Dad suffered from night blindness and didn't see so good driving in the dark. All the way there he was worried sick wondering if it was too late, and when we got to the ASPCA it was closed. I remember being frantic myself we would get there too late.

Dad was still selling clothes out of his car at the time, so he always had a supply with him, and he gave the night watchman a couple of pairs of slacks to let us in. Butch was curled up in a cage. We were all crying, we were so happy to find that dog alive and take him home again.

I never found out if Dad ever said anything about this to my mother or to my brother Harvey in private, but when I was around he acted like nothing ever happened, and only once after that did I see him get mad with Mom. That was years later, after I met Louie, and once again it was over Butch. But that story doesn't belong here, it can wait.

There was no hugging from my mother, never any sign of warmth that I recall, not a pat on the cheek or a happy word to show that anything pleased her. In fact, when I see her face in my memory she's not smiling. Forget about laughing. She refused to watch TV comedy shows, and nobody else was allowed to watch them if she was in the room.

To this day I have no time for people who sit around looking miserable; they remind me of her and how bad she made me feel—and how she made me believe that it was really my fault she was unhappy. It didn't take me long to figure out that the only thing that would make her happy was if I wasn't there.

She didn't slap me or knock me around. She shoved and jabbed at me when she was mad, pulled my hair a lot to the point where I thought of cutting it so she couldn't pull it, but I gave up on that idea because I *hated* the thought of short hair. The fact is, having long hair was about the only thing about my appearance that made me feel good. I didn't like what I saw in the mirror—this was not a pretty little girl looking back at me, this was an ugly, skinny kid with a nose like you might see on a moose. My father's nose is what it was. All through kindergarten and right up until the last six months of high school, when it finally got fixed, this lump on my face was the first thing I noticed when I woke up, the last thing I saw at night.

It was my father who made me think I was beautiful. If we

were home or out together somewhere he would sometimes
be patting my arm, stroking my hair and my face, or kissing
and hugging me, and letting me know that in his eyes I was
perfect. Looking back, I understand that he did this because
he knew I needed the security children can only get from affection. From him I got that security and his unconditional
love, and if it showed only when we were alone at least I
knew he was always there for me and that I would be safe as
long as he lived.

"Come on, Lynda," he used to say, "let's go downstairs
and dance." And we would go down to the basement and put
a 45 on the record player or watch *American Bandstand* on
the TV, and I would pretend I was Ann-Margret or some famous modern rock-and-roll dancer while he sat in the arm-
chair and watched me leap and spin across the room. When
we danced together I felt so happy I could have burst. We
were in our own little world up there on cloud nine. His feet
were so light he was like a butterfly, and he was so graceful
when he moved I could have watched him for hours.

I loved him even more when we danced because I knew
we had something in common, being the low ones on the
family totem pole. "You two are like peas in a pod," my
mother used to say, and she meant it as an insult. When she
said this I always thought, So what, I'm glad I'm like my
father.

I asked him many times, Why doesn't my mother like me?
And the tears would come into his eyes and he would say,
"Sure, she does, your mother *loves* you, she's just tired, that's
all." I wanted to believe this, I tried to believe it because I
couldn't stand to think she didn't love me, but as I grew older
and noticed the difference between the way she treated me
and my brothers I had to face the truth, that in her eyes I was
for whatever reason nothing but a nuisance and a disappointment to her. The way she treated Dad, she must have felt the
same thing about him.

When Dad's mother, Grandma Lustig, was dying over in
Jersey his three brothers, Nat, Joe, and Sam, took turns stay-

ing with her overnight. When it was my father's turn, my
mother told him he couldn't go. They had a fight over it and
I heard her telling him, "I don't care what Nat and Joe do,
you staying there all night does not sit right with me." My
mother argued that my father had children and he shouldn't
go. This time, my father went; this time he stood up to her.
For once he stood up for himself and I was so proud of him
when he left the house that day.

Most of the time, though, my mother called the shots and
his job was to do what she told him. When she disapproved
of his friends, they had to go, no ifs or buts. Years later, after
my parents retired to Florida, we were in a restaurant in
Miami, and Dad saw his old friend and onetime business
partner Joe Cheffo at a table on the other side of the room.
He went to get up to say hello and my mother grabbed his
arm and said, "Don't you dare go over there, I'm telling you
now!" Dad sat down without saying a word. It broke my
heart trying not to look at his face.

She didn't stand by her man, she stood on him. That play,
Death of a Salesman? The way I see it, my gentle father
spent most of his long life dying. Mom ran the house, she
ran his life, just like she tried to run mine until she gave up
on me.

What made her the way she was, I couldn't figure out then
and I can't now. Even after she was dead I couldn't get any
kind of explanation from my father, and when I asked one of
my aunts or uncles if they knew, all they ever said was, Your
mother was one tough lady. Tough? In my book she was just
plain nasty. I had my own name for her. She was the Queen
of Mean.

Maybe I should be grateful to her, because the more she
got at me, the harder I got inside. The more she ignored me,
the less I cared. Maybe I became a bad daughter, I don't
know, but it's hard to see how a little girl of around four or
five can be so bad she can't be helped out of it with a little
bit of caring, which is all I wanted from her. Not getting it
only pulled me down inside and made me feel I was a dis-

appointment not just to her but, even worse, a disappointment to myself. I don't think people used the expression *self-esteem* when I was a kid, but I know what it means, and I can see that my mother for whatever reason didn't just make me think less of myself, she destroyed any chance I ever had of feeling good about myself, either as a girl or as a grown woman. Other women in similar situations turned out differently and grew up strong. I just grew up harder.

If there had been a choice I would sooner have had a loving mother than grow up hard. For me, the trouble with growing up hard made it easier to make all the mistakes I made later on. If your own mother can't show you she loves you, how can you ever hope to like yourself or think that anyone else will ever like you? And why should you care one way or the other?

I must have been around twelve when I found Dad's autograph book from high school. I still have it. It's full of names of the kids he knew, with dopey remarks over the signatures, like, "Two in a hammock attempted to kiss . . . and ended up like this." With both names written upside down. One name stands out because it shows up so many times, and that was Esther Berg. You can see from what she wrote that she was crazy about my father. Everywhere her name appears my mother has written over it or next to it, usually with some kind of sarcastic comment, like, Move over Esther Berg, here comes Sally Dostis! As I grew older I thought, He should have married Esther Berg, she wouldn't have kicked him around the way Mom did. I asked him once, "What happened to this girl Esther Berg," and he smiled and said, "Your mother came along."

CHAPTER 2

Keeping Secrets

Grandma Dostis died in March 1957, when I was ten years old, and by then I had a third brother, Gary, who was born three years after me. Mom and Dad took Gary and me over to Uncle Sam's house to sit shiva for my grandmother. They turned the mirrors to the walls and covered the pictures, with the drapes drawn over the windows. Family members came in and out all day, bringing food and eating what was put out on the tables.

We stayed until dark and my family got ready to go home. Mom wanted me to stay there for the night, which was okay by me because it meant I could do something she wanted me to do and maybe get in her good books for once. Staying the night meant sharing a bedroom with Selma, who was a few years older than me, a distant relative I didn't know too well but sort of looked up to—she was smart and beautiful, and the couple of times I met her she wore the kind of clothes my family could never afford. Spending the night together also meant we could get to know each other better, so I was really looking forward to it.

The bedroom we stayed in had twin beds, and there was a bathroom in the hallway. Selma gave me a pair of her pajamas and watched me while I undressed. I hadn't been in bed long when she said, "Why don't you come over here, we can talk better."

So I got into her bed and in no time she was rubbing up against me in a way I didn't understand except that it felt uncomfortable. Her hands were all over me. I didn't know what to make of it. But I must have thought it was okay because Selma would never in a million years do anything bad to me.

She got out of bed and went into the bathroom. Came back with a toothbrush. "Take off your bottoms," she said, so I did. What do I know? I figured this was a game that big girls play. She started rubbing the bristles up the insides of my legs. It tickled at first and I started giggling. Don't make any noise, she says, they'll hear us downstairs. She started rubbing harder, moving the bristles higher and higher up my leg until she put the brush where I know she shouldn't, ten years old or not. She was jabbing and jabbing and twisting and twisting it inside me until it hurt. I went to jump out of bed, but she was yanking hard on my arm, pulling me back.

"Let me go," I told her, "I don't like this game. I'm going to tell my mother what you did."

I got free of her and ran into the bathroom and locked the door. I felt skeevy, dirty, like I needed a wash, so I poured a bath. Forty-some years later I remember how that bathroom looked. The tub was big and square and magenta, wine colored, with a matching sink held up on shiny chrome legs. I was looking at this, wondering what to do and figuring I had to stay where I was long enough for Selma to go to sleep.

That was the first time in my life I felt really scared.

When I went back into the bedroom she had all the lights

on and was sitting up wide awake with a nasty smirk on her face.

"You ever tell anybody about this and you will be in big trouble," she said. "You think your mother will take your word against mine? She doesn't believe anything you tell her anyway."

She was right. If I told my mother, it could only make trouble—not just for me but for Mom's family and Dad's, because Selma's family was very rich, and in my mother's eyes, if you had money you could do no wrong. I couldn't say anything to anybody without it getting back to her, and if that happened, it would mean a family war, with me as the one who got the blame for setting it off. It didn't matter how I hurt, what mattered was keeping my mouth shut. For years I never told anybody, not even Louie. He would have had to kill someone. So I kept that dirty little secret for most of my life, and now I understand that not telling anyone was the first and probably biggest mistake of my life, because from then on everything got worse at home, and the worst thing was that if I ever stood any chance of feeling good about myself, it went down the drain with the bathwater that night.

I should have gone home and told my mother, "This is what Selma did to me. And by the way, Mom, she said you would call me a liar if I told on her and that you'd take her word for it, not mine. What are you going to do about it, Mom?"

That girl had it all figured out. She knew my mother better than I did, especially when it came to money. Mom would sooner have run herself under a truck than risk upsetting a rich person, at least not somebody like Selma and her family, who might one day throw a few bucks our way or do us some favor we wouldn't get otherwise. And there was another reason that made me keep my mouth shut about Selma—I was terrified they would put me in a home, like I was nuts or something.

At ten I didn't know about sex, I didn't know what sex

was, and even if I had known, I was too young to make any
connection between sex and the way I felt after that night
with Selma. Looking back, I can see how it could have put
me on another track if I had enjoyed the experience, but I
didn't, it confused the hell out of me—frightened me to
death, in fact.

I saw her a few times at family functions over the years,
but there was no talk about what happened that night.
Someone told me she spent some time in hospitals when
she got older but if she did, it's not something I've taken
enough interest to confirm one way or the other. To me she
became a nothing person, and that's how I think of her
now, forty-five years later. Just recently I told a family
member of this incident and she remarked, "Well, maybe
you were playing doctor." I said, "Ten years old or not, she
was thirteen, and I would have known if I was saying yes;
this was by all means rape."

It didn't help that from the time I was little until the time
I left home my mother made me wear Selma's hand-me-
downs. She told me they had top-quality labels and I
should consider myself lucky to have such nice things.
Look, she used to tell people, this is Selma's dress from
Saks, how do you think it looks on Lynda? At the same
time the only shoes I had were the used shoes the customers didn't pick up from the shoe repair man over on
86th Street. When other girls showed off their new shoes at
school I didn't want to look in case somebody said, "Gee,
Lynda, how come you're wearing those crummy old shoes
with your cousin's nice clothes?"

I don't mind admitting I was jealous of the girls at school.
I could never figure out why they were so happy and why
they laughed so much. What's to laugh at? I used to ask myself. At recess I'd go off in a corner and eat my sandwich
while they played their games and flirted with the boys.

Being Jewish in a Brooklyn school with mostly Italian
kids was not an advantage. My best friend, my only friend
at Seth Low Junior High, was a black girl, Barbara Gaskin,

who was one of the kindest and nicest people I ever knew. We took Hebrew together as a second language. The other kids used to see us in the playground and right away they were looking at us and whispering as if we're not there. They were the hip crowd, and Barbara and I were the odd couple. We pretended we didn't notice, but for me it went in deep and it hurt.

Other girls took their girlfriends home or went to their houses and stayed overnight. My mother made it clear she didn't want anybody from the outside in our house. Why? I didn't need to ask. People who live by the golden rule of my way or the highway don't have to explain themselves. Asking my mother to explain something was like asking somebody how many crumbs you get in a loaf of bread. There's no answer, and for her, most of the time there was no answer if she didn't feel like giving you one. I didn't have to ask her how come people didn't come to the house—it's not complicated, it's because she didn't want anyone coming to the house.

I understand now that my mother had created her own world. It had borders, customs, laws, and punishments, and she wasn't about to let anyone cross over while she was on patrol. Some stranger, not knowing any better, might laugh at her or tell her she was full of it with her rules. Like not putting on the lights in the basement, for instance, which was crazy because this was the family TV room, and later on when Mom got a job and Dad started bringing in more money, it also had a pool table in it. I put on the lights to watch TV one time and there are cockroaches everywhere. I'm running up the stairs screaming, "Cockroaches!" and my mother says, "Why did you put the light on"—not, "Okay, let's call in the exterminator."

I think she didn't want anyone there because she didn't want any happiness in the house. I really believe that. No happiness, no laughing, no talking. She wasn't happy, so why should anyone else be happy? Maybe it was that simple. I used to think of my mother as a cross between Bette

Davis and Joan Crawford because their movies were the
only ones she wanted to watch on the TV—those heavy, de-
pressing movies where everybody looked like they wished
they were dead. I swore I would never be like her.

A few times my kid brother, Gary, brought another boy
home when Mom was at work and the three of us hung out
in the basement. In the washing-machine room there was a
safe where my oldest brother, Harvey, kept the silver dollars
he got in tips from the Magic Touch beauty parlor he and
his wife Sandi had on Ocean Parkway. After a while it
turned out that someone had been stealing the coins from
the safe.

I'm not saying Gary or his friend did this, though I know
for sure I didn't, but when my brother Harvey told Mom that
a couple of hundred silver dollars had disappeared, she immediately attacked me. I was the one who got fingered, and
nothing I said changed the situation. My mother blamed me
for that until the day she died.

So there was no way I could take my friend Barbara
Gaskin from Seth Low Junior High or anybody else to our
house—black, white, Jewish, whatever. If I took a black girl
home I don't know what Mom would have done, but I know
I would have had to pay the price, one way or the other. But
Barbara never invited me to her house, either, so maybe her
mother was the same way as mine.

None of this racial business made sense to me then and it
still doesn't. Even so, when it came time later on to choos-
ing between Barbara and people my own color, I went with
the majority, because I was afraid that if I didn't, I would be
even more unpopular.

It's easy to see now that I wasn't just trying to escape
from my mother, I was trying to get away from who I was
to someone different, someone I could like and live with,
someone who was nothing like me. I didn't fit in at home,
I didn't fit in at school—and how much I longed to be one
of the girls, and didn't dare let it show in case they re-
jected me—but most of all I didn't like who I was and I

didn't understand why I was the person I was. So escape from home became the only and most important thing in my life. Blaming my mother or blaming Selma didn't help, and it got to the point where it didn't matter. Getting away and turning myself into somebody else was what mattered to me.

CHAPTER 3

Guilt and Fantasy

I was still at Seth Low Junior High when Mom took some kind of secretarial job in New York. It was with a guy called Mr. B, and if he had another name I never heard it. Mr. B had a business on Broome Street, something to do with printing. A couple of times I asked her to take me there but she let me know that wasn't going to happen, and since he never came to the house, I never got to meet this wonderful Mr. B.

All I knew was that he can do no wrong in Mom's eyes. She never stopped talking about him. Mr. B wore beautiful suits, he had class, he had his own business, he made a lot of money. The way I saw it, it was like she was telling my father, who spent his entire life hustling for a buck any way he could, that he was a loser.

Sometimes, when the weather was bad, Mr. B sent his chauffeured Lincoln to bring her to work. She was gone all day, five days a week, and when she got home late, which happened a lot, my brother Gary and I would get back from school and feed on cold franks, canned tuna, and egg salad. It felt like we lived on this stuff for years.

Was she having a fling with Mr. B? If I didn't know any better, I'd say she was, but I've thought about this question a lot and I think the answer is no. My mother had a lot of respect for money and power—just like me, in fact, when the opportunity came along—but I don't believe she ever confused the two with sex, and neither did I. On top of which, she liked calling the shots, and if Mr. B was everything she claimed he was, maybe he wouldn't have stood for that.

What she got out of her new job was a regular salary, which, combined with Dad's income from his various deals, made a big improvement in family finances. My father was the type of person who liked working all day every day, and now he was starting to get ahead. In the summers, he was working at the Monticello trotter track nights and during the day selling clothes all around the resorts and bungalow colonies in the Catskill Mountains. For once, it wasn't just my two older brothers who were doing all right financially, now it was my parents' turn. Suddenly we had cash hidden behind the walls and stuffed under the carpets in the trunk of the car.

In the old days, when they could afford it, they sometimes rented a summer bungalow in the Catskills. Now we had enough to buy our own place, in Mountaindale, near Woodridge, New York, and from then on until I left home I spent every summer vacation up there, loving every minute of it, not just because it was in the country but because it meant being alone with my father, just the two of us plus my kid brother, Gary, and Butch the dog.

At thirteen, I was making money for myself with a summer job at a place called Mother's Bakery in Fallsburg, helping out behind the counter. Every day I used to hitch rides back and forth to work, driving through hills and quiet forests where everything smelled fresh and piney. That was when it was safe to hitch in the Catskills, because you knew most of the people on the roads, and if it was a stranger, you didn't get in.

To me this place was better than heaven. Brooklyn with all its noise and dirt was maybe a hundred miles away and it felt like a million. Up there, with Dad, I was one happy kid. The only time I saw Mom was when she came up by bus for the weekends, and then we hardly saw her in the house because she went into Woodridge to play mah-jongg with her friends. First thing Monday morning, she was on the bus to go back to the city and work for Mr. B. We used to drive her to the bus stop to see her off. She never once looked back.

I used to dream about staying in the Catskills and never having to see Bensonhurst again. There was nothing for me there. I still didn't have any close friends at school. At home I watched *American Bandstand,* which was a big-deal show for kids at the time, and pretend that my best friends were two of the regular dancers, Justine and Bob, a good-looking couple who in my mind liked me so much they would invite me over to their house to listen to records.

I wanted to be with them, I wanted to be like them, and next to Justine and Bob, I loved Elvis and James Dean, and also Marilyn Monroe, because when I read about them in magazines, I found that they had had a tough time of it as kids, even if they did turn into big stars, so I felt that they would understand me, that we would have something in common.

Most kids live in a fantasy world at some point. They have imaginary friends they talk to, they tell their parents if they've been good or bad and they make up stories about them. I kept my fantasies to myself. I never read books, I couldn't concentrate on the words because my mind was too busy thinking about other things, mainly about the life I would have when I was old enough to leave home. There would be a sports car in it, preferably a Corvette, I was sure of that. There would be a man who would always love and protect me, and we would live in a big house, and our children would go to private schools.

The downside of these fantasies was coming back to reality. Facing the truth was just too painful. When *American Bandstand* ended and my famous friends, Justine and Bob, faded off the screen, I was back where I was. That's when I started to think I would never escape from my mother. There would be no sports car, no loving husband, no big house, and no children in private schools. If I was real lucky I might meet some schlub and spend the rest of my life in a two-family semi-detached house in Brooklyn, like the one I already lived in. I couldn't stand the thought of it.

As a little girl I don't remember ever being moody, but as a teenager it seemed that moods came every day and I didn't know how to shake them. Leave Lynda be, my family would say, she's in one of her moods again. Even Dad couldn't do anything to make these feelings go away. He could fix a lot of things but he couldn't fix me.

I understand now that feeling guilty had something to do with the way I felt, and I was guilty—I was ashamed of something I did to one of the nicest people I'd ever known. When Barbara Gaskin and I left Seth Low and went to Lafayette High together, I cut Barbara out of my life like she had never existed. The only way we could stay friends was for me to hang out with her and the rest of the black kids at Lafayette, and I just couldn't do it. I didn't want to do it, I wanted to start a new life at this school, I wanted to be somebody else and not have to deal with the crap you took from the other white kids for being friendly with a black girl. I wanted to be someone I approved of.

In the South in the early sixties, people may have been marching for freedom, but in Brooklyn in those years, like they used to say, if you're white it's all right and if you're black stay back.

I turned my back on Barbara because I figured it was the only way I could fit in at school. Fat chance. In three years at Lafayette the only girl who invited me to her house was Cathy Lopresti, whose parents had been born without the ability to speak or hear. I don't know if I felt sorry for Cathy because of that or because it made my life seem brighter, but the fact is that her mom and dad seemed a lot happier than my own. They had rigged the telephone and doorbell so that when someone called the lights went on. This fascinated and impressed me. Maybe they couldn't speak or hear, but they sure knew how to laugh.

Too bad I was too wrapped up in my own problems to realize that other people's problems make your own seem like nothing, but when you're a lonely, introverted kid, ugly and unloved, all you can think about is yourself and how you can ever get through the rest of your life when you wake up every morning wishing you were dead.

No matter how hard I tried I couldn't make friends at school. Their fault, my fault, who knows, but I could never get close to the other girls. Sure, I *knew* girls at Lafayette, just like girls knew me, but not as friends—the kind of friends where you go to their houses and they go to yours. How could I go to their houses if I couldn't ask them to mine? I was too ashamed to tell anyone my mother didn't want anyone at the house. For the same reason I couldn't go to parties. The fact is, if I didn't show up for school, nobody would have noticed I wasn't there, and after a while, if I didn't feel like going, I just didn't bother.

I thought I had found a friend in Annette, who got engaged to my brother Arthur. She was maybe twenty when I was fourteen, and when we first met I thought, This is it, this is someone who likes me! In my mind Annette would be a second big sister, like my brother Harvey's wife, Sandi, who I loved because she never turned me away or treated me like I wasn't there. She was much older than me, too, but she was kind and patient, she had a good sense of humor.

With Annette, this didn't happen. Even before she married Arthur she started picking on me, finding fault with everything I did or said. You don't have to be a genius to figure out when someone's talking down to you, like you're some kind of moron, and Annette made me feel that I was just a dumb kid who never got anything right. I didn't mind that so much; what really hurt was when she tried to get between Sandi and me by making snide remarks in front of me, like I wasn't even in the room.

I was a bridesmaid at the wedding in 1961. I still have a picture of me at the ceremony, walking down the aisle with my big nose leading the way. I fainted at the altar. Everything went black and at the same time I felt like I'd been kicked in the stomach. When I woke up Annette was looking down at me like I'm something the garbage man forgot to take away.

In other words, trying to make friends with females wasn't working for me, and although I came up with a bunch of reasons to explain this so far as school was concerned— they didn't like me, they didn't like Jews, they thought I was ugly, they were spoiled and stuck up, they were stupid and so on and so forth—deep inside I felt they didn't like me because there was something wrong with me. I could blame my mother and Selma and now Annette for this, and of course I did, but it didn't change the fact that nobody at that school cared if I was alive or dead. Maybe we didn't have much in common but at least we agreed on that.

CHAPTER 4

Peppermint Twist

Because of her job with Mr. B, my mother never once went to my schools, not to Seth Low Junior High or to my next and last one, Lafayette High on Stillwell Avenue. This was where I joined the Delta Royale sorority in my sophomore year and took up baton twirling because the boys liked to watch and I got pretty good at it. I was pushing myself into school activities and hoping it would help me fit in better. Mostly I wanted to show my mother that her daughter could be good at something. She never even came to watch the rehearsals.

You understand I'm not talking about getting ready for an Ivy League college here. This was Brooklyn in the late fifties and early sixties, and at schools like Lafayette and New Utrecht High, which was no better, you had these twenty-one-year-old wannabes who were still in class because their mothers refused to sign them out. For working parents like that, school was somewhere you put your kids for free all day.

It didn't take long before I figured out that's how my own mother saw it. She didn't ask me about lessons or homework or the books we read in class, and she had no time to go and meet teachers, what with working all day in the city. One time I asked her why she didn't come to functions like open week and she said, I don't have to go, if they want me they can call me.

She had no time to go to the school but she was out just about every night playing gin rummy and mah-jongg with her friends in Canarsie. And because she didn't drive, my father, who's been busting a gut all day, had to take her there and then sit around half the night waiting to go back and bring her home after midnight.

If school didn't matter to her, it didn't matter to me either, so after a while I stopped doing anything. Screw the baton twirling, no more Delta Royale. No more learning. I didn't take pencils, I didn't take books, and if I went to a class I didn't take notes. Eventually I was just walking around the park most of the day or hanging out in Mom and Pop's candy store across the avenue from the school. It was fun hanging out in the neighborhood. The park that Louie would go to was Seth Low Park. We didn't know about gyms then, so the boys would go to the park and do curls and chins on the bars.

I used to wonder why none of the teachers ever came over to Mom and Pop's and dragged us back to class. They must have known we were there, but I suppose they didn't care, either, because not one of them ever came into the place. It was a private club for dropout kids like me who had already given up but didn't know it.

Places like Mom and Pop's were a major fixture in the neighborhood in those years. From the outside, the typical candy store didn't look like much, what with all the signs stuck over the windows and the merchandise piled up on the floor and counters, but that was the way the owners and the customers liked it. Some of the customers, anyway, especially the men who came in to do business that had nothing to do with candy. With the right connections you could back a horse, get rid of a couple of swag furs, or hock a truckload of city cement, including the truck.

I'm not saying Mom and Pop's was any of these, nobody should jump to conclusions here, but for me it was a place to pass the time with the other truants and watch the people come in and out and do their business. I may have been a washout in class but I was always an inquisitive kid, I enjoyed watching the crowd, I wanted to know who was who and what was what.

Some of the people who came into the candy store were guys you had to watch for your own sake, guys like Jimmy Emma and Jerry Pappa, for instance, who were what we called *trumpiniks,* troublemakers. Both of them got kicked out of school. They were hooked up with a gang we knew as the Junior Rampers. If a non-member saw one of that bunch on the street, he crossed over to the other side if he didn't want to get his face rearranged. Back then, Jimmy Emma and Jerry Pappa were the toughest guys in Bensonhurst. When they walked in, life stood still.

Hard to believe, considering everything that came later and the part he played in destroying my family, but at the time Sammy Gravano was with the Rampers, only this was long before I ever laid eyes on him or heard his name. Or maybe I saw him around Mom and Pop's without even knowing it, when he would have been a skinny kid instead of the pumped-up steroid freak he became later on.

Sammy probably hung out with Jimmy Emma. Jimmy was the type of person who, if there wasn't a fight in progress, had to hit someone to make things happen. Everything about him said, Get the fuck outta my way. He was a short guy, like Sammy G, with a round face and dirty blond hair. You could see he worked out. I don't know if they had steroids then but he must have been on something because he didn't look normal. He was like a truck with muscles, and to me he was one scary, scary person. In the neighborhood he was known as a bully, a flat-out dangerous individual. He hated the world and everything in it. He didn't care about old people, young people, he didn't care about cats or dogs, all he cared about was doing and getting whatever Jimmy Emma wanted.

His sidekick, Jerry Pappa, was an okay guy until he started hanging out with Jimmy and copying his ways. They dressed the same—blue jeans and tight T-shirts with a pack of cigarettes rolled up one sleeve and pointy-toe Italian shoes. Jerry was a skinny guy with a normal kind of voice. Jimmy's voice was real deep, the same as Sammy after Sammy started with the drugs.

I was in Mom and Pop's one afternoon with the rest of the cutouts from Lafayette when Jimmy Emma and Jerry Pappa walked in. There was a Wurlitzer jukebox by the wall. It was the kind that had colored bubbles running up tubes in the front. Jimmy got hot about something or somebody, or maybe he just wanted some attention—with him you never knew what set him off—but suddenly he picked up the jukebox and threw it. I was so scared I ran out the door with everyone else before it hit the floor.

Years afterwards, when I was married to Louie already, Jimmy and Jerry were washing their cars on the corner of 79th Street and New Utrecht Avenue and some guys ran up and shot Jimmy Emma stone dead. Jerry Pappa got away in a passing car, but his turn would come.

When I heard what happened, I said to Louie, "Look at this, tough guy meets bullets, tough guy loses. You're nothing against a bullet." And Louie goes, "Yeah, yeah."

He didn't want to hear about it.

I guess that's where I first became aware of that life, at Mom and Pop's. It wasn't just Jimmy Emma and Jerry Pappa. There were older men you would see there and on the corners around Bensonhurst, Italian guys, checking out who was on the street, stepping off the curb to talk to friends who drove by in their cars—big new cars, Cadillacs and Lincolns, polished like they'd just come out of the showroom. It could be the middle of the week and they'd be out there, sharply dressed men of all ages who never seemed to work and had nothing to do but hang out and talk to each other.

To this day I still marvel at how so many of our paths crossed years later, not just mine and Sammy's and Louie's, but others, too. Right in my own neighborhood the stage was being set for one of the most twisted and most murderous true-life nightmares ever to be played out in America, and my husband, our children, and I would get parts as victims.

CHAPTER 5

Sex Ed

Those last couple of years at school took so long to end I felt like somebody must have stopped the clock. Nothing had changed there or at home. If my parents knew I'd stopped going to classes they carried on like always—they never said anything, and neither did anyone at Lafayette High. So I had escaped from school, and now all I had to do was escape from my mother. It sounds ridiculous, thinking about it now, but I figured that my life was about to be turned around, because in 1962, when I was fifteen, I finally got a new nose, courtesy of Dr. Silver, who did the same operation for one of my cousins. My nose was like my father's nose, like a boxer's; it was all over my face. It was certainly not feminine. When I went to see the doctor, he said he was going to change my whole life. When my surgery was over and I took off the bandages, I felt like a new person. It didn't matter about the swelling. I felt beautiful. And I loved my doctor.

Did this transformation make me more popular at school? No. Did the boys come running after me? No. Nothing changed except that for weeks my face looked like it got hit with a shovel. And I was still short, skinny, and flat-chested.

That summer, as usual, I went to our house in the Catskills with Dad, my kid brother, Gary, and our dog, Butch. A guy followed me there, Tommy, who I met in Mom and Pop's. Tommy was maybe four years older than me and had quit Lafayette to get a job driving a moving company truck. He let me know he wanted to see me again, so I sent him a note telling him okay, but I also told him we would have to meet up in the mountains, someplace over by Silver Lake, where my dad couldn't find out.

I was still a virgin at this time and in no hurry to stop being one, so I was careful to let Tommy know this when he showed up in his truck from Nick's Moving and Storage. We spent a couple of hours making out and he kept his hands pretty much to himself. He told me he got caught doing something in Brooklyn and had to go to prison for a while. He wanted me to write to him while he's away and put the letters SWAK on the envelope, meaning "sealed with a kiss."

This idea of writing to someone in prison was so romantic and exciting to me I never got around to asking him what he did to get sent away. I could see him behind bars, reading my letters, missing me, wishing we could be together, and then sitting in his cell and writing back to me and telling me how much he loved me. Well, maybe Tommy wasn't the dashing and protective husband I fantasized about, and it was obvious that with him there would be no Corvette or big house in our future, but I was attracted to the idea that he was more of a man than a boy, and there was comfort in that. He wasn't just there for a quick grope, he liked me for myself, he could see what was in me that others couldn't see.

As things turned out, I never got around to writing him because when I went back to Bensonhurst, I found he had a wife and daughter and lived with them on Cropsey Avenue.

From being with Tommy I found that I preferred the company of men older than me. They had confidence, they didn't act stupid, they knew how to talk. Barry Rosenblum, my sort-of sweetheart at the time, didn't really stand a chance. He was the same age as me. I don't remember exactly where we met but I think it must have been through some kind of school function. He wanted to be a dentist. My mother was always saying what a nice boy he was—she thought he would be perfect for me, which didn't help. If she liked Barry there had to be something wrong with him, or maybe I didn't see any future with a nice guy. My father was the nicest guy in the world and he paid a heavy price for it.

I was still dating Barry when I got into some real trouble, the kind you can't tell anyone about, just like that experience with my cousin Selma, except that this time I couldn't blame anybody but myself for what happened.

For as far back as I remember, I was crazy about cars, and my favorite was—and still is—the Corvette. Everything about Corvettes excited me, I don't know why, but to my way of thinking, when Prince Charming showed up, he would be driving a Corvette and we would cruise around Brooklyn like a couple of Hollywood movie stars.

It must have been the end of 1962 when I met Frankie La Fonda at the Spumoni Gardens candy store over by the Coney Island el. Frankie was in his early twenties, a good-looking tall guy I never saw there before. He had a new blue Corvette and he asked me if I wanted to go for a drive.

I was in that car before he could change his mind, but as I was looking out the window and watching the rain washing the dirty snow off the streets I was also thinking, I don't really want to do this. Then I figured that Frankie's okay, it's not like he was hitting on me, so I stopped worrying and tried to enjoy the ride.

It ended at an apartment building on Ocean Parkway. Frankie said he had to go in and get something, and it could take a while, so I should go with him because he didn't like to leave the car running on idle, which meant I would have to sit in the cold until he came back. I still can't believe that I was stupid enough to go with him, but I did, and the moment we were inside his apartment he locked the door and jumped on me. At first I was too surprised even to fight back. With one arm he had me pinned to the floor and with his free hand he was fumbling with the zipper on his pants.

"You know what a blow job is?" he said. "That's what I want and that's what you're gonna give me."

"What's that?" I said. And when he explained what it meant I almost threw up.

"Either a blow job or you can lie back and relax," he said.

I couldn't do it, all I could do was beg him to get off me and let me go home. I promised I wouldn't tell anybody, which was true, because if my mother found out she would only put the blame on me. I told him I was a virgin and I had my period, which was also true, but it didn't make any difference, he tore off my clothes and forced my legs apart until he got what he wanted and I was no longer a virgin.

I should have screamed or something but I couldn't catch my breath. I was so scared I felt I was choking. I don't remember much about what happened afterwards, how I got home or anything like that, and I didn't tell anyone about that day until I saw a therapist thirty-some years later. Back then it was shameful enough to not be a virgin anymore. But rape was something nobody talked about. It was different back then. You didn't really press charges or anything. Getting raped was one of those secrets that, when it came into my mind I put it away again, I pushed it out and didn't think about it. Back then there was no such thing as date rape. It was usually the victim who got the blame.

This was the second dumbest mistake of my life, not telling anyone. It was like Selma all over again, except that this time I kept quiet because I was ashamed and because I was terrified the shock might kill my father. What my mother would have done, I have no idea and was too scared to find out. I'm sure she would have blamed me, and let's face it, to do what I did—getting in a guy's car and letting him take me to his apartment—I may have been a fifteen-year-old virgin, but growing up where and how I grew up, any Brooklyn girl of that age would have to be dead from the neck up not to understand what she was getting into. But the thing is, I *didn't* understand. And maybe I didn't care because I thought I deserved it.

Did this change the way I felt about men? Sure, it did, but no more than it changed the way I thought about women after Selma. It showed me that some men are worthless creeps and so are some women. Just because I had the bad luck of running into one of each before I knew anything about sex, true sex, not the kind that's forced on you, it didn't make me think I could ever find happiness in sex or could ever trust another human being. In my mind, life was over when people forced you into situations you had no control over. But these experiences taught me that no matter what it took, I would never again allow myself to be forced into sex against my will.

I had to struggle to learn right from wrong. It feels like no one taught me. And at fifty-five I'm still figuring it out. I'm still trying to accommodate my partner, trying to get his acceptance, and this leads me to believe I have a problem with self-esteem. It hurts inside whenever I come across these situations and I keep hoping I will find a cure, but to do that I guess I would have to go back to being ten years old again. My therapist of ten years says we must find out why you keep picking the men who are no good for you. I think—at least I hope—that now, after remembering and writing all this, I will see more clearly why I choose some of the things I do.

CHAPTER 6

Meeting Louie

I met Louie about a year later, January 4, 1964, to be exact. I was about to turn seventeen. It was at a club in Brooklyn called Terry Lee's. I used to go there on Saturdays with a couple of girls from the neighborhood. It had a long, skinny room with a bar down one wall and some tables on the opposite side. The rest of the floor was for dancing.

I noticed these two guys at a table on the other side of the room. One of them wore a black nylon bomber jacket, pointy boots, and what looked like a beret, which flopped down over one eye. He had real thick black hair and some kind of pin holding this dumb flapjack-type hat on his head. He also had a thin mustache, which turned me off right away because I didn't care much for mustaches, especially thin ones. I figured the guy was some kind of New York nutso. I mentioned this to the other two girls, so now we were all trying not to look their way in case we started laughing.

But he was pointing at me, making a gesture like, Come

over here. I looked around, hoping he meant somebody else, but it was me he was looking at. I went over to his table, feeling a bit afraid because of his weird outfit and the way he stared at me, but I figured that we were in a public place with lots of people around. What could happen?

I was feeling pretty sure of myself.

"You want me for something?" I asked him. He smiled.

"Aren't you kind of young to be here?" he said.

He turned to the guy who was with him. "Look at that," he said. "Penny loafers. With real pennies." To me, he said, "I guess you don't come from Coney Island."

He was right about that. In those years, Bensonhurst was like upper class compared to Coney Island, which was a place where you found gangs of greasers looking for trouble. Those Coney Island Italian girls didn't wear penny loafers, they went around in sling-back shoes and tight skirts. That night I was wearing a yellow sweater and brown Glen plaid pants with the brown loafers.

He was still sitting there and I was standing by the table starting to feel stupid. It wasn't as if he asked me to sit down with him and the guy he was with. He was just checking me out, up and down, and he had this little smile, and I could see that behind this fancy front he was a handsome guy with a good strong build on him. Also a bit older than me, five years as it turned out. Then he asked me if I wanted to dance.

"Okay," I say, being cool. "I'm ready."

It felt great right off, he was a fantastic dancer. Instant chemistry—it felt as if we'd been dancing together for years. Even so, at this point I wasn't throwing myself at him, he was just a nice-looking guy who's a great dancer and had a freaky taste in clothes. He told me his name was Louie Milito. Actually, his first name was Liborio, which he didn't like, and to make things more confusing, his parents called him by his middle name, Bernie. I preferred Louie, which was my father's name. These coincidences—the same names, the easy way he moved on the dance floor like my dad—instantly got my attention.

"What kind of work do you do?" I asked him.

"What's it look like I do?"

"Construction? Painter? Carpenter?"

There was something calm and solid about Louie that I'd never known before. I didn't really care what he did. His answer surprised me.

"Hairdresser," he said. "Mermaid Avenue. LouArt Beauty Salon."

This was some place in Coney Island I never heard of.

And I told him how my oldest brother, Harvey, also had a beauty salon in Brooklyn.

We must have danced for hours. The girls I came with had already left, so had Louie's friend. I didn't even see them leave, I was too busy talking and listening. We talked about cars, we talked about work, about the Yankees—my favorite team—we talked about movies and music, we talked about families and I told him about the problems I had with my mother.

He was so easy to be with, and when he spoke he had a way of explaining things. He made you want to listen—and he was a careful listener, too, it wasn't like he was all mouth. What he did was make me laugh a lot. More than that, for the first time I felt someone was taking me seriously and genuinely paying attention, as if he wanted to know what I thought. I knew I was falling for this man. Everything about him made me want to know more about him.

I had been trying to put my finger on what else was different about Louie from other guys I knew and I realized that it was his voice. Some men seem to think that women are impressed by loud and confident talk. Louie wasn't like that. He didn't raise his voice, he spoke clearly but softly. In fact, in all the years we stayed together I don't remember him shouting more than two or three times, and when that happened, you did not want to be there.

I got the impression that he was more than just a hairdresser, because he sure wasn't like any hairdresser I ever

met. For one thing, he was very muscular, too muscular to
be a hairdresser. He looked like he did something very physical. Also he reminded me of Dean Martin. Would Dean
Martin do hair? I don't think so. Hairdressers back then
were either Jewish or feminine. They certainly were not
what Louie was. Also I had the feeling I'd seen him somewhere before.

When he told me he lived with his parents, same as me, I
figured he was single. His house was just a few blocks from
mine. That's when I remembered where I'd seen him.

A couple of years before this, a group of guys used to
meet on the corner of our street and sing close harmony—
doo-wop, we called it.

They were too old for me, but a couple of them had really
hot cars parked on the corner, two-tone street machines
waxed and polished to perfection. I paid more attention to
the cars than to the boys.

They used to sing outside the dry-cleaning place on the
corner of 74th Street and 20th Avenue. Mom came home
complaining one day because somebody had painted a name
on the wall of the dry cleaners. I saw it when I went to
school the next morning. Bernie.

I mentioned this to Louie while we were dancing.

I did that, he said.

And I told him, "Get out of here," and he said, "It's true,
that's me, Mister Doo-wop."

Louie drove me home from Terry Lee's that night. I fell in
love with his car, a '58 black-and-gray Pontiac with black
roll-pleated seats.

I told him not to take me by my house but to stop down
the block because I didn't want my parents seeing him.
When he asked why, I said it was because he's older, because he's Italian and I'm Jewish and my mother
wouldn't like it no how, no way. He laughed and said his
parents were Sicilian and would probably feel the same
about me.

He stopped, we made out. He didn't force himself on me,

he didn't make any moves that frightened me. This was no Frankie La Fonda, and I was happy about that.

I didn't get any bad signals from Louie, I felt safe with him. When I was getting out of the car he asked for my number, so I wrote it down and told him that if he called and one of my parents answered he should say his name was Bernie. Which was kind of stupid because Dad was Jewish and of course his name was Louie also. But I wasn't thinking about that, I was thinking this is someone I like and trust. I didn't want anything to go wrong with this guy. He was the one I wanted, there wasn't a doubt in my mind.

I told my mother that "Bernie" was half Jewish and half Italian, and for a while she fell for it. I also told her we met at a dance at the Jewish Community House over on 79th Street and Bay Parkway, and for a while she believed that too, until he came to our house in the Catskills wearing a gold chain with a large crucifix.

"Couldn't he have found a bigger one?" my mother said.

I don't think she was in favor of Louie or against him, whatever his religion and family background. Like me, she probably welcomed the possibility that I would be leaving her house and we would at last be free of each other. She probably figured that if it wasn't Louie it would be someone else, and if Louie turned out to be the one who took me away, it would be fine with her, and the sooner the better.

I look at myself then and I see a girl so desperate for attention and so confused by her fears, real and imaginary, that she would do anything and take any chance to break away from one life and start another. That girl knew nothing and had no experience of the world except, as she saw it, pain and disappointment. These were real enough, though, and for better or worse they had made me who I was. It's true that I had my father's love and support, but so far as it being there all the time, hugging me or even praising me when my mother was around, well, that never happened. Dad's feelings for me, the proof of his love, came when we were alone, it was measured out and cautious, it wasn't something I could count on seeing at all times—and even if it had been, there was no way it could substitute for the unconditional, powerful love and attention every young woman hopes to find with the man she chooses to spend her life with.

I believed then that for me, Louie Milito was that man. It was what I wanted to believe.

II

1964-1979

CHAPTER 7

Leader of the Pack

Louie started out as a petty thief, sometimes on his own and sometimes working with a couple of friends, Alex Genco and Billy Spezia, who were cousins. Alex was one of those big guys who couldn't control himself. To me it always seemed like he was about to have some kind of seizure, you never knew which way he would jump. But he adored Louie and would do anything for either one of us.

Billy latched on to Louie because Louie was strong and Billy was one of those good-looking weak-minded characters who liked to make trouble as long as he had someone like Louie with him. And Louie would always stand up for Billy because Billy once saved him from drowning after a friend paid them to take his boat out and sink it for the insurance. They began whacking away at the hull with a couple of axes, and just as the boat started to go down, Louie remembered he couldn't swim. Billy half carried him all the way back to the beach.

After that, he was always ready to help Billy, even if it meant getting out of bed in the middle of the night, which he did once when Billy called up from a bar where he'd locked himself in the phone booth and guys were trying to beat the door down after he made a pass at somebody's girl.

We'd been going steady for maybe two months before I found out my hairdresser boyfriend did other kinds of work that just about scared me stiff when I realized it. We were over at Billy's house and Louie said that he and Billy had to go out for a while. They came back an hour later with a ton of women's clothing and dumped it on the couch. I asked Louie where they got it, and he says, "Trunking." Then he explained what it means, which is basically breaking into car trunks and stealing anything that can be turned into cash. Louie and Billy were looking at me to see how I would take this.

In one part of my mind I thought, Get out of here, Lynda, forget about this guy. You don't want to be around these people. You don't want to be a part of this. Go home.

That's what I should have done and I didn't.

Walking out on Louie would mean giving up the idea of having a life of my own. I would have to admit I'd been wrong about him, that I'd made a big mistake. I couldn't do that. Being with Louie meant freedom, and that's all I wanted. He was sure of himself without being cocky about it. He had the strength of will I wish my father had. In fact, it's probably true to say he had all the qualities of character my father had but without the weaknesses. Nobody would ever push Louie Milito around, that was for sure.

I didn't mind that I was still living at home. As long as he was in my life there was a chance of escape, and I could wait for that, and I didn't mind the waiting just as long as I felt there was something to look forward to. The more time the two of us were together, the happier I was. I could tell that Louie felt the same way.

I also knew that day when they came in with the stolen clothing that if I started kicking up a fuss in front of Alex

Genco and Billy Spezia, Louie would have to make a choice between them and me, and I didn't have enough confidence to think he'd pick me over his friends. So I said nothing. I acted like this trunking business was no big deal. Everyone, even Louie's boss in Coney Island who would accept Louie's swag clothing in the beauty parlor, acted like it was no big deal. I didn't want to make waves. Or seem like I wasn't used to anything.

My father used to tell me that sometimes, when they rented sites for his Pig Slide at carnival venues outside the city, the weather was so bad they didn't make enough money to pay the rental, so they'd skip town. Once, my father and one of my uncles hid in a hotel room while people banged on the door, yelling at them to come out and pay what they owed. But they didn't make anything extra. I think what they made was for survival.

Dad was pretty good at cutting corners when he felt he could get away with it. Like a lot of people who grew up poor in the Depression, he did what he had to do to put the food on the table for his family. All his life, all he ever knew was scraping out a living the best way he could. The clothes he sold in the bungalow colonies in the Catskills came from companies in the Garment District. My father was an earner; that was all he knew all his life. Do what you gotta do to earn and take care of your family.

Maybe this was why Louie's "earning" came as no great surprise.

❖   ❖   ❖

Looking back at myself as a kid just turned seventeen, I wonder how come I figured I knew how to handle things when the truth is, like a lot of high school dropouts, I was in many ways dumber than a dead fish—street smart and world foolish. I could make excuses for the way I was—blame my problems on others—but in fact nothing and nobody forced me to stay with Louie.

We even split up for a while that first year, but being away from him only made me want him all the more.

I'd been over to his house to borrow a car to go shopping out on Long Island, and his father gave me the keys for a Pontiac 2+2. Louie was waiting on the sidewalk when I got back to the house. By this time I'd been with him long enough to know when he was angry—he would get what I called that stone-face look, and that's the face I saw that day and would get to know all too well over the years.

"Out of the car!" he said.

I asked him what was wrong.

"You know what you just did? You just took one of the swag cars, dummy! You could have got us all pinched. Get out of my sight, I don't want you around here no more."

I tried to explain but he wasn't listening. He got in the car, rolled up the window, and parked in the alley, leaving me on the sidewalk with a pile of shopping bags. Then he walked right past me and went into the house without a word.

At home I shut myself in my room and stayed there. I let a few days go by, then walked over to his house. Louie's car was in the drive, so I knew he was in, but when I called the house, his mother told me he just left. I couldn't eat or sleep, I just lay on the bed, and every time the phone rang, I picked it up hoping he'd be at the other end. He didn't call.

After about a month, I went out with a couple of girl-friends to Terry Lee's, the place where we first met, and Louie was there with a bunch of guys. He came over to our table like nothing had happened and we started talking.

I was kind of pleased with the way I handled myself that night. There was no apology from him, I didn't cry or ask him to forgive me about the car, I didn't throw myself at him. I was determined to show him—and myself, though I didn't believe it for a moment—that I could be as indifferent to the situation as him even if, inside, I felt like I was about to explode from fear and tension. He looked at me with a half-smile.

"You wanna dance?" he said.

"Maybe."

"You know you do, Lynda."

And five minutes later, wrapped up in his big arms again, my head on his chest, all the tension drained away and there was nobody in the world except for the two of us.

Because he spoke so softly, people who didn't know Louie well made the mistake of thinking he was harmless. I knew better. One night not long after we met, we were in a place in Brooklyn called Warm Beer, Lousy Food, now known as the Crazy Country Club. It was the kind of club where, if you asked for napkins, they would throw you a roll of toilet paper. A guy who'd been sitting near us had now moved over to the bar and he started hitting on me as I was walking to the bathroom. Louie didn't say anything when I returned to the table, but his cold-stone expression told you everything you needed to know. He called the manager over and said, "You see that gentleman by the bar? Would you ask him to come over here please?"

The guy strolled over with this sloppy grin on his face and Louie stood up and punched him hard in the face. He was still on the floor when we left.

"People mistake my kindness for weakness," Louie used to say. I took that as a warning, and from then on I did my best to stay on his good side. I would find out soon enough that no matter how hard I tried, this didn't keep me out of trouble.

I never saw him do anything like that again, not when we were out together, anyway. That wasn't the way he was, he didn't go looking for fights, but if some friend called him up in the middle of the night and said they had a problem, he would be out the door and on his way.

The first time he got mad enough to hit me, we were in the basement of my mother's house. I was at the typewriter doing what we called paperwork, which meant scratching out a couple of the mileage numbers on auto titles with a straight razor and putting in new ones. Louie got the titles from buying wrecks of late-model cars and then stealing the same kind of car so he could use the wreck title to claim new license plates.

This of course is a serious crime today, and it was then, but to me at the time, I had no clue just how much of a risk I was taking with the law. And maybe even if I had known at the time, I guess I would have done anything to be accepted by Louie if it meant escaping from my mother.

Guys would call up from a junkyard in Jersey to say they just got a new wreck in and was it something Louie would be interested in, and for a while that's what he dealt in, but it got to the point where he preferred dealing with theft and recovery cars because they didn't smell as bad as some of the wrecks. Sometimes he stole the cars himself and sometimes he gave the job to friends who took a cut.

He couldn't sell the swag car as legit, but the guys who bought these cars paid maybe a grand for a car worth three or four, which was a good deal. All the buyer had to do was make sure he didn't get pinched, and if he did, he should forget about fingering Louie. Louie always explained this very carefully so the guy understood how this part of the deal worked.

This particular day, when he hit me, I was in the middle of typing in the new numbers when he picked up one of the titles I'd just finished.

"Look what you did here!" he says. "You got the mileage wrong—I'm gonna have to pay another hundred and fifty dollars for a new title!" And he pushed me so hard on the back of the head I fell out of the chair.

"See what you made me do?" he said.

I couldn't think straight. I didn't understand what had happened. Nobody had ever hit me before, not even my mother, and here I was, lying on the floor in her house with the right side of my head feeling like it had been squashed in a vise.

It was usually the right side that took the punishment. Years later a dentist checked my X rays and asked if I had ever been in a car wreck, because to him it looked like the right jaw had suffered bone loss, which sometimes happens in a bad traffic accident. I told the dentist I'd never been in any kind of wreck, unless you counted marriage.

People have asked me why I didn't kick him out of the house immediately, why did I allow myself to stay with this man, who at the time wasn't even my husband. I don't have an answer aside from what I've said before. Partly it was a question of not wanting to admit to myself or to my mother that I'd been wrong about Louie. Partly it was because in some part of my mind I felt maybe I deserved it, not for anything I did wrong but because of this feeling I'd had most of my life that there was something wrong with *me,* and that I deserved punishment. And mostly it was because I didn't want to lose Louie and was too stupid to know any better. I see now that in my desperation to escape from my mother, from all the abuse, from my lousy life, I had lost my self-respect.

All my life people had been telling me I was wrong about this and wrong about that, and I was sick of it—I wanted to prove that I was right and they were wrong. I guess the shrinks would say this comes from some kind of deep insecurity, and maybe it does. But so far as Louie was concerned, I felt there was no choice. I *had* to be right about him. I would *make* it right, whatever it took, and if it turned out I was wrong, I wouldn't admit it.

There was that Louie—vicious and uncontrollable—and there was the other Louie, the one that made me love him so much, there were times when I could have burst with happiness just being with him. This was the side of Louie it was impossible to resist, and this was the side you saw most often. His gentleness, his warmth, his humor. His quietness.

People liked him as soon as they met him. He didn't push himself, he was considerate, he was polite and he paid attention. He was an explainer is what he was, but only when it came to things he knew about and understood all the way through. He wasn't one of those guys who blow words all over the room about subjects they knew nothing about. If there was someone present who knew more than he did, Louie kept quiet and listened. He always paid attention when he was learning something he didn't know.

And he liked to clown around. He couldn't help himself, his weird sense of humor was in him when he was born. Over the years, we had two dogs, both Dobermans. Lady One and Lady Two. Louie could make Lady Two laugh—well, he called it laughing, and she certainly looked as if she were enjoying herself. He used to put his face up to hers and talk nonsense words—oopsie woopsie poopsie, and so on, until she lifted her upper lip and showed him her teeth, with this dopey expression on her face, as if she were smiling at him.

Look at this, he told people who came to the house. You wanna see my dog laugh? And he'd be down on his knees, making Lady laugh.

Louie! Here's a man who would spend an hour taking a splinter out from under my nail. Who told me we were lovers, partners, and friends for life. Who got red roses delivered to the hotel room when we went away for a weekend, candy hearts on Valentine's Day. And when anyone in the family had a birthday, he made sure the four of us were home together for the celebration. On my birthdays I got three cards from him.

Twice a month he took us to watch the Yankees because he knew how much I loved that team, especially Thurman Munson, the Yankee catcher, my personal hero. Late one night, long after I'd gone to sleep, Louie came home and woke me up. He said he'd just heard that Thurman had been killed in an airplane crash and because I was usually the first up in the morning he wanted to tell me himself so that I wouldn't hear it on the radio.

Like all people, Louie was a mixture of good and bad—
sure, worse than bad in his case, but even after our early
years together I wanted to believe what I wanted to be true,
that he put his family first and would always be there for us.
When I think about it now I realize that in many ways I was
just making it easier for him to do what he did. The shrinks
tell me that the word for this is *enabling,* and that's how I see
it. I was Louie's enabler.

I've never known anyone as popular as he was. Years before
he got made with the Gambinos, I used to notice how people
looked at him when we went anywhere, as if they saw something special in him. I knew what it was but I could never figure out how they knew. It's not as if he were a big man
physically. He was good looking and he had a solid build on
him, but he was only around five seven and he didn't swagger
into restaurants like some of the guys we knew, peeling off
hundred-dollar bills for the maître d' and shouting across the
room to let everybody know he was there. That was never
Louie's way of doing things.

His idea of a good time when we first met was going out
to some track in Southampton with Alex Genco and racing
their cars, Louie in his two-tone Pontiac and Alex in his new
Impala. Louie loved to drive fast and he was always coming
home with trophies. He was very competitive. He was the
type of person who enjoyed being number one, as we all do,
but if he lost a race, he didn't get mad at himself, he'd just
go back and try harder the next time.

Most Sundays, when the weather was good, we went out
on the motorcycle. He had two Harleys, a Sportster he raced
out on Long Island, and a candy-red-and-chrome dress bike
we rode in the summer. I thought of Louie as leader of the
pack, after the record that came out that summer. We'd meet
up with maybe twenty or thirty other guys with their girlfriends over by the Cyclone ride on Coney Island. The first

few times they tried to get me to go on the Cyclone, but Louie knew I was afraid of heights, so without making a big deal about it he would tell them to lay off me. They gave up after a while. With Louie next to you, nobody could make you do something you didn't want to.

Coney Island was where we met to figure out where to go for the Sunday ride, the usual choices being Bear Mountain, Washington Square in the Village, or a biker hangout called Bow Wow's out in Valley Stream on Long Island. I preferred the Village because it was closest and because I wasn't crazy about being on a motorcycle for four or five hours in Sunday traffic. The part I didn't like was crossing the Manhattan Bridge to Canal Street and trying not to see the river through the bridge grating, which rattled so loudly I was scared to death all the way across. I'd have my arms wrapped around Louie and keep my eyes shut. He knew the bridge scared me, so he took extra care when we crossed over, squeezing my arms with his elbows to let me know it was okay.

Louie made me feel safe, that's what it was. So did my father, except that with him there was always a limit, because when it came to standing up for me with my mother, I was on my own. In situations like that there was nothing my father could do for me, but with Louie I was never on my own. With him I had someone on my side, someone who loved me the way I was, and if he sometimes lost his temper and knocked me around, which he did, many times, he was still my best friend and my protector, and that's what mattered to me.

I quit school after I turned seventeen in 1964 and got a receptionist job at an employment agency off Times Square. Louie would usually drive in on Mondays, his day off from the LouArt Beauty Salon, and we'd eat at the Automat or grab a deli sandwich and sit in Bryant Park, watching the people. He made up stories, telling me that the guy talking to a tree was a Russian spy reporting back to Moscow, or the lady in the fur coat feeding the pigeons had just escaped from the Women's House of Detention down on Greenwich Avenue and was waiting for her boyfriend to show up so they could go rob a bank.

If you ask me where I went yesterday or what I did when I got there I probably wouldn't remember, but I can see Louie and me in that park back in '64 and it's as if I'm right there right now, just the way it was when it happened. It makes no sense to me how certain details stick in the memory. How come I can see us at the curb on 42nd Street on a hot day in summer, waiting for the light to change so we can go look in the windows at Stern's, the big department store? Louie holding my hand, pulling me out in the street before the lights change, and laughing at me because there's a cop on the corner and I'm scared he'll give us a ticket for jay-walking.

He'd walk me back to work after lunch, we'd stand on the sidewalk for a few minutes, then he'd give me a quick kiss—he was never big on kissing in public—and he didn't want me to be late getting back. The rest of the day I'd be watching until it was time to go home on the BMT back to Bensonhurst and see him again.

In my mind the future was all figured out. We would save up until we had enough money for him to open his own beauty shop. We would get married, buy a house, raise a family, and live a normal life, like everyone else. The thing is, I believed he would stay in the business, because he was a first-class hairdresser. His customers were crazy about him and I know he was proud of his diploma, which he framed and hung on the wall at LouArt's. And for most of the first three years we were together he went to work five days a week, Tuesday through Saturday, without fail. I used to drop by and watch him working, but I had another reason to go see him. Louie was good at making up words, silly words, kind of like a private code we used when other people were around, and during the first year we dated he came up with "pushkanini," which is how he told me he loved me. I'd go over to the salon on a Saturday just to hear him tell me, "Okay, pushkanini," and nobody but the two of us knew what he meant.

It was trivial little things like this that made me believe that underneath everything he wanted the same kind of life for us that I wanted.

There were two problems with the plans in my head, the first being that in the real world, and not in the fantasy world I dreamed about, Louie Milito was a criminal. The second problem was that he enjoyed crime—he had a talent for manipulating money out of people, as he put it, and the more he made from stealing, the better he got at it.

All the time he worked at the LouArt Beauty Salon in the early sixties he was going out trunking, stealing cars, doing paperwork, changing the titles and selling swag to his customers—baby clothes, TVs, menswear, toys, furs, you name it, he could get it. And his boss at LouArt, who was also called Bernie, was in this with Louie right up to his neck.

How Louie and his friends never got pinched in those early days was a miracle to me, because they were pulling off scores every night of the week and making a ton of money. Later on I figured they must have been working with some cops on Cropsey Avenue. In those years in certain Brooklyn neighborhoods, there wasn't anything you couldn't get away with if you knew the right names. So if you get stopped for a traffic violation, and with me it was usually speeding, all you had to do was drop the right name and give the cop a couple of bucks to lose the ticket. We called it settling out of court.

Not all the crooked cops were in Brooklyn. I was home one day after we were married and two huge guys came to the front door with mink coats over their arms. They were very polite. They said they were detectives from the Fifth Precinct in Manhattan. They showed me their badges.

"Sorry to disturb you, Mrs. Milito. Is Louie around?" I told them he was at work and asked if there was a message.

"Tell him we came by with a couple of fur coats he might be interested in. Have him call us."

Louie came home a couple of hours later.

"Look what I found on the front step," he said. He was holding two shiny bullets.

I told him about the cops with the minks and gave him their names and said maybe they dropped the bullets. "Oh, those guys," he said, and laughed.

But I see that I've been getting ahead of the story here, pulling things out of order and putting them where they don't belong. This gets confusing because it's hard to tell what happened when, and for neat freaks like me, who can't stand any kind of mess in the house, things need to be put in order, from start to finish.

I started hanging out at Louie's house in 1964, that first summer we were together. The difference between the Milito house and my family's house was like the difference between rain and sunshine. What with the beagles his father raised in the basement, their house was full of noise and people and talk, Louie's brothers and cousins running in and out, music from the stereo—usually Jimmy Roselli, every Italian's favorite at the time—and always something cooking on the stove.

Louie's grandfather was a true Sicilian, born in Palermo. He lived next door with one of his other daughters and her family. His part of the house was the basement, where he kept canaries and hung salamis over the boiler pipes for aging. Papa, as the Militos called the old man, was always in Louie's house, smoking what we used to call guinea stinkers, these dark little cigars that looked like twigs. He had a dog he called Puppy that slept on the carpet and snored so loudly you had to keep waking him up to hear the conversation.

I never knew what Papa was saying because he talked

mostly Sicilian. And I say he was old, but he was still working a full week as a roofer, and he was as tough as an old leather boot.

By contrast to Louie's home, our house was like a funeral home, but without the flowers. There was a parlor nobody ever used in case it got dirty, not that anybody ever visited much. My mother didn't care for cooking. In fact, Louie got nauseous after eating with us the first time. She poured ketchup over spaghetti and put mayonnaise over the salad, with hot dogs on the same plate, which she cut with an X so they opened up like dog bones.

The first summer we were together he came up to our house in the Catskills for the weekend. My whole family was there, my brothers Harvey, who bought a beauty salon upstate, and Arthur, who was steadily working his way up the executive ladder with my Uncle Sam Dostis.

My kid brother, Gary, who idolized Louie, drove up with us, and I remember being nervous in the car because this was the first time Louie would meet all the family together, and I was worried sick about everything going okay. My mother had already made a couple of comments about him—what did he do for a living, how come he's always got a new car, that kind of thing—but she was on her best behavior that weekend.

Louie and I slept next to each other on cots in the living room. He made me promise to eat his share of the chopped liver and the tuna salad if my mother served it up one more time. Louie was crazy about Jewish food, but not my mother's, when there was too much of it.

His mother, Vincenza, who people called Jenny, was an old-fashioned Italian cook who couldn't make a bad dish. I figured that all Italian families had octopus, squid, spaghetti with artichokes plus figs for Christmas dinner, because that's what we had that first year at Louie's house.

Louie was the oldest of three brothers, the next being Bobby, then Anthony. Bobby started off as a carpenter, but became a hippie and then a writer in New York and changed his name to Sebastian. He eventually drove out to California in his Volkswagen bus. Anthony, as far as I could tell, was basically a garbage man who wanted everything for himself without having to give anything back. It was Louie who got him a place with the Sanitation Department, only to have Anthony complain how cold it was, working the streets in winter. So Louie went back to his connection in Sanitation, who found an inside office job where Anthony sat close to a heater.

In the Milito household he didn't get a lot of respect. When he first started on the garbage detail Papa Milito used to wave a broom at him and shout, "Hey, streeta cleana guy!"

Louie never had any time for the hippie lifestyle but he wasn't the sort to tell people how they should live, and although they were just about as different as two people can be, he and Bobby got into mischief together—nothing criminal, just the kind of stunts that brothers enjoy, like riding around Brooklyn in a convertible. Louie was at the wheel once when he saw two girls on the sidewalk on 76th Street and backed up the car to talk to them. When they drove off, Louie floored the gas pedal thinking he was in drive and could burn some rubber to impress the girls, but he was still in reverse, with the result that he knocked down a fire hydrant and flooded the street.

I called him Louie when we were alone but at home his family called him Bernie, because his father was also called Louie, which made things confusing, to say the least. And to make things even more complicated, his father insisted on calling him Lou!

The Militos had a few acres out on Long Island and Louie Senior and "Bernie/Lou" took me hunting there one day with Maggie, their favorite beagle and best hunting dog. That was the main reason I went with them, to watch Maggie work. It was also the last time they took me, because I refused to get in the car unless they took Maggie out of her cage in the trunk and let her sit on my lap in the backseat.

That day they shot a couple of rabbits and some pheasants and took them home for Jenny, who was just like her oldest son, "Bernie," and would eat anything. Not Louie Senior, though. He wouldn't touch it, he said it was food for savages. I felt the same way. After that, whenever I was at their house I would only eat what he ate because I knew it came from the butcher.

Louie's dad liked to tease me because I was a cleanup fanatic—still am, cannot sit still with dirty dishes on the table. "Hold on to your plates, here comes Lynda," he used to say when he saw me getting up.

Later on, when the children were born, he made up names for both of them. Louis was Lukula and Deena he called Deedy Weedy. And Louie was never Louie to his father, he was always Lou.

Louie Senior was a good man and we took to each other from the start, partly because in some ways he was like my own father, warm and gentle, a get-along kind of guy. But I never did figure out Jenny Milito, Louie's mother. She had a stern face, she wasn't big on smiling. Sometimes I called her Ma, like the rest of the family did, but I couldn't tell if she liked me or not, even when she made me a silver lamé dress, which I treasured for years. We'd be alone in the house when I went around for a fitting, but there wasn't much talk. I wanted to get closer to her, and I sure made the effort, bringing her flowers on her birthday and remembering anniversaries, but it didn't seem to have much effect.

When she introduced me to people, I wasn't just "Bernie's" girlfriend, I was his *Jewish* girlfriend. Then I was his Jewish fiancée. After that, I was her Jewish daughter-in-law. A million times I asked her, "Ma, why can't I just be your daughter-in-law?" She wouldn't answer me. I decided she didn't want to know from nothing.

To her, a Jew was a Jew and that's all there was to it. Plus I wasn't Italian, and in her book, if you weren't Italian there was something missing. She didn't care that I didn't care what I am—and I still don't. The way I see it, only people who don't have a life give a rat's ass about that kind of thing. I didn't look down on the Militos because they were Sicilian, and I tried telling her we all get here by accident, we don't get any choice in the matter, we're all equal, it's how it is, and she'd start crossing herself and talking to herself and muttering, like she just saw Satan or a ghost coming up the steps.

But I still called her Mom.

She and Louie Senior worked in a Brooklyn sweatshop, like a lot of people we knew. She was a seamstress and Louie's dad was a presser. So far as I know he never turned a dishonest dollar, but Louie's mother was another story. I've been in their house when she'd be poking Louie in the guts and telling him, "Bernie, Why don't you get me a new toaster? We need a color TV for the living room. See if you can pick up a nice vacuum for your mother, the kind you don't have to bend over to switch on."

Louie said she would steal a red-hot stove if she could get someone to help her lift it.

He wasn't afraid of his mother—Louie was never afraid of anyone—but he felt responsible for her and for his father, and he just loved giving them things they couldn't get on their own. He never missed birthdays or special holidays. I still don't know for sure how they could have bought the little piece of land they had out on Long Island, but I don't see how they could have found the money to buy it on what they took home from the sweatshop. I don't know. Maybe they had money from somewhere else. Anything is possible.

Who owned what was always a complicated business in our life. Louie never filed an income tax return, never wrote a check, and as far as I know, never had a bank account. Later on, when the money started coming in, everything we ever bought in the way of property—houses, office buildings, and so on and so forth—had someone else's name on the papers, not ours, and the names usually belonged to someone either in Louie's family or mine. But again, that's getting a long way ahead of the story—in the early sixties, even though I knew

Louie had two lives, one criminal and one legit, I was still young enough to hope that over time he would give up the first and focus on the second. Young enough? Make it stupid enough.

For the first few years we were together I believed he would stay in the beauty business because he was good at it and because that's what he said he wanted to do. And that's mostly what he did, but the time came when I could see he was getting fed up with the work. He told me he didn't like washing old ladies' hair because he could feel all the bumps on their heads. He complained about his boss, Bernie—Brooklyn was full of Bernies!—who kept him late on Saturday nights and made him do complicated jobs that took hours to set up and finish. Plus he was starting to screw up.

One of the salon sinks got clogged. Bernie poured some Draino down the hole, then soaked up what was left in the sink with a rag. Louie didn't know this, and he used the same rag to wipe some black dye off the head of one of his best customers, a lady who owned Carolina's, a restaurant in Coney Island, and when he went to rinse it her hair fell out in clumps. She stayed bald for months. Louie was so upset with himself he didn't stop worrying about it for weeks.

Another customer might have called in the lawyers, but this lady was one of Louie's most loyal regulars, and when Bernie offered to fire him for what had happened she told him that if he did any such thing she and all her friends would never come back.

Louie did my hair at the salon every Saturday. At that time I had what we called a beehive, like what just about every other girl in the country had in the sixties. Louie was a bee-hive expert. You'd be in and out of his chair in half an hour. First the wash, then the dryer, then about twenty minutes of him back-combing and teasing to make the shape, and finally half a can of hairspray to hold it in place. A Louie beehive was good for a week.

One Saturday, just when Louie was about to leave for the day, Bernie told him he had to stay late because a customer had booked a last-minute appointment for a special hair treatment. Louie explained that we had plans for that night, which we did, but Bernie brushed that off. Louie flipped, pulled his diploma off the wall, and walked out. That was the end of Louie Milito, lady's hairdresser.

By now we had rented a small apartment over on Brigham Street in Sheepshead Bay. It was a ground-floor one-bedroom with a garage—Louie always had to have a garage so he could fix the cars. We still lived at home. Our parents didn't know about the place, it was just somewhere to go and be alone. I was worried my mother would find out about it, but when I told her she couldn't have been happier, because she was just as anxious for me to leave her house as I was, on top of which she and Dad were planning to move into a small apartment of their own in Canarsie, and there would be enough room in it for only my kid brother, Gary, who would live in the basement. So there would be no room for me, anyway. I could have cared less.

For months she had been going on at me about Louie, anyway: Is he serious about you? When are you getting engaged? Is he going to marry you?

I hadn't said anything about this to Louie before because I figured it was none of her business, but when I did tell him, he took me right over to Bontate's Jewelry Store so I could get measured for an engagement ring. The store was owned by a man I will call John Bontate, an older guy who I never saw before but made a big fuss over Louie when we went in. I didn't pay much attention to this because most people made a fuss over Louie, but it seemed pretty clear that they were old friends.

I wanted a 1-carat diamond, which to me at the time was a huge stone. Louie wouldn't hear of it. Wanting to impress my mother, he ordered a 2.25-carat in a ring that cost almost two thousand dollars! A big chunk of change in the sixties.

A lot of things happened that summer. For one thing, I'm pretty sure this was when Louie started building his connection with the Gambino Mafia family—not as a made member, you understand, it was too early for that, but as someone worth watching, the kind of stand-up guy they could take into the membership when they figured he was ready—and I guess the connection must have come either through John Bontate, who was in fact a made man and a captain with the Gambinos, or maybe it came through some other Gambino old-timer, possibly a guy we can call Benny Lima.

Benny had a son called Sal, who was about the same age as Louie and would eventually play a small part in our lives. And John Bontate had a younger son, too. In fact, he had quite a few sons, but the one we came to know best was Sonny, a lady's man who liked to impress people with his knowledge, which wasn't much, as it happened.

The four of us, Louie and me and Sonny and his latest girlfriend, were driving home from the Copa one night after seeing Tom Jones. As usual they had given us seats right up close to the stage, so close that when Tom went off I took the glass he'd left on the piano and slipped it into my purse.

"That Tom Jones guy is a real conosewer," Sonny said.

Louie looked at him.

"What's that?" he said.

"A conosewer. You know, somebody who has good taste. Like me. I'm a conosewer."

"Boy, are you dumb," Louie said. "You mean a connoisseur."

"Yeah, that's right. You got it. Conosewer."

CHAPTER
8

Take a Favor, Give a Favor

It was some time during the mid-sixties that Bontate
Senior and Benny Lima pulled off a big favor for the Milito
family, and like most of these things, it happened in a round-
about way.

That summer we started going to a new club under the el
in Bensonhurst. Later it turned into a gay bar, but when we
first went, it was a private club with a bar, a DJ, and a dance
floor. The owners were one of the Bontate brothers,
Leonard, and John Bontate was a silent partner. They had a
third guy with them called Mickey the Mutt. At first I figured he was an owner too because he acted the big shot and
treated Louie as if he were a celebrity, but after a while it
turned out that he was a junkie who worked for Bontate's
family as a gofer and sometimes helped out at John's jewelry store.

Did I understand any of this at the time? No. Did I know
that John Bontate and Benny were made men with the

Gambino crime family? No, not yet. I didn't yet know what a made man was. I didn't even know there was a Gambino family. Or any crime families. The Bonannos. The Luccheses, the Colombos, the Genoveses. Who knew about any of this except for cops and the men actually involved in organized crime? Maybe if I'd read the papers and knew about the gang wars that broke out every now and then all over New York and especially in Brooklyn, leaving bodies dumped on the streets, maybe I would have figured it out. The only time I ever read the papers was to check out the employment classifieds.

So I was just another high school dropout with a boyfriend—now my fiancé—who I knew was stealing and into some shady dealings but who I loved without reservation and who I believed (with the dopey, dreamy faith of any typical teenage girl) I could help go straight. We really could have a fairy-tale marriage; I would just ride out the storm.

Years afterwards I asked Louie why he never told me who these men were and how they lived, and he said he was worried that I would leave him because I didn't approve. Well, he was right about that. It would have frightened the life out of me. But the way I felt about him then, I can't say for sure that I would have left him. For who and for what? There would be many times later on when I wished I was dead and times when I tried to kill myself, when I begged him to kill me, but all of this came when it was too late to change anything.

So for years I figured John Bontate was just a jeweler and the other men Louie brought home or we met at nightclubs and restaurants or weddings and confirmations were just local guys no different from any others you saw on the streets.

But there was a big difference. It was Benny who helped one of Louie's aunts, who also worked in a sweatshop, get a new job after they laid her off a month before she would have qualified for a pension. I don't have a clue what he did, or how he did it, but he arranged for Louie's aunt to get another four weeks on the payroll, and the Militos had been grateful to Benny ever since. Men like Benny and John Bontate had the power to grant favors that could change someone's life. You want something from the city, you need to lose a traffic ticket or build an extension onto the back of your house without any trouble from the building inspectors, you go see someone like Benny and John, and they make your problem disappear.

That's what they did for Louie that summer—not for Louie personally but for Louie's friend Nunzio when Nunzio got his papers from the draft board. We learned about this when we went to Nunzio's house one night and found his mother in the kitchen, sobbing and hysterical. She could hardly get her breath. "They're sending Nunzio to that Vietnam place! They want to kill my Nunzio! Louie, you have to do something!"

I guess Louie must have made a call, because the next day he came up with $2,500 in cash and went to a club in Bensonhurst to meet John Bontate, who took him to Benny. According to Louie, Benny said to tell his mother to relax, they would take care of his problem with the draft board. Back then favors were important.

Like an idiot, when Louie told me about this, I asked him what Benny did for a living, and he gives me this look that makes it plain that I don't need to know. "Benny is a skipper, like John Bontate," he says.

"Skipper?" I said. "You mean like a boat captain?"

And he said it's something like that, and I should shut up about things that are not my business.

Nunzio went to see a doctor in Bensonhurst who gave him a 4F certificate for flat feet.

So Louie got a favor and Nunzio got a pass, which now meant—as Louie explained it many years later—that it's Louie, not Nunzio, who owed the Gambinos a favor in return. I know Louie was not officially hooked up at this time, he's not even an associate, he's not in any crew, but that didn't count. What mattered was that he owes them and all they have to do is wait until it's time to collect. Take a favor, owe a favor. That's how it works. This first favor was how it all got started.

What doubled the favor in this case is that when my friend Rita found out how Louie got a pass for Nunzio, she came to the apartment to see if he could fix things for her fiancé, Mario, which he did, through Bontate and Benny again, using the same doctor, whose name I don't remember except it was Italian.

So, like I say, a lot happened that summer.

I got to wear my engagement ring for maybe a couple of months before Louie told me I had to lose it.

"What are you, crazy?" I asked him.

"You'll get another ring later, a bigger one," he said. "This one has to go."

He wanted me to go to Macy's to try on some clothes and then go back to the store a couple of hours later and tell the clerk I lost the ring in the dressing room. Also to be sure the clerk noticed the ring before I went in the dressing room. I told him no way will I do this. It's bad enough he's still out trunking and fixing up stolen cars, but I didn't want any part of something like this, where I could get pinched.

He laughed in my face. "Pinch you for what? Saying you lost something in the store? You think it makes any difference to Macy's what happened to the ring? All you want out of them is a lost property report. Don't give me any argument about this. Do what you're told."

I rode the subway into Manhattan, and when I got off at 34th Street I was so nervous I nearly got run over by a police car. One of the cops sticks his head out the window and shouts something about my ass, and I turned away because I didn't want him to make my face, but they were driving along next to me, real slow, so I had to cross back over the street behind them and start walking down Broadway, away from Macy's.

I did everything Louie asked. It was easy. The woman behind the counter saw the ring and started going on about how her daughter just got a two-carat diamond from her boyfriend and how my boyfriend must really like me a lot to give me an even bigger one. If you only knew, I thought. I tried on a pile of tops and pants in the dressing room, left the store, sat in a coffee shop for a while and went back to tell them about my missing ring, which was in my bra. The whole thing made me feel like throwing up, I was so scared. My heart was hammering so hard I thought I would faint, but everything happened the way Louie said it would. A Macy's supervisor searched the dressing room, looked in the clothes I'd tried on, and found nothing. I signed the lost property form and went home.

About a month went by and Louie got a check for $1,875 from the insurance company. My ring went back to Bontate's Jewelry, and John put the stone in a new setting.

"How come it's a straight swap?" I asked Louie. You didn't have to be a genius to figure out he shared the check with John. Louie's reply to this was one I would hear a lot over the years whenever he wanted to shut me up.

I ask Louie how come it's a straight swap with the rings and he tells me what he always says when he wants me to shut me up.

"You're Jewish, you wouldn't understand."

A lot of things I didn't understand. Poor Mickey the Mutt, the Bontates' gofer, got killed three years after I met him. Some valuable pieces from the store were missing, and Mickey got the blame, what with him being a junkie and everything. Louie told me they found him dead in the trunk of a car. I asked him what happened and he said Mickey died of what Louie called an "expedited overdose," plus he had two holes in the back of his head.

I may have been young, I was certainly stupid, but I was starting to put two and two together and getting four. And most of what I found out came from Louie, who always told me never to speak to anyone about his business or his friends' business, and never under any circumstances to ask him about things that didn't concern me—and bit by bit over the years it was Louie who told me just about everything I shouldn't know about. Everything except for the murders, which he either flat out refused to discuss, or he would hit me or walk out of the house and stay out for hours. In a way, I think he was pouring his guilt or his problems onto me. Maybe he thought I could try and make it right. Or maybe he wanted someone to at least try to make him walk the straight and narrow.

If you were a man, he used to say, you would be dangerous.

It was Louie who told me a long time after he stopped doing it that he had been out on scores for John Bontate, stealing back jewelry from Bontate's customers, selling them, and splitting the take with John. He was coming home with diamond necklaces and platinum watches. One of my sisters-in-law bought several diamonds. Louie told her he got them at discount from Bontate Jewelry.

I never did fall for that one. I asked him afterwards, "Where did these diamonds come from? You stole them, right? All of this stuff is swag, don't tell me any different."

And he said, "Ah, don't worry about it, nobody's losing nothing, it's all insured."

This is where Sammy Gravano first came into my life, not personally, you understand. The fact is I didn't even know he was in it, because I still hadn't met him and I can't even be certain that I ever saw him at Mom and Pop's candy store years before this. But now Sammy was like what they call an offstage presence—he was in my life because he was working the Bontate scores with Louie. This isn't something Louie told me at the time, it was many years afterwards. They were together when they broke into a house on Bedford Avenue where nobody was supposed to be home. Years later I was questioned about that: I was asked if I knew that while Louie was opening the safe, the old lady woke up and Sammy put a pillow over her face until she stopped breathing.

Killing that old lady was one murder Sammy never mentioned when he finally rolled over for the feds. And I didn't know.

Not that Louie was any better. I've always wondered who killed Mickey the Mutt. I know Louie met with Mickey the night he disappeared—he told me when he left the house that he had to see him about some business. He never once mentioned his name again, and the only time I brought it up, he said Mickey was a no-good junkie who couldn't be trusted to keep his mouth shut, and sooner or later somebody had to kill him. By then I could pretty much read Louie's face. You could tell this was one of those things he didn't want to talk about anymore.

I don't have any excuses for what I did with Louie. Maybe I didn't do any burglarizing or trunking, but I helped him with the paperwork for the cars, and even if I was still working five days a week in the city and earning my own money, I was also living off what he made from stealing and walking around with the new ring we got after the insurance score.

Guys would call the apartment. "Tell Louie I need a red Porsche," or "Ask him if he can fix me up with a white Corvette." He and Sonny would go driving around looking for swag cars to match up with the fake titles and sometimes I'd be in the backseat while they wired up the car and drove it back to our garage.

All of it bothered me, only I didn't want to think about it. A thousand times he must have told me, "Lynda, you worry too much. You're giving yourself problems. Relax. You think I don't know what I'm doing here? You think I'm not careful?"

I didn't worry enough to do anything, that was the problem. I kept on hoping it would disappear.

The telephone scam started when he came home with a pay phone that looked like it had been ripped off a wall someplace, because it had wires hanging out the back. As usual I asked him what the hell he thought he was doing now, and as usual he told me to shut up and pay attention. Then he emptied a big brown paper sack onto the table.

"I got a present for you," he said. "Your new hobby."

It was a box of paints, brushes, and some boards with out-lines of pictures drawn on them. Pictures of mountains, seashores, ships, castles, flowers, and so on and so forth, and they were broken up into sections with numbers all over the pages. To myself I'm thinking, What the hell is this?

"I'm going to be working at home for a while," he says. "It means concentrating. No talking. No TV. No music. You're the one who's always saying you could be some kind of artist—this here will help you pass the time." I guess he was trying to keep me busy, distract me.

It was true, I had always liked color and design. But I knew nothing about art, I'd never even thought about the possibility of going to an art school. In fact, I'm not even sure if I knew such places existed when I was growing up. Where I come from, growing up was about getting a job after school, marrying someone who worked for a living, and then raising a family between us.

"What's this?" I go. "Painting by the numbers? I don't have any time for this shit."

Anyway, I was sitting at the table looking at this pay phone on the kitchen table and thinking that if he's going around rip-ping public telephones off the wall he has to be nuts. But that's not what he had in mind.

When you put coins in a pay phone they fall in the money box, which is behind a little door or cover plate on the front. The telephone company puts special locks on these cover plates. Louie's idea was to open the doors and take out the money boxes, which are just sitting there loose, not even bolted in or anything.

I was listening to this and not believing it.

"This is illegal," I told him.

"It's white-collar crime," he said. "It's not stealing, it's manipulating money out of people. If the telephone com-pany don't want people taking the change, why are they put-ting it out there?"

You couldn't argue with this guy.

In some ways Louie was highly intelligent. Sure, he could make incredibly stupid mistakes, and he made many of them, but he was also a perfectionist in his work, and when it came to scheming he was in a class of his own. By the time he stopped working the swag car scam he was using a silver dollar and a rubber mallet to make an official-looking seal on the paperwork. You couldn't get away with that now but in those less sophisticated years I don't recall anyone questioning it. He also made his own notary stamps. He bought perfectly forged titles, fifty at a time, and sold them for $150 each. For metal VIN plates, which he made himself, he also got $150. VIN is a vehicle identification plate. It's located at the bottom of the front windshield on the driver's side. The VIN plate conincides with the numbers on the motor. Louie would take a number punch to the plate and a sledgehammer to the motor to make both sets of numbers match. He knew how to fix things when they broke. That was one of his talents, taking pieces of metal and making something useful out of them. He made all his own tools and the picks had to be precise.

For the pay phone score he needed hard steel picks to open the locks. He made these out of Allen wrenches and spent close to three months working nights in the garage at Brigham Street, in Sheepshead Bay, Brooklyn, grinding and filing them down, heating them with a blowtorch and bending up the ends with a vise. You'd go in there and find him inspecting the finished picks with a magnifying glass and then tossing the piece out because it wasn't right.

By now we had a heap of cover-plate locks and he'd sit at the kitchen table with a pick inside a lock, trying to get it open. I wasn't allowed to talk or make any noise while he did this. He needed to concentrate on listening to the tumblers fall inside the locks. No music, no TV, no radio. The phone had to be off the hook so nobody could call in. If I wanted to talk to anyone I had to go out. Mostly I was sitting at the table filling in the stupid numbers on the paintings, which I got pretty good at after a while. In fact, after I finished the first bunch I started doing movie star collages, which was basically sticking photographs of my favorites onto pictures I painted myself without using the numbers.

Every night he had his head jammed against a cover plate, listening and poking around with the picks. You could hear it clicking a couple of times, then the pick would snap and he'd go back to the garage and start over.

When I told him I was fed up with painting he bought me a couple of parakeets, Lulu and Bobo, and pretty soon they knew how to perch on my fingers and walk around the house, just like little people. They could fly but for some reason they liked walking more. They also liked being with Louie when he came in from the garage, and that's what I remember best from that time: him working with the picks and the two birds sitting on his head and bobbing up and down until I was laughing so hard he would get mad and the birds would both take off and start squawking at him from the other side of the room.

So we had a few laughs while he worked on the boxes, but the only money coming in at this time was from my new job as a showroom assistant for Lucy Bongiorno, who was a dress designer for Adrian Tabin on Broadway at 39th Street. I had to stop with the employment agency because they wanted me to run around some of the worst neighborhoods in New York City collecting unpaid bills from their deadbeat clients, and after a couple of times being scared half to death doing that, I figured I should quit while I was still breathing.

Louie wasn't bringing anything into the house while he worked on the locks, which made me happy because it meant he wasn't out stealing, and for a while I started kidding myself that if the pay phone score didn't work out, he might decide it was time to give up on crime and go legit. Maybe in the car business, because both of us were good with cars and we could make money from cars without doing anything illegal.

Or if not cars, he could get into something he always told me he wanted to be—a veterinarian. I would support him while he trained to be a vet, I would support him at anything he tried. "Forget about it," he said. "I don't have the education, I'm too old to go back to school."

Years later, a therapist told me that this kind of thinking on my part is what they call wishful thinking, and is almost as useful to a person as not thinking at all. Maybe if somebody had told me this thirty years earlier, my life would have turned out differently, although considering that thirty years earlier I never paid any attention to advice I didn't want to hear, I doubt it.

Louie didn't quit with the locks. He never quit with anything once he got started. The only reason he didn't go out and start picking the phones sooner was because he wasn't ready yet, he didn't feel he was fast enough. His plan was to get into the booth, pick the lock, and take out the box with the money, and he figured he would be good enough when he could do this in a minute or less.

One night I got home from work and he was waiting in the kitchen with his coat on.

"Look at this," he said. He had maybe a half dozen cover plates spread out on the table and he'd opened the locks on every one of them.

I remember being tired out that day. My boss, Lucy Bongiorno, had me showing dresses for customers in the morning and running around on errands the rest of the day, so all I wanted to do was order in some pizza, watch TV, and go to bed. We had buyers coming in from out of town early the next morning and Lucy wanted me there when they arrived.

"Keep your coat on," Louie says, "you're coming out with me. I need you to watch out while I pick these phones."

I told Louie I wasn't leaving the house. Helping out with paperwork on the swag titles was bad enough, but at least it wasn't something you did on the street or somewhere else in public. The idea of standing outside a place while Louie was inside robbing it scared me to death. I told him to get one of his friends to go, I couldn't do it.

"I don't want to hear that shit," he says. "Either you come with me or you can get the fuck out of here right now."

That was the thing with Louie: When he started getting that hard look on his face, you never knew what to expect. I was scared more of him than I was of us getting pinched, and he knew it. He also knew I had nowhere to go. And most of my friends were the wives or girlfriends of his friends, so I couldn't turn to them. I had already figured out that when you move in those circles and a couple splits up, it's the woman who gets shut out, not the man.

So that was my first night out picking phones with Louie. It wasn't hard work. In those days most of the pay phones around New York had folding doors. If you closed the door all the way the light went on. Louie picked the phones in the dark, keeping the door half-open so the light stayed off, and I stood outside with my back to the door. If someone came too close and looked like they wanted to use the phone I had to say, "We gotta go," which was the signal for him to leave.

He was bringing home maybe ten or twelve money boxes every time we went out. If the box wasn't full or mostly full he left it there and closed up the box so the telephone company guy couldn't tell someone had been screwing with the lock.

Maybe stealing money boxes out of pay phones doesn't sound like such a big deal, but Louie always said it was a lot safer than robbing banks, which he considered one of the dumbest crimes there is, on account of the risk. And we're not talking small change here with the telephones—on a typical day he's bringing home over a thousand dollars and he's doing that around four times a week, sometimes more. Two hours' work every day and sixty seconds or less to get the box out. This was no white-collar crime, this was flat-out robbery, and I knew that if Louie got caught he would be in serious trouble.

He was working in Jersey, in all five boroughs of New York, and sometimes in Connecticut and Pennsylvania. Being his lookout wasn't the only job he gave me. I also had to spend two or three hours a night wrapping up coins. The wrappers came in three colors I will never forget: blue for nickels, green for dimes, and orange for quarters. After a while I got so fast I'd be sitting on the floor, watching TV and separating the coins into heaps then dropping them into the wrapper and tucking in the ends. We had a red sculptured-type wall-to-wall carpet in the living room with a gold rug by the couch. The rug got such a bad stain on it from the coins and the print off the wrappers that we had to keep shifting the couch over it so it wouldn't show, and in the end we threw out the rug because it ran out of clean parts.

The only problem with the telephones was getting rid of the coins, which were coming in faster than they were going out. We had rolls stacked up in the closets, in the refrigerator, inside the furniture—they were everywhere. Louie found a couple of guys at Brooklyn banks who were friends of friends in the neighborhood. They took most of the coins and gave him back bills. The rest he changed all over New York where he knew the people in candy stores, car washes, diners, gas stations, and Laundromats. He didn't ever deal with anyone he didn't know.

Basically we had a lot of paper money stashed away at different places, including in his mother's attic in a leather briefcase. I don't think she knew it was up there; I don't think anybody except us ever knew about it, just as nobody except us knew he was out picking phones. And the coins came in useful, too. I was driving on the Belt Parkway one morning when a patrol car pulled me over for speeding. It was the same cop I mentioned before, the one from the Six Two Precinct who didn't mind settling things out of court. I gave him a five-dollar roll of dimes and drove home.

Louie bought a bunch of coin catalogs and collection books, which had holes in the pages for rare coins, and he sorted these out from the change after washing them in battery acid. So now he was a coin collector. All the time he

was robbing phones he was dying to find a three-legged buf-
falo nickel, but never did.

Louie was still a long way from being a made man with the
Gambinos at the time he was picking phones, even though
he was probably making his stripes, getting a name for himself, by handing over a percentage of the take. By the time
he got out of the phone scam he'd been pinched twice for
burglar tools and locked up in Riker's Island and the Manhattan Correctional Center. My guess is that he probably
killed people even before he got in with the Gambinos. In
fact, I don't doubt it, since nobody gets straightened out with
a Mafia family without killing at least once.

So I figure he was turning over money to the Gambinos long
before Carlo Gambino took him in as a soldier—the Nose,
that's what Louie called the old man, except he used a long Italian word I don't remember and never could pronounce. This
was filtered through Bontate and a lot of money went to the
Nose. I would go to take a few rolls of quarters to buy something for the apartment or for myself, and Louie would make
me put it back. "You can't touch that. That money's got somebody's name on it." Or he'd tell me to put a few hundred bucks
together because he had to give a bag of cash to some guy for
the Nose, so I'd count it out and he'd be out the door with it.

Louie wasn't in the Mafia yet, he was just paying his way
up the ladder.

It was around this time that we started seeing a lot more of
the Bontate family. They lived in a big house right on the
Brooklyn waterfront, and just about every Sunday we went
there for dinner, which started late in the afternoon and lasted
most of the night. At the table, it was John Bontate, his wife,
Carol, their two sons, then Louie, me, and Carol's mother,

who everyone calls Grandma, and her brother when he's sober. Uncle Patsy slept in the basement, and Louie and the Bontate boys were always creeping around down there and scaring the hell out of him for laughs, which struck me as mean. I asked Louie to quit it but he didn't take any notice.

We always sat in the same places, with John at the head of the table. Being the only females at the table, Carol, Grandma, and me didn't count, it was the men who did most of the talking, which was mostly about cars and food and people with Italian names I never heard of.

I sure liked Carol Bontate. She was one of the kindest and smartest women I ever knew, and we hit it off immediately. I only wish my mother could have been more like her. Carol never talked down to people, she didn't put on airs, she was just a good person, and I really enjoyed being with her. Also she was completely different from her husband; she was more dignified for one thing. John dressed beautifully and reminded me of Vic Damone, but for all his polish and handsome face he sometimes acted more like a big kid than a man with two grown sons.

Louie worshiped him. He was like a puppy dog waiting to be taken out for a walk. It kind of surprised me, seeing how he buttered him up. "Gee, John, that sauce you made is fantastic! Lynda, you gotta get the recipe for this."

I thought, Who's he kidding? The first meal I cooked for Louie was southern fried chicken, which made him so sick he stayed in bed three days. After that he did the cooking and cleaned up afterwards, and the only time I went near the kitchen after that was to heat water for the coffee. Now all of a sudden he wants recipes?

This was a side of Louie I'd never seen before. He'd follow Bontate around in the kitchen while the old man cooked dinner—he was the cook in that house, or he was on Sundays, anyway—and Louie would be listening to every word, as if Bontate were the pope or the president, which to Louie he probably was because by then he had to know that John was made with the Gambino people.

One Sunday, it must have been sometime in 1965, the two of us were alone in the dining room and all the men were out in the kitchen. Carol Bontate tried telling me what I was getting into.

She stood up and closed the door.

"Lynda, I have to tell you something. Between you and me, okay? And please don't take it the wrong way, and don't say anything to nobody. You must promise that."

"Okay. Sure. What?"

I couldn't help wondering what was coming. Carol was a lot older than me, and because I never heard a dumb word out of her mouth, I had a lot of respect for her opinions. Now she's got a very serious look on her face.

"You don't belong here. You and Louie should stay away from my husband."

We were sitting on the couch and she was holding both my hands, looking straight at me. I didn't know what to make of the situation. I didn't know what to say.

"Why?"

"Look, for all I know, Louie's a very nice guy, and I can see you're crazy about him. But if he's anything like my husband, you're not going to want this kind of life. You deserve more. It's no way to live if you want children. It's not good for them, it's not good for you. I'm telling you. It just destroys everything."

I didn't have any idea what she meant. This kind of life? What was wrong with it? The Bontates had it all, as far as I could see. Money, a big house, cars, businesses. John Bontate was an important and successful businessman. He got a lot of respect from people. He knew how to make things happen. He had power and influence. To me it looked as if the Bontate family life was a big-time success. I thought, What else is there?

Carol Bontate was very smart. She must have known a whole lot more about Louie's dealings with her husband and his sons than I did. Her warning went straight in one ear and out the other.

CHAPTER 9

What Do You Know, You're Jewish

Louie was nuts about guns and hunting, they were among his biggest passions. He must have subscribed to every gun and hunting magazine in America—and he kept every copy, even after the kids were born. Nobody was allowed to touch those magazines.

When he went hunting he usually took a crossbow with him plus a collection of knives and guns. The knives were for skinning deer and cutting up the meat, which he sometimes did in the woods before coming home. Most often he'd bring the deer home and skin it in his mother's garage. He killed a deer once with the bow, and it made me feel sick when he told me. When he barbecued the meat I couldn't eat it. I told him it would be like eating Bambi.

"Ah, what do you know, you're Jewish."

We used to go to a Brooklyn carhop joint at 86th Street and 7th Avenue called Mitchell's where you sit in the car and the girl brings food on a tray. Louie had been having some kind of beef with Doc, the guy who ran Mitchell's. It wasn't serious, just some back-and-forth about Louie's friends and why didn't they quit scaring the girls by driving their cars at them and why the service at Mitchell's took a decline. The arguments had been going on for a while and Louie wanted to put Doc in his place. One weekend he shot a black bear in the Adirondacks, and, with Butchie Hollywood's help, they managed to stuff it into the trunk of Doc's car, which was parked around the back. Then Louie took the air out of Doc's tires. Louie was laughing so hard I thought he would give himself a heart attack. People who were there when Doc went to take his jack out of the trunk to fix the flat said his cursing could be heard all the way to Coney Island.

We were married November 23, 1966, in the chambers of Judge Hyman Barshay of the New York State Supreme Court. We didn't tell our families about the wedding, so it was just the two of us plus Sonny, who stood up for Louie, and Sonny's ex-girlfriend, Carla Mancini, who before this used to be Mickey the Mutt's girlfriend. Carla stood up for me.

It wasn't the dream wedding I'd wanted, with a bridal gown and bridesmaids, a banquet and an orchestra with hundreds of guests, but that was okay by me because now that I was married I was officially out of my mother's house, and that's all I cared about. And it was okay with Louie, too. We both knew that a big wedding meant family problems because of the difference in our religions. It would have been his mother wanting the church and a Catholic wedding, my family wanting the chapel in the catering hall and a Jewish service. Who needed it? But I have to say I was disappointed anyway, and for one reason only—that I didn't get to dance with my father at my wedding, which I know would have made me so proud and made him so happy.

No sooner do we sign the papers in the judge's chambers than Louie takes off with his friends to go hunting in Pennsylvania. We would go to Florida for a couple of weeks' honeymoon afterwards.

I went back to work with Lucy Bongiorno, showing dresses for the customers, which was something Louie always laughed at because he said I was too skinny to be a model. "You got Biafra arms," he used to say, and when I asked him what this meant, he said that Biafra was a place in Africa where everyone was starving. He made me eat Carnation Instant Breakfasts and heavy cream, which he brought home by the case, but it made no difference, my weight stayed the same, at around ninety-eight pounds.

Maybe three days before the wedding, an attorney we knew, Charlie Lo Bianco, called up the apartment and asked for Louie. I wasn't paying much attention to Louie's end of the conversation but I noticed he went very quiet after he picked up the phone. He was just nodding his head and listening. When he hung up I asked if there was a problem, and he said some woman had told the police she saw him shoot a guy in a bar. She picked his photograph out of a book at the Six Two Precinct station.

I just looked at him.

"Don't worry about it, Charlie's taking care of it. He's putting a squash on the deal."

"What's a squash?" I asked him, and he said it's when someone changes their mind.

"Did you do it?" I said.

"I didn't do nothing, she's got me mixed up with someone else."

Then he goes into the bedroom and tells me to bring out the Tupperware container where we keep the sugar, which I did. He came back in the room with an automatic pistol and buried it under the sugar.

He was doing this, he said, in case the cops broke into the place while we're on our honeymoon.

I was so gullible I didn't even make a connection with the gun and the phone call from Charlie Lo Bianco, or maybe I made the connection and put it in the box in my brain where

I kept other stuff I was too scared to ask Louie about—like the ruby-and-diamond set of cuff links and tie tack that Charlie bought afterwards for Louie. What was that for? Who cared? It went in the box along with everything else I didn't want to think about too hard. My priority was to make it work with Louie. All I cared about was the wedding, our honeymoon, and our marriage.

Charlie called again the day before the wedding. I was alone in the apartment.

"Have Louie call me," he said. "Tell him the witness changed her mind."

We never talked about this again. I knew better. You could go so far with questions and then you could go too far and you had a serious problem. So I didn't say anything, but I've always wondered why, if Louie had no criminal record up until that point, and he always swore he didn't, how come the cops had his picture in a book? And I didn't ask him about that, either.

My therapist tells me I wasn't in denial, I was way past it, and she's right. I never tried to find out the truth about the case against Louie, if there was a case. I could have called Charlie to see if there was more to it than Louie told me, and of course there had to be more, but I didn't. And even if I had called Louie and he flat out told me—or someone else told me—that he was a murderer, would I have left him then? I don't know, but I guess I would have refused to believe it. You don't believe what you can't bring yourself to believe, but somewhere in my mind I must have accepted it as a possibility and then put it in that box in my brain with everything else I didn't want to think about. What would you do if you loved a man with all your heart, like I loved Louie, and somebody told you he was a killer? What would you do?

My way of dealing with it was to pretend that I could handle everything. The hardest part was trying not to notice that I was in over my head.

❖   ❖   ❖

Right after he got back from his hunting trip we drove to Florida in a two-tone Buick Electra 225, what we called a Deuce and a Quarter, a real workhorse of a car. One of the guys stole it for our wedding present and Louie changed the title and tags. Before leaving Brooklyn he threw his hunting rifles plus a .38 and a .45 in the trunk, so now we had a trunk-load of guns. His plan was to go and shoot deer and alligators in the Everglades.

We stopped at my parents' house and I put a note on my father's pillow, telling him I was sorry we didn't tell them before about getting married, and saying how I'd call when we get back from Florida. I asked Louie if he wanted to go by his house and tell his family, and he said to forget about it. He didn't need to explain why, it would have been the last thing his mother wanted to hear, and knowing that just cut right into me.

We no sooner came out of the Jersey side of the Holland Tunnel than he pulled into a rest area and parks near a couple of pay phones on the side of a building. He had the money boxes out in no time, and shoved them inside his jacket, and we were back on the turnpike heading south. I was furious with him and didn't show it. He would have said I was trying to jinx him, make him screw up so he couldn't concentrate, and this would have made him mad.

Louie lived in dread of being jinxed—he was the most superstitious man I ever knew. He wore one of those Italian good-luck horns around his neck to ward off evil spirits. He avoided black cats and ladders, and on the dashboard of our car—the car we drove to Florida on our honeymoon—there was a little metal box of Jewish doodads of some kind that he found in one of his other swag cars.

I said nothing about taking the money out of the boxes. But that's how we paid for the honeymoon, robbing pay phones.

In Virginia I made him call home to tell his mother about the marriage.

How did she take it? I asked him when he came back to the car. Was she surprised? Is she happy?

Louie wasn't saying anything, so I asked him again.

What did she say?

"She told me I should take one of the guns out the trunk, shoot you, and then blow my brains out."

I thought my mother was hard. Compared to Louie's mother, she was a cream puff. I felt like throwing up in the car. To say such a thing! Here we were, just married, and I'm thinking, This is it, I'm free of the past, now we have a new life stretching out in front of us, it's something to celebrate, and even if we did get married without our families present, they had to understand we were happy about what we'd done and I figured they would be happy for us. So I couldn't understand his mother's response—how she must have hated me for marrying her favorite son! I stared out the window and blinked back the tears, squeezing my eyes shut to keep them from running down my face. We didn't talk for a long while. After about a hundred miles, Louie said, You okay? and I told him I was fine.

We checked in at the Holiday Inn in Miami carrying $1,600 in coins and some special hunting boots and hunting clothes he bought at one of those army surplus stores. Nothing weighed less than twenty pounds. Louie was on the phone the minute we get in the room, calling up information to get a guide for the Everglades. Then he remembered some Bensonhurst guy who moved down to Florida, Ray Zuto, so he called him up and the next thing you know we're driving up to their house in Dania, near Fort Lauderdale.

The place was so scuzzy inside I didn't know what to say. You go into a stranger's house and you want to be polite and say something nice about the place, but this one looked like somebody drove a truck through it. The guy was a mechanic, so he was all greasy from being under cars all day, and although his wife tried to be nice, she didn't smell too good, plus both of them were way older than Louie and me, so we didn't have much to talk about after we said hello. I guess they were having a tough time.

Usually this kind of situation would make me so uncomfortable I would have to leave, but I found I didn't care. Now I was content. I wasn't Louie's girlfriend anymore. I wasn't this kid who some of his friends in Brooklyn called "Jailbait" whenever they saw me. I was Mrs. Louie Milito, I was crazy about my husband, and if he was a thief and a murderer, there was nothing I could do to change that. Ray and Anna Zuto were friends of his, the first we met together after the wedding. I could see that Louie was proud to introduce me to them as his wife. And he was my husband for better and for worse, and I wasn't worried about anything or anyone else.

We were up at five the next morning to go meet the guide for the Everglades. This was the last place I wanted to be, but Louie wasn't taking no for an answer. He was still pissed off about the previous night, our so-called first night out on the town. The drinking age in Miami was twenty-one and I was nineteen. We were bounced out of a nightclub after I gave them my driver's license. For all I know it may have been the same in Brooklyn, but in the clubs we went to back home, nobody cared about our age. But every place we tried to get into in Miami, they turned us away because I was too young.

I guess Louie must have been expecting a night of romance back in the hotel, but for some reason I had a tickle in my throat and couldn't stop coughing. I coughed so hard he couldn't get to sleep, and in the end he pushed me out of the bed and told me to stay in the bathroom for the night and keep the door shut. I cried myself to sleep.

This was a long way from the honeymoon of my dreams. This was the side of Louie that I hated. And that scared me.

I don't care if I never see the Everglades again. Nothing but sky, water and mud and a few trees in the middle of a big swamp. I was there twice on the honeymoon and that's too much for any normal person who's not crazy about open-air situations. The Catskills, okay, you have your forest and your mountains and so forth. There are stores and houses, with roads and traffic. There are people to look at in the Catskills. In the Everglades there is nothing to look at, and Louie, who cheered up as soon as we got there, was trying to tell me it's the most beautiful place in the world. I couldn't see it.

For one thing, he made me wear the army surplus outfit he read about in a magazine article about hunting in the Everglades. It's for protection, he said. I was wearing leggings, boots with loafers inside the boots, a bomber jacket, wool pants because of the mosquitoes, which never showed, as it happens, and I also had a fall tied into my hair. On top of which I had to carry all the bullets and shells in the jacket pockets because I was the only one of us who could swim.

We drove a million miles with the guide in a swamp buggy because it seems that there was a drought in the Everglades that year and the water wasn't where they normally keep it. And when we found some water, the guide told Louie he couldn't take the both of us on his airboat at the same time because he didn't count on Louie showing up with all the guns and equipment he brought with him. They left me and a couple of the guns in the truck while the guide dropped Louie off on some rocks and then came back for me.

Before we got there I could hear Louie yelling. This was followed by a lot of gunfire. It sounded as if he were in a war. He was shouting, almost screaming. "Get me out of here!" There were snakes all over the rocks, water moccasins, Louie told me afterwards, and some were dead and some were still crawling around. Louie was still shooting at them with a couple of pistols when he jumped on the airboat, which almost immediately got stuck in the mud, forcing him and the guide to get out and push it until we could get it started again.

For Louie this was the biggest adventure of his life; he

loved every minute. I hated it. I was listening to him making
arrangements with the guide to do it again the next day and
I thought, I'm staying by the hotel pool.

But that was another thing with Louie. When he was
happy and having a good time he wanted me to be with him.
I did, too, because I loved being with him—most of the time,
anyway. I just wasn't the type of girl who liked guns, hunting, and running around in swamps and woods like he did.
Maybe he thought if I tried harder I would get to enjoy being
outside, and because I wanted to please him I didn't make a
big thing out of it at four the next morning when he tells me
it's time to go meet the guide again.

The second time we went it's worse than before, it was like
a rerun of yesterday except we went on a swamp buggy,
which sunk into the mud ten yards from where we'd started
out, so now we had to walk to some special tree where the
guide says he made some kind of platform in the branches
for people to shoot ducks from. We walked for hours. My
feet were getting sucked under. Louie and the guide were
way ahead of me. The sun came up and I was wearing the
same outfit as yesterday but with extra bullets in the pockets. I was sweating to death.

I couldn't walk another step. I found a place where the
mud wasn't too deep, sat down and took off the bomber
jacket and the boots and the wool pants which I wore over
shorts. Louie came running back.

"Are you okay?" he says.

"Am I okay? I'm fucking dying here."

I must have looked like the creature out of the Black La-
goon. He was so anxious it made me stop being mad at him.

"Come on, baby, it's not far. I'll help you."

When we reached the special tree with the duck shooting
platform it turned out to be a really skinny tree with climb-
ing pegs stuck in the sides. Louie turned to me and said,

"Lynda, climb the tree and point where the deer is." I told him no way. I was afraid of heights. Louie puts two guns over his shoulders. The tree bent over from the weight. I was laughing my ass off and he's looking at me and getting closer to the ground because the tree's folding up. That's when the guide said he didn't think this was a good idea, and partly from his slow southern accent and also because of the sight of Louie hanging almost upside down on the tree, it put me into a fit of hysterics that kept breaking out all the way back to the hotel. Louie really didn't think it was funny, he was paying for this.

So those were my two trips to the Everglades.

Louie went on his own a couple of days before we drove back home. I stayed at the hotel and spent most of the day around the pool. At about six that night he called from the lobby and said he needed some help with a deer he'd shot. He had already skinned it, cut it up, and put the meat in a big cooler, which he left outside the hotel. He wanted me to carry the thing through the lobby and upstairs in the elevator because the cooler had sprung a leak and he was too embarrassed to be seen carrying it.

In the end Louie had to carry it, anyway, because I couldn't lift it off the floor, so he had me walking in front, trying to shield him while the cooler dripped blood all across the carpet of the lobby, which was filled with people staring at us.

Up in the room he called a bellboy, gave him ten dollars, and asked for ten buckets of ice and a sack of salt. Also tinfoil and big black garbage bags. Then he dumped the ice in the bathtub, scraped the rest of the fur off the meat, wrapped all the pieces in tinfoil with salt inside, and covered them with ice. I don't know what the maids thought when they came to clean the bathroom, but I sure was glad we checked out before they arrived.

Louie bought a new cooler and filled it with dry ice for the drive back to New York. All the way home he picked telephones again, but he was in a hurry, so we didn't stop too

Louie listened to this, he's nodding his head like he understood, then he gave me a backhand and I was on the floor. My head was spinning, I couldn't see straight. It felt as if someone had hit me with a bag of hammers. Louie walked out of the house.

This was the second time I remember him hitting me, and just like the first time, in my mother's basement when I screwed up with the car paperwork, I asked myself: I'm the one here who's in the wrong?

I didn't know what to do for the best. There was nobody I could call. I didn't want any of our friends to know, and there was no going home to my mother. There was no way out of this situation that I could see. I've been married for maybe a month to a man who I'm crazy about and who at the same time frightens me to death, and I don't know what to do about any of it.

Living with Louie was like riding a roller coaster—it wasn't the ups and downs that scared me so much as the fear that the car would jump the tracks and take us both with it.

There was half a bottle of scotch in the kitchen. I'd never been a drinker but that night I emptied what was left in the bottle. I don't know what I was thinking. Maybe I was hoping it would kill me. Except for my job, which I loved because Lucy treated me so kindly, I felt like I didn't have any control over my life. Suddenly—and it was very sudden, I was shocked by how quickly it had happened—I felt there was nothing in my life that I wanted, including life itself.

Somehow I ended up in the bathtub with all my clothes on and I was still there when Louie got back and woke me up. It must have been almost daylight. I had thrown up on myself. My arms were all bruised and scratched up and I couldn't think straight.

"What the fuck you been doing?" he said. "I got some change you have to roll up."

Then he brushed his teeth and went to bed.

I fell asleep sorting out the coins and putting them into the wrappers.

There were no apologies from Louie when he woke up hours later. I was used to that by now. Neither one of us said a word about what had happened. You can say, Well, this woman's pathetic, she hasn't got the guts to stand up for herself. And you would be right. I didn't. I thought I was pretty tough in my own way but I was finding out that my strength was useless, because it was mostly about proving that I was right and everyone else was wrong. I *had* to be right about getting married when I did and marrying the man I did. I refused even to consider the possibility that I was wrong about that, just as I refused to believe that I couldn't make a success out of a marriage that was already beginning to look more and more like a death trap.

As I think about it now, it may have been that Louie was testing me to see how much I could take, which sounds insane, but I can't think of any other reason why he behaved the way he did—the violence all mixed up with the love and the sweet, gentle kindness that was so much more a part of his everyday nature—to explain why he stayed with me. And if there was a test, I must have passed it, because for the next twenty-some years, the only times we were separated was when he was in prison. He stayed with me, I stayed with him. Anything else would have been unthinkable to either one of us. Both of our parents had stayed together, as unhappy as they were. Back then you just stayed put.

We both wanted children. I wanted them because they would bring more life into the house. I wanted someone else there when Louie was out at all hours of the night. Maybe it sounds kind of dumb, but I also thought a baby would be company for Lady, the world's softest Doberman. And I'm sure I hoped having a child would make the marriage stronger, and I'm also sure I didn't share these thoughts with Louie. But he agreed that we should start a family, and from then on he stopped wearing condoms, which was our normal method of birth control. I didn't use the pill because Louie said it hadn't been perfected yet and he was afraid it might give me cancer or some other terrible disease. I remember when Louie and I were together intimately for the first time. I had to cover up the fact that I wasn't a virgin because of the rape with Frankie La Fonda. I had to make sure Louie and I first slept together when I was on my monthly cycle. I had to make it so that it looked like I was a virgin, so that there would be no mention of why I wasn't. And it took a lot of thinking on my part to hide it from Louie. To this day, I never told him.

I got pregnant in August 1967, the year after the wedding. Louie was as pleased as I was, but that didn't mean the testing was over.

"You want the money for that baby to be born in a hospital, you have to come and work watch-out with me for the phones," Louie said.

The thought of driving all over the city and standing watch while he broke into pay phones scared me to death. I told him I couldn't do it. What if I get caught? I said. What if I end up having the baby in prison?

"Lynda! Stop putting the jinx on everything! It won't happen. And if it does, you'll have the baby in prison."

I was terrified. I begged him not to make me go with him.

"I'm telling you, you want this baby born in the hospital, you gotta help earn the money. End of story."

I gave up the day job with Lucy Bongiorno. The way Louie was working the phones, he was out almost every night of the week until two or three in the morning. That's how it was all through that winter, with me expecting he would get pinched every time he went out. When I was eight months pregnant I told him he shouldn't do it anymore, but he continued with guys he knew.

Our daughter, Deena, was born at Maimonides Hospital in Borough Park, Brooklyn, in April 1968. They had to use the forceps on her, so she came out bruised, with a black eye. When Louie arrived he took one look and yelled at the nurses, "That's not my baby!"

But she was, and maybe because of the way she looked

when he first saw her, he felt she needed special care and attention.

Louie was a good father. By that I don't mean he took the baby with him whenever he went out, because he didn't start doing that until Deena was about three, but he played with her and he paid attention to her if I left them alone in the house. He refused flat out to change diapers.

"I don't want to see any of that," he used to say. "That's your job." Louie had a weak stomach.

One day when I had to go to the store and Deena had been suffering from a severe diaper rash, he asked me to take off the diaper and leave her nude on the rubberized sheet in the crib. "She had a little accident," he said when I came home, "but I dried her off."

And he had, too, so, like I said, Louie paid attention to the baby instead of just sitting on the couch watching TV while I was out. Once Louie got mad with me over the baby after I gave her a toy phone to play with.

"What are you, stupid?" he goes. "Look what you did here!"

Somehow she had managed to wrap the plastic telephone cord around her neck.

We had moved from Brigham Street to an apartment on Bellini Terrace a couple of years after we got married. By this time there was a lot of money hidden all over the apartment, so when the place downstairs got robbed Louie immediately found a bigger and more secure apartment over on East 92nd Street in Flatbush. Deena would have been around six months then.

About a year and a half before Deena was born, we bought the first of our two Dobermans, Lady One, who we got from a retired cop in New Jersey who raised dogs and, for a cop, was a nice guy. I didn't want a big dog, I wanted something small and cute, like a toy poodle. "You can forget about that," Louie said. "I'm not going out in public with no fucking poodle."

So we got Lady, a big soft Doberman puppy that looked like it wanted to rip your face off but in reality was scared of her own shadow. The parakeets made her life hell. When she first came home she used to run away from them and hide under the bed, howling.

I called her Lady because she was beautiful and gentle and because for a big dog she was very dainty. Didn't eat like a pig, didn't tear up the place or bark all night. If you can say a dog has good manners, Lady had more than her share.

You couldn't get any closer to an animal than the two of us were. I used to tell her my troubles and she'd look at me as if she understood every word I said. If I cried she cried with me. People say somebody means the world to them, and that's how it was with Lady—and with Deena, after she was born. The three of us were a private and perfect world. And the two of them loved each other as much as I loved them. Louie, too. That was our family—him and me, our baby, Deena, Lady the dog, and the two parakeets. When Louie started doing his trick with Lady, making her laugh, the birds went crazy and Deena and me couldn't stop screaming from happiness.

But even with all of this, Louie kept working the phones.

His regular lookout became Allie Boy, who Louie had known for years from the neighborhood. Nobody would describe Allie as the world's neatest dresser, and the fact that he was bald and wore long sideburns didn't help, but he was loyal to Louie, which was what counted. Louie tried to teach him how to pick pay-phone locks, but Allie lacked the concentration, and I think his hearing and the size of his fingers made it difficult.

This was not how Allie Boy saw himself. He took his crime seriously. When he was out robbing he took a police radio scanner; in fact, he had it with him the night he went to Queens with Louie the first time Louie got pinched picking phones. My guess is that he had the radio tuned to the world series when the cops showed up.

They had Lady with them that night. Louie said it was necessary, because if the cops stopped him he could say he was walking the dog. I was dead against this. I knew Allie would take care of Lady if there was a problem, because he liked animals, and so did Louie, no question, but if something happened to my dog I could never forgive him, and I didn't want to run the risk of being put in that position. So when Louie told me he was taking Lady with them, I said he couldn't.

"Shut the fuck up," he said, "we're taking the dog."

I was asleep in bed when Allie Boy called. He's shouting down the phone, "Lynda! Lynda! Louie got pinched! You gotta call up that bail bondsman guy Al Newman and get him out!"

"What about Lady?" I said. "Where's my dog?" And Allie Boy tells me he just heard over the scanner that the cops put out an all-points bulletin to shoot the dog on sight.

"Lynda! They're saying your dog's an attack-trained Doberman!"

I didn't want to hear any more. I was so angry I was screaming. "Fuck Louie! I'm not talking to anyone until I get my dog home." Then I hung up.

I went back to bed and turned on the TV. It was one in the morning. I couldn't call Al Newman because I didn't know where to get him at that time of the night. That could wait until morning, and Louie would have to stay in jail. There was no other choice. If Lady got lost or killed because of Louie screwing up, that was the end of us, as far as I was concerned. And it might have been the end except that just when it was getting light the next morning, I heard Allie at the front door, and there was Lady with her tongue hanging out, like she's just run fifty miles.

I clearly remember asking him, "What took you so long?" And he said he waited with Lady in the car because he didn't want her loose on the streets in case the police shot her.

I was still pissed with the both of them, him and Louie. "Thank you," I said. "For once you were thinking."

The good news for Louie was that when he got pinched he didn't have any money boxes from the phones with him, which could mean big problems if they tied him in with all the phones he'd been looting over the past year or so, and I don't remember now whether he hadn't started work yet that night or if he'd gotten rid of them before the police showed up. The bad news was that they had him on the burglar-tools charge, and for this, what with him already being known from once before, when he got off with probation, he would have to do some time.

He got six months in Riker's Island. In New York and Jersey in those years, six months usually meant four months, and he got out after two when they sent him to a halfway house. I left Deena with Louie's mother when I went to see him. I couldn't leave her with my parents because they didn't know about Louie getting arrested. His mother took the news with a grain of salt. She could care less when she hears he's locked up. "Tell him not to expect any visits from me," she said. I passed this on to Louie, thinking it might help straighten him out, because he always showed his mother a lot of respect. All he said was, "That's her problem."

I couldn't sleep the night before going to Riker's, so I was already a nervous wreck when I left the house. Everything about that place scared me.

They don't let you drive to the prison, you have to take a special bus from Manhattan, and Louie's friend Ray Genco drove me to the bus stop and waited there until I got back. The whole experience was a nightmare to me. On the bus there were always a few hacks going on duty and they looked at you like you're lower than the lowest form of life. It's not bad enough you've got someone in prison, the guards wanted you to know that anyone connected to an inmate was just as guilty as the inmate.

You felt like an inmate. There were wire screens on the bus windows, so anyone looking from the outside figured that everyone on the bus was a degenerate criminal. And every time I went to Riker's, I was the only white person on the bus and I figured from the way the other people talked and dressed that they were mostly hookers and drug dealers. Actually, nobody talked, they just yelled and screamed from the time they got on until they got off.

I was too scared to look at anybody. I used to sit all the way at the back so I could jump out the emergency exit in case of trouble.

You walked into the place, and right away the hacks are on your case. Get over here, lady. Move over there, lady. You ask them a question and they don't answer. I asked one of the guards what the prisoners do during the day, and he comes back with, Nothing you need to know about, lady. This ain't no kindergarten!

You couldn't take in stuff from home or from the laundry. It had to be new from the store and sealed in packaging the way it came from the store. Some of the people brought clean underwear and socks for their relatives, but the guards tossed them out.

I was crying the first time I went into the visitors' room to see Louie but I didn't want him to notice, so I stayed outside for a while to clean up. He came into the room in dungaree pants and a T-shirt, and we sat across from each other at a table in a room full of people laughing and crying. To me it was like a crazy house in a movie.

The brave act didn't fool him. He didn't mention it in the visitors' room but that night he called me collect and said, "What were you upset about today? What's the matter?" And I told him I was scared because the prison was on an island and I was worried about something happening to him if they had a riot or something and he might not get away or he would drown in the river because he couldn't swim.

He wasn't mad with me, he said I didn't have to come back again if that's how I felt, so I stopped going after a few more visits. Louie put Ray Genco's name on the visitor list in my place.

Someone gave me the name of a woman at the Jewish Federation in Manhattan. I called her and put Louie down for the foundation's prison work-release program. She was very kind. She said she would take care of it and get back to me. But when she called, she said there was nothing they could do for Louie because he was written up as an organized-crime figure.

This really pissed me off. I gave her an earful about Hasidic diamond traders and how they controlled the market by jacking up prices. I asked her, Isn't that organized crime? The poor woman had to be thinking she was dealing with a lunatic.

"I'm sorry, Mrs. Milito, we can't help your husband."

I called Judge Hyman Barshay, the judge who married us. His secretary said she couldn't put me through to the judge but she would give him the information, and if he could do anything she would let me know. I didn't hear from her again, but a couple of weeks later Louie called to say they were transferring him to a hotel in Harlem, which was like a halfway house. Ray Genco took him a big can of Raid because the room was full of cockroaches.

He was supposed to stay in the hotel seven nights a week, but pretty soon he was sneaking home on the weekends in his Cadillac and doing pretty much the same as he was before the arrest. I told him, "Louie, if you get pinched this time, you won't be looking at any six months or halfway houses."

We knew a guy, I'll call him Danny. He was a legitimate businessman who owned a couple of gas stations and auto-parts shops around Brooklyn. I called Danny and told him we had a problem but I couldn't talk about it over the phone. He came to the house with $5,000 wrapped up in rubber bands because he figured I needed money, and he tried to make me take it even when I told him all I wanted was a letter saying he would give Louie a job, which he did. But nothing changed. When Louie wasn't working for Danny he was still going out nights trunking and dealing in swag cars, just like before.

I think the fact that he went to prison maybe in some way made me stronger or angrier or at least less scared of him than I was before, and I know it shook him up, because when I told him I would leave him and take Deena if he didn't go straight, instead of losing it and smacking me in the face, he goes, "Yeah, it's something to think about. But what can I do, I don't know anything else but this."

I told him, "Look at Ray Genco. He's got a store in Staten Island where he sells jeans. Get a hold of Ray and make a connection with the guy who supplies Ray."

That rat! He turned Louie down flat. He told him if he wanted to open a store he'd have to buy his stock through him and take a dollar a pair for his trouble. It was like take it or leave it.

Louie was so mad when he came home I thought he would punch holes in the wall. "After everything I did for that guy," he says. Which was true, because Louie taught Ray how to pick phones, and Ray got so good at it he called up the New York Telephone Company and offered to stop robbing them for a onetime payment of $50,000.

The end result is that Louie for the next couple of years made money from trunking, making up fake paperwork for the wrecks he got from scrap yards, and using the new titles for stolen cars.

All my threats turned to nothing. I didn't leave him like I said I would. There was no going back, the bridges had been burned already and we both knew it. And for a few years he never raised his hand against me.

By now he's making steady money, not so much as he got from the phones, maybe, but enough so he can pass money up the Gambino family pipeline, like he did before he went away. This was not something he talked about but I knew he was doing it—not why he did it, because at this point I still didn't know that he was paying them off to make a name for himself as an earner. It's not like we sat down together and he told me, Lynda, I have to give money to these guys so I can join the Mafia! A word that was never mentioned in our house, by the way.

In many ways Louie was a traditional Sicilian all the way through—he knew what he had to do to earn his stripes with the Gambinos and he kept his mouth shut while he did it. At least he did in those years, when he was still keeping everything from me.

By 1970, it was pretty obvious to me that we were meeting more and more important people at social functions, and it was also obvious that they regarded Louie with considerable respect. Confirmations, weddings, funerals—they were mostly the same faces, the well-dressed men and women seated around big tables, with enormous ice carvings and floral arrangements on a central table, and a couple of orchestras taking turns. Louie and me would take our seats, and men from all over the room would stop by our table to take him aside and embrace him. I have to say the cheek-kissing thing turned me off, it didn't seem right, it wasn't my idea of manly behavior. What do you know? Louie used to say, as usual. You're Jewish.

We were at the wedding of Camille Colucci and Tommy Spero, which must have been around 1971, maybe even the year before, I don't recall, but for a lot of reasons it wasn't like the typical wedding.

I knew Camille's first husband, Joe Colucci, from when I was at Lafayette High. For a while Joe's sister Jackie and me both belonged to the Delta Royales sorority, which was basically a bunch of girls in blue-and-white baseball jackets talking about boys and hair. A couple of times when I was still at school I was over by Jackie's house and met her brother Joe, who was around Louie's age. Joe was a standout handsome guy who knew it but turned it into a joke, like he didn't want anybody thinking he took himself seriously.

He was also very much on the tough side, but this was something I don't remember hearing about until after I was married to Louie and starting to learn more about who was who in that life and what they did. There were stories about Joe being connected with the Colombo people, and we would see him at clubs and so forth, usually with different girls and a couple of Colombo guys.

This was about the time when Joe Colombo, the head of the family, set up his Italian Anti-Defamation League and started marching outside of the FBI offices and newspapers in Manhattan to get them and the movie and TV people to stop using the word *Mafia*. Joe Colombo I met once at a barbecue at someone's house, and to me he seemed like a gentlemanly person, well dressed and soft-spoken, and we ran into him another time when he made a stop at our table in a restaurant in Little Italy.

Joe Colucci went to these Colombo rallies in New York. So did Louie, who joined in because a lot of his friends went and also because, like them, he figured it was a joke. But some people didn't see anything funny in the idea. Joe Colombo was a good man, but he was bringing attention to something he should have kept quiet about, and because of it he got shot in the head at one of his rallies and spent the rest of his life dribbling down his pajamas.

Louie was at the rally. He comes racing into the house and turns on the TV to see if there's anything new about the shooting. He couldn't believe such a thing would happen to someone like Joe Colombo—he told me he always figured people in Joe's position were sheltered from that kind of problem, and he said that the black photographer guy who they claim shot Joe and who was instantly killed by other guys in the crowd was basically set up and had nothing to do with it—but who knows.

"Louie," I told him, "the same thing could happen to you."

"Nah, not in a million years."

Joe Colucci got murdered earlier that same year, 1970, and there was no mystery about who killed him and why. Joe had settled down in his own way and married Camille, who was so beautiful and had such a gorgeous figure on her that every woman was jealous of her—she was just perfect, from her thick black hair to her showgirl legs. She was something you would look at. Guys couldn't stop staring at her, and one in particular, a thief called Tommy Spero, wanted her for himself. The result is that her husband, Joe Colucci, ended up dead, and Tommy Spero married Camille.

According to Sammy, the only reason Joe was killed was so that Tommy could marry his widow, and this wasn't difficult to arrange, since both Tommy's uncle and I think his father were made men with one of the New York families. All three of them got killed eventually.

Years later, Sammy Gravano told the world he shot Joe Colucci in the back of the head while they were driving around listening to a Beatles song, with Tommy Spero at the wheel. Tommy was just a soft-spoken kinda young-looking guy. At first I thought Tommy must have borrowed a pair of balls from somebody that night, because to me he was a baby-faced wimp who never got anywhere without his uncle, Shorty Spero, pulling him along. I guess you can't judge a book by its cover.

At her wedding, Camille wore a tight white gown and looked like she'd stepped off the cover of a magazine. People at the reception afterwards were standing around laughing their asses off. I said to Louie, What's the big joke here? You wouldn't understand, he said. Now I know. To them it was nothing but a joke how the groom got the bride. I think everyone knew.

They should have saved the money they spent on the reception. Everyone knew why Joe died, just like everyone knew this marriage would last all of fifteen minutes, which is about the time it took Camille to figure out that Tommy Spero was a waste of space in her life and kicked him out of it.

I didn't pay much attention to their problems, I had other things to worry about.

CHAPTER 10

All in the Family

I was now going on five months pregnant with a new baby and starting to feel that everything was getting on top of me again. I felt like I was being sucked down. It was hard to breathe normally. It was bad enough, him taking too many chances and sometimes making me part of what he did to the point where more than once I felt my own life was on the line—now I was scared of maybe being arrested myself, and that brought back all the old fears about giving birth in prison.

For some time I had been angry with Louie over a property he bought in Pennsylvania for hunting. To me this was an investment that made no sense. It was all trees and creeks and so forth, there were no houses or buildings. To Louie it was paradise because of the deer and other animals and birds he liked shooting at.

Louie had a crew come in and build a new road of red shale, nine hundred feet long from the main road to the top of a hill where he placed a big mobile home. At night he liked to drink wine and watch the fire. I tried but it didn't do much for me. He could stand outside for hours, watching birds and clouds.

"Look at this, Lynda, isn't it beautiful?" he used to say.

I couldn't see it. Everywhere you looked there was nothing but open space with trees and bugs. Lots of bugs. And you couldn't even hear traffic, so for me it was hard to feel comfortable out there in all that nothing. As a kid I had loved being in the Catskills, but now I had lost my taste for the country. My heart was in the city.

What's so beautiful? I'm thinking. How can a person want to be in a place like this?

We could have used that money to buy a house on Staten Island, which I had been begging him to do since we had Deena, but he came up with one excuse after another.

"Lynda, say I'm pinched again, what if I have to go away? I'm not putting my name on no papers for a house. We don't need a house yet."

I told Louie that with a house he would always have a garage instead of having to rent one when we lived in apartments without garages. We could have a backyard. Deena was growing into a beautiful little girl, and she lived to be outdoors, just like her father. If we had a backyard, she and Lady would have somewhere to play together. I knew about a place out on Staten Island that would be perfect.

The more I talked about this, the madder he got.

First it's the threats. No shouting, just that soft voice coming out of that hard face.

"How would you like to be fertilizer for tomatoes?"

We started on about the Staten Island house one day, and one word led to the next, and I was running for the bathroom to lock myself in when he grabbed me by the throat and held me against the wall with my feet off the floor. I couldn't breathe.

"See your neck," he says. "I could snap it in a second."

I heard that kind of thing too many times—how he could

break my arms and take my head off at the neck, how he could bury me in the woods and tell my father I ran away and left him. It got to the point where I was putting my face up against his fist, daring him to hit me, and I didn't care when he did. He's two hundred pounds of mostly muscle and I'm less than half that. Go on, I used to tell him, do your worst.

But I was still scared of Louie. After he grabbed me by the throat, I panicked. His grip was so powerful I thought he would squeeze the breath out of me. I didn't understand why he couldn't control this part of him, and I certainly did not deserve this, I started to think.

The fear made me do something I didn't believe I would ever do, no matter what.

I called my mother and told her the truth, that Louie had been hitting me and could I come and stay with them for a while. I was crying and begging her at the same time. Deena and I could sleep on the floor, I said, it didn't matter just so long as I could get out and be safe until the new baby was born. My mother listened carefully and said, "You have a baby already and there's another one on the way. Now you come to me with your problems? You stay with your husband. There's no room here, we don't want no babies here. You made your bed, now you can lie in it."

Thanks, Mom. It's just like they say, a girl's best friend is her mother.

From this I decided the only choice short of killing myself was to lose the baby. Five months pregnant or not, I didn't care. I wasn't going to bring another baby into my life.

For the next week I spent hours lifting the vacuum cleaner over my head until I couldn't hold it up any more. I lifted and dragged heavy furniture around the apartment. I don't know if any of this is what gave me a miscarriage, but something did it, because Louie came home and found me throwing up in the bathroom and there's blood and water all over the floor. It scared the hell out of him.

He took me to the Maimonides Hospital, and when the doctor arrived, Louie was so desperate he's almost on his knees to the doctor to save my life.

"Do me a favor," he said. "I don't care about this baby. The person who comes first here is my wife. Please make sure nothing happens to her."

There was no time to climb on the delivery table. I was conscious but I wasn't feeling a thing on account of being stuffed with painkillers. They held me over some kind of basin on the floor and I felt the baby come out in a splash. It was a girl. She was alive. One of the nurses took her away and another nurse came back a few minutes later to say she was sorry but the baby was dead. They put me on Valium and I stayed hooked on the stuff for the next nine months.

I have to say that Louie was a different man after the miscarriage. For a while, anyway—a very short while. With him, nothing lasted forever, the good or the bad. But for a couple of weeks he went out of his way to be kind, to be patient. Over and over he told me that the thought of losing me was unbearable to him. There would be tears in his eyes. I didn't have a doubt in my mind that he meant it. But, like I said, you got the bad as well, and the bad wasn't always him knocking me around. The three of us, him and me and Deena, could be sitting at home around the kitchen table, laughing our heads off about something, he would get a phone call and when he hung up, his face and voice and even the way he stood would change, and he'd be out of the door, saying he'd be back when he got back.

Whenever he got one of these calls the whole atmosphere changed. It seemed to me that the tension in the room spread to every part of the house. I could feel it in my body. Young as she was, even Deena knew that something was wrong. That's when I used to get out the games or the paints and try to take her mind off it—mine, too, but my brain was going like a jackhammer, wondering where he was and what he was doing and when—and if—he would come back to us.

More and more I was starting to think about the if question. What if he left one day and didn't come back to us?

By now we also had a house. Out of the blue one day in 1971, Louie said let's go see that place on Staten Island you keep talking about. It was at 552 Arlene Street, a two-story-high ranch, with a vestibule and a big room for guests on the ground floor. It had a staircase with a wrought-iron railing leading from the ground floor to the top floor and the rest of the rooms.

There were two reasons why he finally agreed to buy the place. Number one, I found $12,000 in stock certificates which he never told me about. They were in a drawer in the bedroom. So that was the end of one of his arguments, that we can't afford the down payment. The number-two reason is because when we go to see the house on Arlene Street, the real estate agent turns out to be a guy called Jumbo, who is an old friend of Louie's, and Jumbo was the kind of salesman who could sell you the clothes you're wearing for three times what you paid for them and make you feel he's helped you out. Between Jumbo and me, Louie didn't stand a chance.

Owning your own house changes everything. For me it was as if the world opened up. I designed a fireplace for the ground-floor vestibule and converted the downstairs den into a guest room with its own bathroom. Upstairs we had three bedrooms, a living room, dining room, kitchen, and bathroom. To make the backyard bigger we bought an adjoining piece of property from the builder, so there was plenty of space for Deena to play in.

You couldn't have wished for better neighbors than ours, Herman W. and his wife, Gloria, who were a couple of years older than us. They were religious Jews who kept a kosher house and had a son and two daughters. Herman owned his own taxi, which he drove in Manhattan. He and Louie got along like a couple of brothers. We were constantly in each other's houses, we ate out together, and went to the movies together, and at least once the four of us took a vacation in upstate New York.

That house was our home for seventeen years, much of it a living hell, and if it hadn't been for the kindness and friendship of our neighbors, Herman and Gloria, it would have been a hundred times worse.

Wherever we lived, I used any excuse to have a party, and we had plenty at the house on Arlene. For a while, with the sound of people enjoying themselves, the laughter and music, I could dress up and forget the problems I couldn't stand thinking about. That's why other people have parties, I guess, but most of them don't have the same kind of worries I had, of their husband going to prison or being killed, and these had become fears that never left me and I couldn't talk about with anyone, not my family or even my closest friends, whether they were in the life or out of it. And that's how I thought about it now—the Life. Parties were just a way of temporary escape from it.

My parents had retired and moved to Florida by now, so we rarely saw them unless we flew down there or they came to us and stayed in the guest room on their way to or from visiting one of my brothers, which they did every summer. My mother and I were as far apart as ever and would remain that way for the rest of her life, but that didn't matter much to me, because my only interest was in spending time with my father, and if my mother had to be there, too, I could deal with it as long as it lasted.

Louie never gave up on trying to make peace between the both of us. He didn't sit us down together and make us talk about the problem, that wasn't his way, and I don't suppose either one of us would have done it, anyway. Instead he did his best to make her feel welcome by playing cards with her and buttering her up in any way he could, hoping that this would help make the situation between the two of us easier. For whatever reasons, it didn't.

Living at Arlene Street was when Louie started holding his "meetings." Maybe four or five of his crew would stop by, sit around the dining room table for hours, and talk about who knew what while I stayed in another part of the house or took Deena out shopping. Or we'd go visit his mother or somebody.

Sometimes the men who came to these meetings were strangers to me, and some of them I either knew or had seen around at clubs or various functions. This particular day they were all strangers to me, and I was in one of the bedrooms when I heard Louie calling out for Inez, our cleaning woman, to come into the dining room. I wanted to know why, so I hung around the door when she went in. Inez was around sixty years old. She came to the house three times a week. That day as always when she came to the house she was dressed for a hard day's work and wore a *schmatta* or some kind of rag over pin curlers.

I heard Louie say, "Gentlemen, I want you to meet my wife."

"Oh, Mr. Lou," Inez goes, "you and your jokes!"

Everyone in the room, including Inez, was laughing, and nobody laughed louder than Louie.

Which was another thing about this man—he would do just about anything to make people laugh, even if it meant making a fool of himself. But that was only in private. There was no clowning around with Louie Milito when he was out and about in public.

He had a whole list of sayings he never stopped repeating. Don't mistake my kindness for weakness, and A leopard never changes its spots. Another was, I keep my enemies close to me—his friend Ray Genco surprised Louie after Ray tried to stiff him in the deal with the jeans.

He told me, "I will never forgive Ray for that." But Ray and his wife, Natalie, came to the house all the time, not because Louie wanted them but because Natalie was my friend and I wasn't about to cut her out of my life.

She was one of two very pretty sisters, the other being

Karen. Both were friends of mine. They also had a brother, whose name I don't remember.

Their father had a mental problem and a drinking problem, he was in and out of prison and loony bins for one thing or another, usually for violence of some kind. He also drank too much and once he shot his girlfriend, did time for it, and came home. Natalie and her sister couldn't wait to get out of the house, and married early. They had always taken care of their family from early on. Both of them got married to the first man they met—their first boyfriends, one to a weight lifter, another to a muscle man who ended up stabbing a wiseguy with a screwdriver while on meds for a chemical imbalance. The time would come when I saved his life after Louie was ordered to kill him, but at this point that day was a long way off.

Natalie was a close friend. She married Ray Genco for the same reason her sister got married—all the wrong reasons— to get away from their overcrowded house and lunatic father. Back then you stayed with your first love, but when Natalie married Ray, I knew she couldn't have made a worse mistake.

They both used to come over to the house on Saturday nights for pizza, and the four of us would play Scrabble afterwards. Ray couldn't stand losing, especially to me or Louie. To him that stupid game was a holy war. If he thought he was losing he would start screaming, as if he was in pain, and he'd be sitting at the board figuring out a move while the rest of us watched TV. Louie would say, "We're getting tired, Ray. Go home, you lost already."

He just couldn't give up. One time he got stuck with an X and couldn't figure out where to put it. One night after they went home I called him up and told him I knew where he could have put his X, and when I gave him the word he said he was coming right over and picking up where we left off. Louie had to tell him to forget about it.

Ray's main problem was how he treated Natalie—he used that lovely girl as a punching bag. He was harder on her than

Louie was with me. Louie hit me maybe twenty times in all the years we were together. Ray was maybe six feet and knocked Natalie around so much she was lucky he didn't kill her. He was a beast.

Natalie's brother, the one whose name I forget, used to run a bakery in Bensonhurst for his sister Karen, who had made enough money somewhere along the line to buy the place and a couple of dozen apartments in a building in Brooklyn. The brother was a gambler, not with the bookies but with cards, and he owed money. He and his girlfriend had just pulled up outside the bakery one morning when somebody stuck a gun through the car window and put a bullet in his head.

Natalie went crazy. She called me the same day, begging me to ask Louie if he could find out who killed him. I told her she should call Louie and ask him herself, which she did, every day for the next two weeks. He couldn't tell her anything or, if he could, he didn't. I don't think he had anything to do with her brother's murder, but when her calls didn't stop, he refused to talk to her and made it clear that he didn't want to hear anything more about it. "Tell her to stop making a noise about this here," he told me. "Tell her to shut up."

She called the house one night. This time it was because Ray had beaten her up again. She could hardly speak. "I have to leave him," she said, "I can't take any more of this. He's going to kill me if I stay."

"Pack your bags," I told her. "Get out."

An hour later she called from a bar down the block to say she had left the house with her baby daughter and was never going back to him.

Natalie eventually got a divorce. She met another guy who was completely outside the life and who, from everything she told me later, was just a good man with a steady job. Last I heard about Ray Genco, he was living in his car. He used to call us up and say people were after him. I doubt if anyone even knew or cared if he was alive.

I know it's ironic that I could advise Natalie Genco what to do and not do it myself. But I had my reasons. Natalie had a big, close family to turn to. They had always stood by her even if none of the men in the family wanted to mess with Ray, who was bigger and meaner than all of them. Her family helped her with money, they took it in turns looking after her and the baby after she left Ray. I didn't have anyone like that except people who were also Louie's friends and wouldn't dare take sides, and on top of this, I believed with all my heart that if I humiliated him by leaving he would forget everything he ever said about loving me and wanting us to stay together. He would find me and I would never be seen alive again.

I could tell Natalie to do something I couldn't do myself and at the same time wish it was me, running away and taking Deena with me.

CHAPTER 11

Straightened Out

By early 1973 I was pregnant again, and in October of that year gave birth to our son, Louis. The name was Louie's idea, not mine. I asked him, "How many Louies do we need in this family? We already got my father, we got your father, and you, we got at least five more Louies we know—enough with the Louies already, I want him to be Robert."

I figured he would go for Robert because his brother is a Robert, but he wouldn't buy it. That's how we do it in the old country, he says; in the old country the son takes the father's name. So my son became Louis, and that's the name I've always used for him—Louis, not Louie. Robert is his middle name.

I think 1973 was the same year Louie got pinched for burglar tools again. Like I said, with him there were things he tells me and things he didn't, and one thing he didn't tell me was how he was working the phone scam again. This time he was using John Bontate as lookout. They were driving around Philadelphia in John's car, and when the cops called in the license plate, it came up OC, for "organized crime." Louie called up from the jail in Philly—I was so mad I hung up on him.

Carol Bontate was also furious with her husband. She was steaming when she called the house. "I don't know how John has the nerve to do this to me," she goes. "He should be ashamed of himself. It's beneath him, robbing pay phones. He doesn't need this!"

Carol was a smart woman, but maybe she didn't know the whole truth about her husband.

John looked and lived like a successful businessman, but the truth is he was too kind and a little hopeless when it came to the details, or that's what Louie told me. For a wiseguy he wasn't so smart when it came to himself. When he wasn't getting robbed behind his back he was lending money to guys he never saw again, or investing in businesses that died before they got started, or he let his friends take the jewelry for no money, just a promise. He ended up with not enough dollars to cover the nut for feeding his family and running the jewelry business.

He should have known better than to go to Philly with Louie, and Louie should have been smart enough to know he shouldn't take chances in another state, what with his record in New York.

The police found the burglar tools in the car when they pulled them over. Louie for some reason did not get fingered for OC.

"It's a bail deal, no big thing," he tells me over the phone. "I'll be home in the morning."

For months the attorneys did what they could to make the case disappear. Someone must have been working very hard in the background—Louie thought it was probably the feds, trying to make themselves look good—because in the end his lawyers couldn't get the charges tossed out, and he and Bontate had to go back and stand trial.

In the courtroom the judge mixed the both of them up and

started addressing Louie as Bontate and Bontate as Louie and telling Louie at the top of his voice he should be ashamed of himself for leading an old man into organized crime. Louie didn't think it was funny. "The guy was pointing his finger at me and saying how sorry he was for John and telling me I'm some kind of vicious criminal who deserved to be locked up for life."

It got worse when the judge figures out who was who. He told John he would see to it that he would go to prison until he was dead. Louie came home after one session and said he was afraid the judge would bury the both of them.

It all came to nothing . . . well, it was more than nothing, but it was better than what could have happened. They got probation and no time. Somebody reached out to one of the family bosses in Philadelphia, and he reached a lawyer who knew how to work the courts and the law. The fees came to $6,000, every penny of which came out of Louie's pocket, since it was his score that went wrong.

I was just happy that Louie didn't have to go away for this pinch. I didn't know that he was already into Bontate for a couple of favors. Now he owed one to the bosses in Philadelphia as well. These were favors that ten years later Louie would eventually have to pay back in blood, and not his blood.

I was no longer trying to keep up with him. Most of the time when he was home, well, he wasn't home. He would come back five nights a week just before it got light. Louie had a routine. At six o'clock the whole family had to be at the table for dinner. Saturday nights were our night out. That was the way he wanted it, and it was a schedule that hardly ever changed, except now and again, when the two of us went away for a long weekend and left Deena and Louis with Louie's mother.

With Bontate out of the phone-scam picture, he got Enrico Arnato to go with him as watchout, which surprised me, because Enrico was also an older man we'd known for quite a few years and, judging from the way he and his family lived, I always figured he had it pretty good. They had a mansion in Queens—at least to me it was a mansion, what with all the big rooms, expensive furniture, and the white grand piano in the living room. But, like old man Bontate, Enrico was in a jam and needed a temporary cash transplant to see him through a dry patch, or at least that's what Louie said. How Enrico made his money and whether he was straightened out with the Gambinos or just some guy on the fringes, I never found out and didn't want to know. I figured he must have been someone, because Louie always showed him a lot of respect.

The partnership in the phone scam didn't last long. The phone company came up with new locks that Louie couldn't open to save his life. They had chrome-plated cover plates on the front instead of the old black plates. Louie brought one home and spent weeks driving us all crazy, making new picks and getting nowhere. He tried everything he knew, and in the end he couldn't do it. Now they were putting in the new phones all over the city. That was how the phone scam ended. I didn't tell him, but I was really pleased when he told me he was quitting. Louie was disgusted, but for once, instead of taking out his frustration on me, like he sometimes did when things didn't go according to plan, he accepted it. From now on, until he took up shylocking, he stayed with the old routines, trunking and doing paperwork for swag cars. Eventually we would also get into legitimate car sales—or they would have been legit if he hadn't started clocking the cars and getting pinched for it. Clocking means turning back the mileage on the odometers. For this he would get six months' state time in Jersey and four years federal. But all of that was a few years down the road; in fact, it was close to the end of the road for Louie. In the meantime he was making a lot of money, more than I'd ever seen, and once again he was passing a percentage to his captains and bosses in the Gambinos.

In the life, this was called making turn-ins. When you made money, you turned in a share to the family you worked for. A lot of people who ended up in car trunks with bullets in the head were guys who didn't make their turn-ins. It was a rule Louie never broke.

My guess is Louie got straightened out with the Gambinos in 1977. He didn't tell me, just like I didn't tell him a girl-friend had already told me. She heard about it with her own ears. I don't want to put her name here, she doesn't need any more grief in her life. Let's say her name is Patty.

We used to hang out with her and her husband, who was basically a loser who never got made but knew Louie all his life and liked him because Louie helped him get out of a lot of difficulties over the years. Him I will call Joey, because for all I know he is still on the streets and would not like to see his name in print.

Patty called the house one night to shoot the breeze, which we did when the guys were out, meaning most nights.

"How about Louie?" she said.

"What about Louie?"

"He was over our place and he told Joey he just got made with the Gambinos. They had a ceremony and he took an oath and everything. You know, the Mafia."

"That's bullshit," I said. "Mafia! He never said anything to me. What you talking about, ceremony?"

"Three days ago. He can't tell you about it, he's not sup-posed to tell anybody."

I didn't want to hear this and I didn't believe it. I didn't want to believe it. At the same time, so far as I know, Patty never lied about anything in all the years we knew each other. Some people tell you things because they want to make trouble or because they want you to think they are im-portant for things they know you don't. She was not like that, she was too honest and too smart to play those games.

I didn't believe it and I told her she must have made a mis-take.

I'd been in their little one-bedroom apartment, so I asked her where she was and where Louie and Joey were. She said she was in the living room and they were in the kitchen, and when she heard Joey getting excited she couldn't help listening to find out why. That's when she heard Louie saying how proud he was to be honored. He was laughing and saying how much it stings when they cut his finger too deep and he was dripping blood all over his shoes.

"That's it?" I said. "That doesn't mean a thing. It's bullshit."

But now Patty was getting worried she spoke out of turn and she made me promise not to say anything to anyone. Like I would dare.

Patty wasn't the only one who told me about Louie getting hooked up with the Gambinos. We had a friend who had known Louie since they were both teenagers hanging out on the street in Bensonhurst. I can't use his name, either. I'll call him Gene B, and he's not with the Mafia—in fact, so far as I know he has no criminal record—but he and Louie had been tight all their lives and stayed that way until Louie's death. I ran into Gene at a gas station right after Patty called me.

"Hey, Lynda, things look pretty good for Louie, huh?"

"What do you mean?"

"You know, him getting straightened out with the guys?"

"I don't know what you're talking about."

"Yeah, you do. I just saw him. He told me he was in a new situation and if I had any problem of any kind I should go to him and he would fix it. Anything. He said he was in with some big people now. The best."

"Gene, you're crazy."

As far as I was concerned, this was more stuff to hide in that compartment in my brain, the one with the DENIAL label on top. I never spoke of it again to Patty or Gene, and they never mentioned it to me. I didn't tell them Louie had been wearing a Band-Aid on the first finger of his right hand for the past couple of days. He told me he cut it when he picked up a piece of broken glass by mistake.

So now Louie was part of the Gambinos. As far as I could tell he was still basically making money from stealing. A lot of money, true, because mostly we lived well and had money for just about anything we wanted so long as we worked, but the fact remained that my husband, made man or not, was still doing what he did from the time we met—manipulating people out of their money.

Did I know for sure then that he was also a killer? No. But if it's true that the only way you get to be a made man with the Mafia is after you kill somebody, then I guess there can't be much argument about it. Louie was now straightened out with the Gambinos, and without knowing it, so were the rest of us, his children and me.

When I first met Louie, his friends called him Louie Lobo, the Lone Wolf, because they thought of him as a loner. He didn't answer to anybody. He was his own man. That all went out the window when he joined the Gambinos. After that, he didn't belong to himself or his wife and children. In reality he was no better off than a man locked up in maximum security trying to pretend to himself he was free. As a made man, Louie was free to do what they told him he could do—that's how free he was. He couldn't get out and we couldn't get out. All four of us were locked up together.

There was nothing my family could do for me or the two children, even if they wanted to, and it had long since been clear that my parents and brothers couldn't or wouldn't help because of the risk to themselves.

Even if I tried to get away with the kids, there was no place we could be safe from being found. In any case, Deena and Louis would never leave their father, no matter what. He doted on both of them and they adored him. Once he hit Deena with a bag of potatoes when she was giving me some lip, but apart from that, I don't remember him ever hitting the kids. He gave them just about anything they wanted. He was constantly taking them out, playing the clown for them, listening to their troubles and advising them.

I accused Louie once of not caring about his family. Why hit me and not be around when we need you? Then for a while I wasn't so sure. Why did "business" always seem to come first? Now, years later, I know he did care about us and he certainly loved us. I think about it a lot now, how Louie was.

When he played with the kids he was always kissing them.

"Enough with the kissing!" I used to tell him. "You kissed them already."

Deena couldn't get enough of his attention. She was daddy's little princess, and to her Louie was God and Santa Claus rolled into one.

My son was more reserved. Louis was uncomfortable with affection from the time he was a toddler, as if he were holding something back. I used to think maybe Louie thought of his son as being more Jewish, more like me—not like Deena, who went around handing out pictures of saints to people and had a date with Louie's mother for church every Sunday. And I'm glad she did, because I think Deena's religion helped her in her adult life.

Louie took Louis hunting with him from the time he was around five and for years afterwards. He thought that going out in the country with a gun, shooting birds and animals, would give the boy more confidence. Discipline, too, maybe, since he was a great believer in that—Army type discipline, where you do what you're told.

Louie himself was in the reserves for six months before we met, and anything to do with the military was a big deal with him. He was always telling the kid to respect veterans, which to me personally was a joke, considering how a lot of so-called tough guys we knew paid out thousands of dollars to avoid military service. Naturally I didn't point this out to Louie. He had a sense of humor, but not when his friends were part of the joke.

His idea of being funny was singing Army songs to Louis when they were out hunting. One day the boy came home crying. Louie had told him that if the Army told a soldier to kill his mother he had to follow orders and kill her.

"I don't want to sing the 'kill Mommy' song anymore," he said.

That was the last time I let him go hunting with his father.

When the *Godfather* movie came out, Louie got a copy and watched it like six thousand times. It was like a searchlight had lit up on something he had always believed in but had never seen the proof of before. He couldn't pull himself away from the TV, he couldn't stop watching that stupid movie. A dozen times he told me, "This movie is fantastic!" He was amazed that the people who made it knew so much. All our friends were watching it.

I heard Louie on the phone one day and he was talking about Marlon Brando and Al Pacino and how everyone connected to this film was a genius, because for the first time the public was finding out that organized crime people are not just lowlife gangsters and mental defectives, but men who live by respect and honor. I couldn't believe my ears.

They were trading books with each other. Louie bought the *Godfather* book and swapped it with John Bontate for *The Sicilian,* which he said was more realistic than *The Last Don* and better than *The Brotherhood* and so on and so forth, and the guys who came to the house were all acting like *Godfather* actors, kissing and hugging even more than they did before and coming out with lines from the movie. A couple of them started learning Italian.

Frankie de Cicco was an important guy with the Gambinos and one of Louie's favorite people. I always respected Frankie for his brains and for the way he treated Louie, but he was like the rest of them when it came to this movie. Louie and Frank watched it in the den and Frankie came upstairs looking like he's just seen God.

I saw that movie and it made me nauseous. Louie thought

it was close to reality, but I didn't. Back then I laughed at all that, like it was a farce. Louie used to say I didn't know any better because I was Jewish.

The thing I *can* say is similar is how beautifully Louie and his friends dressed. Oh, they were suave and debonair, impeccably dressed in all their Italian knits. They were handsome gentlemen, always with manners and calling women "Mrs." and "Miss." They were respectful around the women. They could have been movie actors, like the Rat Pack. That's who they reminded me of—Sinatra and his crew. Dapper and polite like that. Louie would buy the same style of shoe in every color. Not a button was ever undone, there were never any creases. And they always, always wore shirts with French cuffs, never those with the buttons around their wrists. And gold cuff links. Their top coats were either camel or black. They were the sharpest men around. Back then, it wasn't like how they show men on *The Sopranos*. The men would never be as fat as Tony Soprano. The men took care of themselves and looked good. Louie and the family weren't sloppy like Tony; they'd never go for that.

Old man Carlo Gambino died in his bed in the fall of 1975 and the papers called him the Mafia Boss of Bosses. This was ridiculous to me. Here's a little old guy who looks like he's almost too frail to stand up and they say he's Mr. Big? Louie went to the funeral to pay his respects, but not me. I have never been big on funerals.

With Carlo gone, his brother-in-law, Paul Castellano, took over and he was now the main boss so far as Louie and the rest of the Gambino men are concerned. Again, I didn't know about this when it happened. What I do know is that Paul lived in a big house on a 3.5-acre lot at the top of Todt Hill in Staten Island, and on the holidays Louie always took him a box of Italian pastries. From Paul he gets nothing, which was par for the course with Paul.

Louie told me how much he respected Paul for being an old-fashioned guy with old-fashioned values, the same as himself. At the same time he complained that Paul was not somebody who gave much back except to tell Louie how proud he was of him, and how he loved him like a son, which he should, considering Paul took a fat percentage of everything Louie made.

Sometimes I wondered what Louie would have done if I'd told him I knew about him getting straightened out with the Gambinos. I never did. A part of me didn't believe it and it was too frightening to think about. For all I knew, he could kill me for even mentioning it. He might think I would tell someone else or go to one of my friends, like John Bontate's wife, Carol, and discuss it with her. I also still didn't want to think it was true, and if it was true, it could come back on me and on Patty and Joey in ways I didn't care to think about.

But by this time I didn't have any illusions worth holding on to. I knew who Louie was and how he lived, and I knew that most of the people we mixed with were the same as him—full-time criminals with Italian names. I used to call them the vowel people when we were first together but he didn't find it amusing, so I stopped.

The swag car business was just about boiling over. He couldn't keep up with the demand, and now that he was making his turn-ins to the bosses again, he was feeling better about himself. Turn-ins came every Tuesday night when he used to meet John Bontate at a club in Bensonhurst and hand over a bag of cash.

I asked him, What is it with these turn-ins? Why do you have to give these guys money? What did they ever do for you? And he explained as usual to keep my big mouth shut and stop getting on his nerves with dumb questions.

That was another one of his favorite sayings: "You ever hear the expression, 'Loose lips sink ships'?"

At this time, except for the Bontates and the men who came to meetings at the house, we stopped hanging out with a lot of the people we used to see. Herman and Gloria next door, we still spent time with them, but they were outside the life, and if they had any curiosity about Louie and what he did for a living, they never showed it. Being around them made me feel we had a normal life.

This was one of the changes in our lives after Louie got straightened out, cutting ourselves off from people. I realize now that this was how he wanted it. He didn't want new people unless they were introduced to him by his most trusted friends, meaning the people he did business with. It was understood that I could not bring anyone new home without telling him first. He had to know their names, where they came from, who their family was, what kind of work they did, and how long did I know them, and if he didn't like the answers he would tell me he didn't want them in the house and I should meet them somewhere else.

He taught me to be that way, not to trust nobody, not to get too close to people, not even a woman, and the result is I still have no real close female friends now and probably never will. I won't say I like it that way, because I don't, but I don't see it changing and it's something I cried about more than once when I wished there was another woman to talk to.

Men, no problem, I always got along fine with the men in Louie's crowd. They liked him so they liked me. If new guys stopped by the house, I used to listen to their voices, trying to guess if it was this one or that one who called the house leaving messages.

People called day and night.

Have Louie call Tommy D at the he-knows-where. Tell Louie okay on what he talked to the fat man about. Louie needs to call the guy he was with at the club on Tuesday night. He'll understand. It's important. Tell Louie the three guys in New York say to forget about it and call the skinny guy. He'll know. It's important.

All messages were important.

Some calls he made to me were in the same kind of code. "Listen, Lynda. Remember that guy we met wearing the dungaree blue jacket the other night? I have a very important instruction you must follow. Go under our bed and take out the package. The smaller of the two. Give it to the guy when he comes to the house."

I never questioned him. Following Louie's orders was part of what I was expected to do.

When he was home he was never off the phone. It was nothing to have a phone bill of five or six hundred dollars a month, a lot of money in the seventies. And he couldn't pass a phone without calling the house. If he was out somewhere, he'd call ten times a day to ask if we needed something from the store, and did Jimmy or Sally or Mickey call in yet.

"You want me to bring you back a pastrami sandwich? What about the kids, ask the kids what they want."

He called me, he called Deena, and he called Louis. When he saw a phone, he had to call that very second, he couldn't help it. I used to tell him, You got terminal telephonitis. He talked with both hands. I could imagine him at the other end of the line, how he would be waving his arms around all the time he's talking. I told him if he had to sit on his hands he would be speechless.

I enjoyed hanging out with the guys because I liked watching Louie with them. I began to notice that younger men especially started treating him with the same respect he showed John Bontate, and like any wife, I was proud to think people looked up to my husband. I just took it for granted that people treated him with respect because he was a man who never wasted a word and wasn't all the time playing the big shot. A lot of them probably didn't even know that he was moving up in the life.

About the only friend of Louie's I never liked being around was the one who became his best and closest friend. Sammy Gravano. Maybe I blotted it out from my memory and maybe I just don't remember, but in the ten years I'd been with Louie, I don't recall that he ever mentioned Sammy, and suddenly it turns out he's known Sammy since they were kids and now Sammy is becoming a fixture in our lives.

One reason I didn't like this was because I knew how his

mind worked. A guy we knew—I have to call him Stan, which isn't his name—told me how Sammy enjoyed hurting people with his fists. He liked to pick fights with strangers who looked at him for too long or stood in his way in a bar. Stan was sitting in Stan's office with Sammy one time and another guy showed up with a trunkload of marijuana in his car he said was worth $300,000. When he went back out to the car to fetch something, Sammy said, "This jerk's got a wad of cash on him. Let's whack him when he comes back, take the money and the dope. We could roll him up in the carpet and chop him up somewhere."

Stan, who was no killer, told Sammy he didn't want any part of it.

So almost from the start I figured Sammy was the kind of person who didn't care what he did and liked to get other people to join in. And this scared me, because if Louie enjoyed his company, which it sure seemed like he did, who knows what the both of them could do together? This only goes to show how ignorant I was of that life. By this time, for all I knew, Louie and Sammy had already started killing together.

I know there are wives who feel maybe threatened when their husbands get too close to another guy. That was never my problem. Sammy was my problem. I didn't like Sammy's face, I didn't like his voice, I didn't like the way he sucked up to Louie, and I couldn't understand why he never looked me in the eye for more than a split second. I can't explain it but I felt from the beginning that he resented Louie and could in some way hurt him. Even now, finding his name in the papers or hearing it mentioned on TV makes me feel sick to my stomach.

The first time I remember seeing him was when he showed up with Allie Boy at our house on Arlene Street. Louie was out in front. The three of them talked for a while and I could see Louie and Sammy knew each other from the way they acted together, with the hugging and the kissing on the cheeks, and then Sammy was backing his car up the

drive and taking some tires out of the trunk, which he rolled
into our garage. They were big new tires, probably off a
Caddy or a Lincoln.

"Who's the guy with Allie Boy?" I asked Louie after they
left.

"Some kid from the neighborhood. Sammy Gravano. You
don't know him, he's one of Sal's friends." This Sal being
the son of Benny Lima.

We started seeing more of Sammy and then his girlfriend,
Debra Scibetta, who later became his wife and is one of the
few women I ever liked and trusted. Our two kids and their
two, Karen and Gerard, went to school together and were in
and out of both houses as they grew up. Debra I liked a lot,
but from the start I just couldn't feel good about Sammy and
had to keep my opinions to myself. Louie made that plain.
The first time I made a crack about Sammy he said, "Lynda!
I don't wanna hear that! You will not go around disrespecting Sammy!"

It was Louie who told Deena and Louis that when he
came to the house they were to call him Uncle Sammy, and
that's what he became from then on.

One thing about Louie, he never put me down in public or
ordered me about. Sammy Gravano was the opposite. The
four of us would eat at the Dakota Diner on Staten Island
now and then. I never looked forward to it. It was all I
could do to keep quiet when Sammy started. "Put some
ketchup on my fries, Debra. Give me a napkin. Get the
waitress over here. Debra! This fork's dirty, go bring me
another one."

I couldn't say anything in these situations—criticizing
Sammy in front of his wife and Louie would be asking for
trouble. But inside it made me boil to think that Louie would
get ideas from this and start treating me in public the same
way this moron treated *his* wife.

I felt so sorry for Debbie, who never complained but just quietly went along with it.

The bottom line was that Louie loved Sammy. So did Deena and Louis. In our house it was Uncle Sammy this, Uncle Sammy that. I got sick of hearing it. "Hey, Ma, Uncle Sammy's here!" And they'd welcome him with open arms and climb all over him as if he were Santa Claus. Deena thought he was the greatest thing since cream cheese—it made me sick to think of it.

And Sammy knew how I felt about him—he got a kick out of it. He knew how to get my goat. I was alone in the house once when he showed up at the front door. He had his pants open and his hand down them stuffing his shirt inside. In front of a woman! I couldn't believe he would pull a stunt like this. I slammed the door in his face.

It made me sick knowing Louie wouldn't believe me if I told him what had happened. Or he would blame me for causing it. In his eyes I could never be right where Sammy was concerned, and I always figured Sammy knew it and enjoyed it.

Having this man in my life was like having a disease in my brain. Sammy was coming by the house three, four times a day, and sometimes he and Louie would drive somewhere or they would walk around the block and talk. There would be times when even Louie got tired of him. Sometimes he'd come in fuming.

"He's not going to listen to me, that fucking Polack! I swear he has the Napoleon complex sometimes. I actually wish he was taller than me."

"Listen about what?" I'd ask him, but he just waved his hand, as if he were too disgusted to talk about it.

Louie called him a Polack because Sammy didn't look typically Italian, with his dirty blond hair and blue eyes. More than once when there was a problem with cops, his looks let him disappear into the crowd and it would be Louie, whose face told another story, who would take the pinch.

The more Sammy buttered up Louie, the more I despised him.

He shows up at the house one morning when Louie was out and said he had to have a transporter plate right away because he needed to move a car somewhere. As soon as I opened the door he was peering over my shoulder at the hall table, where we kept the plate. I told him he couldn't have it because he wasn't a registered dealer. If he got stopped we would have a problem with the DMV and the cops. We could lose our dealer license. "Wait until Louie comes home," I said, "see what he thinks."

"Don't worry about it," he said, grabbed the plate off the table, and took off.

Louie went ballistic when he saw it was missing.

"Where's the plate? You know we're moving all those cars tomorrow."

I told him Sammy had it.

"Did I tell you to give Sammy a plate? Who the fuck are you to give Sammy the plate? How do I know what he's doing with it—he could be using it for a heist. Did you think about that, you fucking moron?"

I started shaking—I was too scared to look at him. Don't look him in the eye, I used to tell myself, as if that would stop him from hitting me.

As I said before, we had a wrought-iron railing on the stairs at the house on Arlene. Louie yanked it out of the floor at the bottom steps and twisted it cockeyed. Deena and Louis were at the top of the stairs, watching and listening. Louie picked me up by one shoulder, held me off the floor with one hand, and with the other gave me a hard backhand and let me drop. The kids saw this and ran to their rooms, screaming. Louie stood over me, yelling.

"You see what you did here? You see what you made me do, what you made my kids see?"

I stayed on the floor. Louie came out in the hall a few minutes later, carrying a bag and his hunting guns. He came home with a deer a couple of days later. The plate was back on the hall table. We didn't talk about what had happened.

As he got older, Louis used to say, "Hide in the closet, Ma! Then Daddy can't find you!"

Louie used to say that if you kept your enemies close to you, you could see what they were doing and make a move before they did. Didn't do him much good in the end, considering how things turned out, but in his world, being ready to make the first move could sometimes be the difference between living and not living.

Not long after Louie came home from Trenton, he hired a Staten Island carpenter to fix a leak in the roof of our place in Pennsylvania. Louie asked his friend Vito to check on the work afterwards to make sure the carpenter did a thorough job. Vito called in to say it wasn't, and advised Louie not to pay.

The carpenter showed up on a Sunday morning to collect his money. Deena and Louis were playing outside when he pulled up in his truck. Louie was working on a car in the driveway.

He was a young guy, this carpenter. I don't know his name and I wasn't paying much attention when he arrived because I was watching the kids. But I knew that, based on Vito's advice, there could be a problem when he showed up.

I saw the guy get out of his truck and approach Louie. Everything looked okay, they're talking and walking, and then Louie put an arm over the guy's shoulders. They're standing outside the open garage door. But something doesn't feel right to me. This was not good. I felt my stomach jump. I shouted for the kids to come back in the house, but they had already taken off down the block. Suddenly the carpenter broke free of Louie, and the next thing I knew he's running back from his truck, swinging a hammer.

This was not a small guy, he was a few inches taller than Louie and a lot younger.

Without taking his eyes off him, Louie reached into the garage with one hand and came out holding an ax. I saw the ax come up and hit the carpenter on the side of his face. His ear was hanging off and there was blood on the grass and the driveway. He took off running up the street, with one hand holding his ear on.

Louie jumped in his car and drove in the other direction. Five minutes later he called from Ray's house. He sounded completely relaxed, like someone taking it easy in a recliner chair.

"Call Sammy," he said. "Tell him what happened and have him go see Albert to speak to that kid."

At this time Albert was the local goon in Travis, where the carpenter lived.

By the time Albert located the carpenter, he'd been to the police to file charges. He had a bandage around his head. Albert had known the kid all his life. He told him that there had been a misunderstanding, that Louie wanted to pay him for his work and everything could be straightened out if he and Louie met. The two of them drove to the Holiday Inn where Louie was waiting, along with Ray and Sammy. They had a couple of drinks, Louie paid the $400 bill for the roof work, and everybody went home. But first he made sure the carpenter went to the police and dropped the charges.

This whole thing made me sick to my stomach. He took an ax to a man's head with no more thought than a kid kicking a soda can across the street. It must have been the way he killed animals when he was out hunting. Easily, without fuss, as if it were just an everyday thing—and I knew without having to think twice that if he could do such a thing, then he could do it to a man the same way. I didn't want to know that, I didn't want to think it was possible. But the incident made me sick to my stomach. When he came home I asked him, "What do you think this does for Deena and Louis when they see blood all over the front of the house? What would happen to them if you had killed that man?"

He didn't say anything, he went back to working on his car in the driveway.

CHAPTER 12

A Person Would Have to Be in a Coma

People have told me that in the Mafia there's a bunch of rules about how made men are supposed to behave with the wives of other made men. The basic rule is that they have to keep their distance. Now, I don't claim to be any expert about Mafia rules and regulations except for what I picked up from Louie, and this was very little, since I wasn't supposed to know about Louie's connections, anyway, and on top of this, what he said on this subject was always kind of vague. Certain men had to be respected and others had to be respected a lot, that was the general idea. Even pretending to respect someone like Sammy Gravano made me feel like choking.

I think Sammy wanted to get close to Louie before he left the Colombos and joined the Gambinos because the top Gambino men respected and liked Louie. Which was no surprise, considering the money he made for them. Sammy wanted to share Louie's limelight.

It got worse when he switched from the Colombos to the Gambinos. After that—and I don't know how he did it—he gradually worked himself into a position with the Gambino captains that somehow enabled Sammy to pull Louie's strings even when the two of us left town for a vacation.

One time we took a long weekend in Miami, leaving the kids in the house with Inez. The phone in the room rang about an hour after we checked in and I picked it up. It was John Bontate, looking for Louie. Louie listened for a couple of minutes. John did all the talking, with Louie saying, Okay, okay, okay. Then he hung up.

"I have to go meet Sammy in Puerto Rico."

"Now? We only just got here. What am I supposed to do?"

"Stay here, go home. Do what you want. I have to go."

We took a cab to the airport. He flew to San Juan and I went back to New York. He came home three days later and he didn't look too happy. His mouth was tight and he walked around the house looking as if he wanted to break something. I think that if I'd asked him what happened in Puerto Rico he would have flattened me. He was in one of those moods. I have no idea what he and Sammy did together on that trip.

Over the next year or so they worked together just about daily, doing who knew what. Sammy tells a story in his book about how he and Louie once got into a fight with some bikers and Louie killed one with a sawed-off shotgun. Well, Louie had a lot of guns, that's for sure, including a submachine gun—an Uzi, I think it was—but I never saw him with any sawed-off shotgun. Which doesn't mean the biker story isn't true. It's not like he came in the house and said, "Lynda, I had to whack a guy with a sawed-off, what's for dinner?"

But the longer we were together, the easier it became to read his moods. You knew that something had happened when he came home and just sat quietly on the couch, flicking the channels with the remote and not watching anything. Not talking was the giveaway, because usually he couldn't shut up. We talked all the time wherever we were—at home, in the car, on the phone, on planes, on the beach, in the hotel—we never stopped talking.

When he was quiet and tense it usually took a few days before he could relax.

That's when I used to ask him if he was okay and he would look surprised and say, "Everything's fine, you hear me complaining?"

❖   ❖   ❖

Eventually there would be many reasons why I didn't like Sammy, and the biggest reason why I never got to trust him was because too many people around Sammy Gravano died bleeding. Billy Stagg, for one.

Some years after Sammy showed up with the tires, I was in bed one night when I heard Louie come in the house. Normally after he's out late he goes straight to the kitchen and fixes himself something hot, but this time there was no sound of pans banging around. I got out of bed and found him sitting at the kitchen table. He was wearing his brown suit and a yellow shirt, which had spots of blood on it. I thought he'd been in a fight.

"Billy Stagg's dead," he said.

Billy? This was horrible news. I loved this kid, he always made me feel good when he came by the house. He was a wonderful guy: Okay, he was also a thief from Coney Island, but basically Billy Stagg was a nobody who never hurt anyone, who had no ambitions to get hooked up with any outfit. He was just a skinny, fair-haired, young guy who we had known all the way back from the days of Mitchell's Drive-In.

"What happened?" I asked Louie.

"They shot him, what the fuck you think happened to him? I don't know who it was, I didn't see it. We were at Doc's. He said hello, I turn around, there's a shot and he's lying on the floor. I don't want to talk about it."

That's all I got from Louie. Conversation closed. I've

asked myself a thousand times, Did Louie do it? I don't know. He had blood spots on his clothes, he had to be right there when it happened.

Last time I saw Billy Stagg, Sammy Gravano was selling him swag tires for Billy's Lincoln. Sammy had a share in Doc's, the club where Billy was killed. Billy had a piece, too, but Sammy didn't have any money to speak of at the time, so I don't see how he could have owned any part of it. Back then, everyone had a piece of this or a piece of that, so who knows—maybe Sammy had a piece of Doc's, too— there was no way of proving it one way or the other because in most cases nobody filed income tax returns, so whatever you owned you had to put the deeds in somebody else's name, not your own.

Looking back on what happened to Billy, I figure that Sammy was jealous of his friendship with Louie. Louie put money in Billy's pockets for doing odd jobs, and Sammy didn't like that—he didn't like anyone getting too close to Louie. I think he resented Billy because he was popular with Louie's friends, because he was liked and accepted, he had that kind of personality. Not like Sammy, who was never what you would call popular among the guys. What Louie saw in him I still haven't figured out and never will.

"Why would anyone kill Billy? He never did any harm to anyone."

Louie said nothing. He took off the suit and the shirt and handed them to me.

I put them in a plastic bag and dropped the bag in the garbage.

Billy Stagg was dead and Louie was so upset, he didn't sleep for days. He sent word out to find out who killed him, but never found out. Billy's murder really hit home with Louie; he wasn't himself, he wasn't the same for about a year. The night Louie came home and told me about Billy's death he was in a foul mood. The only other thing he said about it was, "My friend died within a couple of feet of me. How am I supposed to feel?"

My father's dad and mom—they were warm and wonderful people.

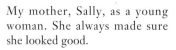

My father, Louie Lustig, as a young man. So handsome and always kind to everyone.

My mother, Sally, as a young woman. She always made sure she looked good.

My house at 2023 74th Street, in Bensonhurst, Brooklyn, where I grew up. We lived on the left side of the two-family home.

My family at my brother Harvey's bar mitzvah. My underwear was showing and my mother never fixed it. Mom, Arthur at eleven, Dad, me at three, and Harvey at thirteen.

Happy days from my childhood.

At fourteen, I was a bridesmaid at the wedding of my brother Arthur to his wife, Annette. I had my old nose here, and I fainted when I was walking down the aisle.

This was Louie's favorite picture of me. I was sixteen years old.

I was sixteen years old and a bridesmaid at the wedding of Louie's brother Sebastian. This was after my nose job; I loved my new nose!

Our marriage certificate. Louie and I were married by New York State Supreme Court justice Hyman Barshay; John Bontate made the arrangements, and Sonny and Carla Mancini came as witnesses. At the end of the ceremony, Louie was in a rush to get to his hunting trip, and Judge Barshay said, "There's a fine if you don't kiss the bride!"

This is the house where Louie grew up—1843 76th Street in Bensonhurst, Brooklyn. Louie slept in the dining room in a hideaway bed. They lived on the right side of this two-family home.

Louie had such a warm smile.

Louie and me with my brothers and sisters-in-law.

Me and Louie. I was five months pregnant with Deena.

My children: Deena was born in 1968, and Louis was born in 1973. Growing up, they were very close.

At the home of our neighbors, Herman and Gloria, on Arlene Street in Staten Island. Louis, me, and Louie.

Louis and Deena in our Todt Hill, Staten Island, house. This was our first year without Louie; he was in Allenwood Federal Prison in Pennsylvania.

Me, Deena, and Louis at Deena's wedding in 1990. Every guest shed tears when Deena and I sang "You Light Up My Life." Louie, who had disappeared two years earlier, was there in spirit.

Me and two of my three brothers at Deena's wedding in 1990.
Gary, my younger brother, me,
and Harvey, the oldest. My
older brother Arthur wasn't at
the wedding.

Mom and Dad at Mom's
seventy-fifth birthday party,
which I organized.

Me and my current man, Jay.

I couldn't be sure about anything anymore. Sometimes when Louie talked to me, I wished he didn't. There was the husband I knew and had loved for years, who let our kids run circles around him, who could be so considerate and funny when he was with us, and then there was this other man, a terrible stranger. This was the one sitting in our kitchen that night.

CHAPTER 13

The Charge Is Murder

I wish I could say it made me feel good to know that a couple of times I was able to stop people I knew from being hurt or maybe killed by Louie. I'll admit I felt good then, as if by saving someone's life without them knowing about it I did something I could be proud of. But I don't feel the same now, I don't feel good about anything I did then, even when it was good.

My friend Karen—Natalie's sister—married a man called Sally Bufalino. He wasn't connected and so far as I know he never worked, he couldn't work. He became sick and was living at home. He heard voices and thought he was being followed. Sally's the one who jumped on one of Louie's wiseguy friends with a screwdriver, stabbing him until he collapsed.

After the man came out of the hospital Louie asked me where Karen lived. He said he needed to talk to Sally. I was suspicious immediately.

"Why do you have to do that?" I asked him. He said it made no difference why, he just had to find Sally and talk to him.

"I can't do that," I said. "I don't know what you've got on your mind but I'm not going to be part of it. Sally's a sick man, he needs help, not punishment."

He said it's important he get hold of him.

"You're not going to find out from me," I said, and he knew I meant it.

I once told this story to someone, who said, Why didn't Louie just go and ask somebody else where they lived? Well, it's not that simple. In the life, you talk to the people you need to talk with to find out what you need to know. Louie could ask me where Karen and Sally lived because he knew Karen and me were friends. If he had asked some other friend of theirs, that person could have gotten suspicious, too, and warned Sally to watch out because Louie was looking for him. He knew I wouldn't do that—what he didn't figure on was that I wouldn't tell him.

Last I heard, Sally is alive, under doctor's care and doing fine.

Many years after this, I was on vacation in Florida, on the beach alone one day, and met two friends of ours we knew from Brooklyn. Scott and Lucy, I'll call them here. They had left town very suddenly some years before and were as happy to see me as I was to see them. I had been to school with Lucy and had known her before she married Scott, and Scott and Louie knew each other from the time they were kids in Bensonhurst. Right away they invited me to bring Louie over to their place for drinks that evening, and maybe the four of us could go out for dinner afterwards.

I thought Louie would be pleased. Big mistake.

"I can't do that!" he said. "Sammy told me to stay away from Scott—he's got this new cigarette boat and they say he's smuggling dope from the Bahamas."

We did go to their house for dinner once but the atmosphere was real tense, so we didn't go back. A long time afterwards, after Louie was killed, I called Scott and said, "I guess you heard the news," and right away he just broke down crying over the phone. The first thing he said when he got his breath was, "How are the kids handling it?"

I told him the truth, that for the three of us it was like the world had ended. But here again, I'm running ahead of myself. The worst was yet to come.

All the time we'd been together, Louie loved to dance. He wasn't showing off, he was just naturally good at it. Mambo, cha-cha, rock and roll, twist, ballroom dancing—whatever, he would be out on the floor the moment the music started. That all came to an end after he got made with the Gambinos—at least it did at any public function we went to. At home, at family parties, okay, it was like old times, but at weddings and other social occasions when the bosses and his guys would be there, he stayed in his chair like a statue. I asked him the first time, What the hell is this? Why aren't we out there? And he said it would be disrespecting himself to get up and dance. People in my position don't do that, he said, we don't make spectacles of ourselves. Are you kidding or what? I asked him. What position? He said, You don't understand, you're Jewish. And what's that got to do with the price of eggs? I said, like I always did when he came up with that old line. And like always, he took no notice.

I thought, If only these people could have seen Louie at home the other night. Dancing around our living room with a brush pretending it was a microphone, and singing Elvis numbers. Doing his Dean Martin impression in the shower.

Disrespecting himself? Here he was, moving up in the biggest Mafia family in the country and he's going out pulling scores a juvenile delinquent would pass up. To him it didn't matter. What mattered was holding up the traditions of showing respect and loyalty.

Him and his crackpot traditions!

He believed that if he wore his best clothes when he was working, the cops would be less likely to stop him than if he dressed like a slob. One night when he goes out with Sammy and Allie Boy to steal spare wheels of all things, he's wearing his green outfit, an Italian double-breasted suit, knit sweater, and new shoes. It was raining, so he took an umbrella.

He drove his new Cadillac that night. First stop the club, to pick up Sammy and Allie. According to what Louie told me afterwards, it was Benny Lima's club, Benny being part of the deal. The plan was for Sammy and Allie to steal spare tires from the expensive cars they expected to find while Louie stood as watchout at the top of the ramp leading down to the garage, which was under a block of luxury apartments in Staten Island.

Louie was walking up and down in the rain, holding the umbrella over himself, when a bunch of angry people came up the ramp holding shotguns on Sammy and Allie Boy. The police arrived and all three of them were pinched and locked up.

I don't know how, because he never explained how, but the cops dropped the charges against Sammy and Allie Boy and focused instead on Louie, who got written up as the ringleader because of the way he was dressed. He got another six months on Riker's Island. That wasn't the worst of it. He was now registered as a known felon connected to organized crime, and as far as the cops were concerned, Louie Milito would be OC for the rest of his life.

Getting pinched didn't stop him from working. Not once did he ever say, Well, Lynda, it looks like they're right, crime doesn't pay, I'd better go get a job. All through the early seventies he made a good living from bogus paperwork and who knew what else. Stealing, of course. Louie would aim for the top and take what he got. For all I knew he could have been involved in airport heists, bullion robberies, house burglary, stock fraud, and whatever else the Gambinos did in those years—everything, in fact, except for the drug trade, which he hated with a passion.

It may sound naïve to say this, but I don't think he ever got into that business. It disgusted him, it went against the tradition, and, knowing how old-fashioned he was in so many ways and how much he valued traditions, I have no reason not to believe him. Let's face it, he got pinched for just about everything he ever did in crime, so it's likely that if he'd been in drugs he would have got pinched for that, too. But that was one charge the cops never made against him or even questioned him about. I would have heard about it, that's for sure, because in all the years we were together there wasn't a charge made against Louie that I didn't hear about, either from him or from his lawyers. I knew his lawyers and they knew I paid attention. They used to tell him, Hey, Louie, next time you come back, make sure you bring Lynda.

Lawyers played a big part in our lives in the mid-seventies, after he was arrested for the 1969 murder of two men, the Dunn brothers. Of all the nightmares I had to deal with in those years, this was the one that came closest to finishing me off.

It began when Louie told me there was a problem coming up for him. He's not sure what it is but it involves an old friend of his, Michael Hardy, who Louie says has turned stool pigeon.

Louie used to rave about this man, what a stand-up guy he was and so on. In the papers later on they said Hardy was basically a psycho serial killer who worked for cash, but Louie didn't see it like that. He told me Michael Hardy was basically a man's man because he had heart, but Louie later found out he stole hundreds of cars and murdered a lot of people, including one he strangled in prison in Mexico.

I remembered Hardy because he was half Irish and half Jewish. He was like a lot of Louie's friends who came to the house. You look at them and out of all the words in the English language, the last one they remind you of is the word *kind.* These were hard, hard faces, and his was one of the hardest. Frankly, it scared me just looking at him.

Michael Hardy had a big build on him and one of those Fu Manchu mustaches men wore in those years. He reminded me of Meat Loaf, that scuzzy-looking seventies rock-and-roll singer. Hardy looked like Meat Loaf on a bad day. A couple of times he stopped by the house, once with Sammy Gravano, when they stayed outside talking to Louie on the sidewalk, and another time when he came in for coffee. He didn't talk much and I got the impression that taking showers wasn't one of his priorities. But he was polite enough—he always called me Mrs. Milito.

I asked Louie, What kind of problem do you have with Michael Hardy? And he says from what he hears it looks like Hardy rolled on him and Sammy and Allie Boy. Also on another guy we know, Larry Martieri, who Louie knew from the car business and was also some kind of hotshot producer in the record business. I knew this Larry guy, fast talker to me, always looked more Jewish than Italian. Once or twice we went to his house, a beautiful place in Sea Gate, Brooklyn.

"Who says Michael Hardy's got something on you or anyone else?" I asked him.

"Larry Martieri," he said. "Larry says Hardy is talking to the Brooklyn District Attorney. Larry thinks it is connected with an old beef he has with Hardy, who used to work for Larry as a gofer. Larry had to let him go on account of his attitude, which was not good."

Living with Louie showed me that some of the people he brings to the house or we meet at weddings and clubs and such like need to be locked in a rubber room for the rest of their natural life, and Michael Hardy was a prime example. Many of the men in his life ran around spreading vicious rumors just for fun, which was maybe the case here. As far as I knew from Louie, the only business he ever had with Michael Hardy was selling him swag tires, but I wouldn't be surprised if he'd worked with him on scores he never told me about.

"It's probably all rumors," I said. "It's probably nothing."

My parents were staying with us on their regular trip north when we found out it wasn't rumors. One morning at around four o'clock, I heard someone beating on the door downstairs. It made the front of the house shake. Louie said, "Go down and see who it is. Look through the peephole, don't open the door."

He got out of bed and stood on the landing at the top of the stairs. My dog, Lady, followed me down.

Men were talking outside. It was too dark to see much through the peephole.

"Who is it?"

"Police! Open the door!"

"Why should I?"

"We have a warrant to arrest Liborio Milito."

"He's not here. He's gone to see some friends upstate."

"Lady, we know he's in the house. Open the door."

I looked up at the landing. Louie said, "They're in the yard, they're all around the house, they've got shotguns. Let them in."

My mother was hard of hearing, she slept through this, but my father woke up and came out into the vestibule. "It's okay," I told him, "go back to bed."

I told the cops through the door that my parents were staying with me and please would they come and wait in the garage, which they did. Lady was lying at my feet. One of the cops said, "You better put that dog away before I blow its head off."

"You do that," I told him, "and you'll have a big problem with me."

That was when Louie came down the stairs.

"Are you Liborio Milito?"

"Yes."

They told him he is under arrest for a double homicide in the murder of two men in Coney Island. The Dunn brothers. They read him his rights, put the cuffs on, and took him outside. I was standing there, watching this, wondering who the

Dunn brothers were, how come they're arresting Louie, and what happens now?

"I'll call you later," he said as they put him in the car.

By now it was getting light. Half the street was awake and standing on the sidewalk. I slammed the door, went upstairs, and threw up. Later I heard that at the same moment the cops put the cuffs on Louie, they also pinched Allie Boy, Larry Martieri, and Sammy Gravano.

It was a school day for Deena but I didn't want her to go, I wanted her and Louis, who was still a baby, at home with me. Louie called after a couple of hours and said to bring the deed for our house to Al Newman, the bail bondsman. That meant I had to tell my mother, who we put on the deed as owner.

Mom went into a yelling fit when she heard this. She's not worried about Louie or me or her grandchildren.

"You don't give up the deeds to the house no matter what!"

Mom always traveled with her most valuable papers, so I knew she had the deed to the house with her. I told her, "You have to come with me, Mom, you have to come to Al Newman's office and sign over the deed. We have to get Louie home."

She refused.

We're going backwards and forwards on this—she won't budge. Finally my father got into it, and for once he didn't hold back. "I don't want to hear any more of this," he said. "Sally, go with Lynda, take the papers to the bail bond office and sign the house over."

From this we posted a bond, and after a few days of keeping Louie downtown, they let him out. He said he had nothing to do with killing the Dunn brothers, he never heard of the Dunn brothers. He thought the whole thing was a setup aimed at Larry Martieri by Michael Hardy over some personal beef they had, and for some reason, maybe to make his case stronger, Hardy had dragged Louie and Sammy and Allie Boy into it, knowing they were the only three he would be leery of.

"Lynda, I swear to God," he said, "I didn't kill these guys. You must believe me. None of us are involved in this thing. It's a bullshit charge."

I believed him. By now I didn't have any illusions about Louie. But I had been with him for ten years when the Dunn brothers situation came up, and by then I was pretty confident I could tell when he was lying and when he wasn't. With the Dunn brothers I just didn't think he was lying.

A couple of years would pass before the trial. While they waited, Louie and Sammy were out robbing to raise money for lawyers. My response to all of this—the murder charges and how Louie was now making things worse for himself by taking chances when he had to know the cops were watching him night and day—was to drive myself close to another breakdown.

I was having a breathing problem, getting that drowning feeling again, like it was before the miscarriage. The embarrassment over the arrest, everyone watching, my parents being there, the fight over the deeds, and the news all over the papers. I felt disgusted with Louie—with this life we had, my life, and I couldn't do a thing.

He didn't care about his family or what happened to us. He wanted the children when he wanted the children and he wanted me when he wanted me, and when he didn't want me he would leave and I'd be there when he came back.

I had a pain in my head that wouldn't go away. It felt like there was a hammer banging inside of my skull. It was so intense it doubled me over on the floor. Excedrin and tranquilizers didn't help. Louie got scared and took me to the emergency room at St. Vincent's on Staten Island. The doctor diagnosed it as a stomach ulcer. I was running a temperature that wouldn't come down. My brain wasn't working properly, there were thoughts coming and going so fast they didn't stay in one place long enough for me to figure out what they were. Everything I could see seemed to be pulling away into the distance.

One thing I do remember: a dream about Bontate's wife, Carol, and how she once warned me about staying with Louie and getting mixed up in the life. In the dream, we were sitting on a big yacht in some tropical place and Carol was gripping my hands with hers, staring into my eyes. *You have to get out, Lynda. Lynda, this life is not for you. Lynda, you must not marry Louie.*

Louie came to St. Vincent's every day, with flowers. He looked pretty sorry for himself. Once, when he was sitting by the bed, he said, "People like me shouldn't have a family." I thought, *Now* you tell me.

They kept me at the hospital for a week and fed me on a drip tube, and when I got home I told him we have a problem. I think we should face it before I get real sick. I think we should get a divorce.

I never thought I would say it.

"You say that word one more time," he said, and he was very calm about it, "and I'll put you in a box ten feet under and tell your father you ran off with some guy to South America." He could make a threat like that and the next minute put his arms around me and say the best thing that ever happened to him was meeting me and how sorry he was about everything that I had gone through. You should have married a Jewish lawyer, he would say, not somebody like me. Then my soft side would always give in.

Like all full-time criminals, finding the perfect long-running money-making business was his biggest ambition, something that would bring in millions forever. I don't understand how their minds work, people like Louie. Maybe dreaming about money schemes kept him from thinking about the trial for the murder of the Dunn brothers, even though running around from lawyer to lawyer, trying to find the one he trusted most, kept him occupied three or four days a week.

Louie was picky about lawyers. He didn't want a mob lawyer. Mob lawyers are usually very bright guys, but in front of the wrong judge their reputation can hurt their clients. Louie wanted someone who didn't have that kind of reputation. Somebody sent him to a lawyer I will call Abe Roth, who according to Louie was a top-quality attorney who was greatly respected in all the right places for his skill and integrity.

"Did you like him?" I asked Louie afterwards.

"Yeah, he's a regular Brooks Brothers guy. He wants seventy-five hundred dollars for a retainer."

I gave him the money, in cash, which he took back to Roth, only to be asked to cough up another $7,500 on the next visit. The money wasn't a problem. What bothered Louie was the question Roth asked: Did you kill the Dunn brothers?

Louie kept the conversation going out of politeness, but the lawyer's question and his tone of voice rubbed him the wrong way. In Louie's mind, it was as if Roth had already made up his mind about his guilt and was just jerking him around to see what he could get out of him.

When he came home he told me about the meeting and asked for my opinion. "Why am I hiring a lawyer who thinks I did it?" he said. "Why isn't he starting out giving me the representation I need, that I didn't do it?"

I told him to find another lawyer. This was not the right guy to defend him in a murder trial. He should forget about Roth and find another lawyer, which is how he ended up with Gus Newman. Gus took $10,000. Now Louie was bitching about the $7,500 we gave to Abe Roth. I told him to let it go, just make out it never happened.

"But I only saw him the one time," Louie said, "and he didn't do a thing except ask me if I did the murders. Lynda, what do you think we should do?"

I told him, "Look, there's no thinking necessary here, forget the seventy-five hundred. You need to ask yourself how much is your freedom worth? Roth's out of the picture," I said. "You're going with Jack Evseroff and Gus Newman, which you should have done in the first place, and we'll see what happens."

Both men had outstanding reputations as criminal lawyers. Jack I didn't know so well, but Gus was a man I admired, a combination of a Harvard professor and a character out of a Shakespeare play. He was a big tall guy with a beard and he always put on a theatrical show in the courtroom. Juries loved him. If this case was a setup, as Louie swore it was, Gus and Jack would tear Michael Hardy to shreds when they got him on the witness stand. Meanwhile, Hardy was living under government protection.

At this time Louie would have all his business meetings at the Staten Island Holiday Inn. One day Louie got there early, before his meeting, and called me. I could hear the panic in his voice.

"Lynda! You're not gonna believe what happened! Michael Hardy just walked in with two detectives. He's got his girlfriend and a poodle with him."

I told him he should call Gus Newman's office right away, explain the situation, and get the hell out of the Holiday Inn. If the cops guarding Hardy saw Louie, he could get pinched just for being there. Being cops, they could make up some story that Louie was following Hardy, which could look real bad in the trial. It turns out that Louie was the only one that Michael Hardy was afraid of, so when he saw him in the hotel, Hardy had a fit. He must have told the cops that Louie was there. Gus called soon after Louie came home. The judge wanted to see the two of them in his chambers, first thing in the morning, which they did. The judge was livid! He told Louie to stay away from Hardy.

Great, I thought, now he's on the wrong side of the judge before the trial even starts. He'll be lucky if he gets off with three hundred years. It felt like I had a red-hot rock in my stomach.

It must have been a couple of months after I got out of the hospital that Louie tells me he's found the deal to end all deals—that multimillion-dollar score that every criminal dreams about, and this one was even more special because it was mostly legal. He met a man we can call Bob Jameson who was some kind of hotshot commodities broker in Wall Street.

I never heard of commodities before but Louie says it's like legal stealing if you work it right. Fat Bob, as he called Jameson, has come up with a guy who corners the market in some kind of grain called triticale, which Louie says is like rice, only cheaper.

Oh sure, I'm thinking. Now he's an expert on Wall Street. But I'm also wondering if this time, even if it doesn't turn out to be everything Louie says it is, maybe it could lead to something totally legitimate. I was hoping and praying that it would turn out to be exactly that.

There can't be many people who don't know there are wiseguys in just about every regular business there is—and by wiseguys I mean made men, powerful men, people who have killed and gotten away with it and work every day, just like regular people. I don't mean they're nine-to-fivers who go to the office by subway. People at their level usually are higher than that or own the company or they put in a relative to front it. Anyone who thinks wiseguys just sit around figuring out who needs to get whacked next has been seeing too many movies. The whole purpose of the Mafia is to make as much money as possible and not get caught doing it.

For all his mistakes, Louie had the brains to do well in business. He knew how to talk and listen, he was quick to learn, and he made a good impression by his looks and presence. He had natural charisma. And after I met Bob Jameson, I could understand why Jameson wanted to make a partnership with him—because Louie was everything Jameson wasn't.

We called him Fat Bob, but in fact he weighed only about 150 pounds. He came to the house with his wife, Jennifer, a very quiet and nicely dressed lady who you can tell from the way she talked was not from Brooklyn. In fact, at first I thought she was speaking a foreign language. She wore her hair in one long braid wrapped around her head and looked like the type of girl who grew up on a farm with braces on her teeth and ponies.

I figured it was best to go along with this triticale scheme and see where it went. One of Louie's associates also came in on it. Frankie the Cop, who was always coming over to the house for meetings and was basically a fixture in our crowd and a very laid-back, friendly man who they say got kicked out of the NYPD for being a junkie. Frankie dropped $7,500 in the partnership, and so did Louie, so it was a three-way deal.

Fat Bob puts on a large front about his major-league connections in Washington, dropping hints about how he knows this senator here and that one over there and how they call him up at home for advice. This was all wasted on me, but Louie, who watched the news every night as if he can't get enough of it, was very impressed. He was convinced that Jameson was in the CIA. And maybe he was, judging by what he did for Louie when the time came to put the triticale deal on the road.

I noticed that when Fat Bob spoke to me, he made a point of talking up to me, not down, asking me what I thought about the situation in some country I never heard of. After a while I started thinking he did this probably because he figured out I had him pegged as a number-one bullshit artist, and he wanted me to feel good about him because for whatever reason, he needed Louie and me on his side. And I suspect he may have respected me or had a thing for me, which he showed in little ways when his wife and Louie were somewhere else. Or maybe this was part of his plan to get me to go along—with a guy like this, who can tell what he wants and why he wants it?

The next thing we hear, we have to get passports to make a trip to Norway with the Jamesons. I never had a passport before, I never went anywhere you need passports. Louie also. I asked him, What's in Norway? and he told me this was a big opportunity for the both of us, because Fat Bob had connections with some Egyptians in Washington, and through them he got hooked up with the Egyptian ambassador in Norway, and since Louie is his business partner, we had to go with the Jamesons and help sell the Egyptians on the triticale deal.

I was listening to this and wondering if Louie had finally lost his brains. "Did you forget we have two kids?" I asked him. Deena was then about six and Louis was less than a year old. I also reminded him about the Dunn brothers case. There was no way they would let him leave the country before trial and sentencing.

"Don't worry about it," he says. Fat Bob went to see somebody who pulled a few strings and issued a special permit putting Louie in Bob's custody while we were away. He showed me the paper—it was just like he said, and it was signed, stamped, and dated from some office in Washington. What office I don't remember, I just remember it looked very official.

I told him I wasn't getting a passport and I was definitely not going to Norway.

"You are part of the deal," he says. "Bob needs the both of us there."

A week later we took off to Oslo, Norway. Our regular baby-sitter, Eileen, moved into the house to look after the kids. On the plane it was just me and Louie with the Jamesons. All the way across the ocean Louie is reading up on triticale from a bunch of papers Fat Bob gives him and he's making notes. Frankie the Cop didn't come. He stayed behind because Fat Bob said he didn't trust him and didn't want him on the trip, which worked out for the best, because Frankie fell back into drugs just before we left and was in no state to go anywhere.

We flew first class on a 747 with an upstairs lounge. There was a guy playing the piano. Louie and the Jamesons were scarfing up the champagne and caviar, two things I have no taste for. At the Oslo airport, a chauffeur picked us up and took us to the Grand Hotel, where me and Louie are booked into a suite. The bedroom had a balcony on it. Louie was out there even before we unpacked. He pretended he was Mussolini, throwing his arms up in the air and shouting in Italian to the Norwegians down on the street.

Most days Louie and Fat Bob ran around meeting Arabs, while I went sightseeing and shopping with Jennifer. I took her to the Sonja Henie Museum, which was fascinating to me because I loved her ice-skating movies when I was a kid. But I got the feeling Jennifer didn't get much out of it. And one morning all four of us went to some kind of Viking museum where Louie bought a bunch of old silver coins and a pair of Viking cuff links.

Our second night there, we go to a party at the Egyptian embassy. This was in a huge room with chairs and tables around the walls and a high table at one end with a ton of food on it. They had a band and people were dancing. At one point a woman came over to our table, and Jameson made a big fuss over her and introduced her as the sister of the Egyptian ambassador. Then she started patting Louie down, frisking him like she was a cop!

"I hear you're a professional, if you know what I mean," she goes, and I'm thinking, Who is this? What have we got into here?

I was also thinking Jameson must have a big mouth on him and any minute Louie will get up and put his fist in it—but Louie said nothing and he did nothing, he just sat there, smiling. I was too shocked to speak. The way I saw it anything you said would be the wrong thing. Then a guy comes over in a tux and a red sash. The wine waiter, I thought. He asked me to dance.

I didn't move. Louie never liked me to dance with other men. I could see him starting to stiffen up in his chair. Fat Bob leaned over and said it would be an insult to refuse. The man in the tux was the Egyptian ambassador. I didn't want to seem rude, so I looked at Louie, who gave me a nod to say it was okay. The ambassador spoke excellent English and was also a pretty funny guy who made harmless little jokes that made me laugh a lot, probably too much, judging by the black looks I got from Louie, who never stopped staring at us. We had one dance, and then the ambassador walked me over to the table, shook hands with everybody, and went back to the head table.

Louie didn't talk on the way back to the hotel. In the room he was pacing up and down. "Why do you have to dress like that?" he said.

I already knew better than to go out with him in a dress that showed too much skin. At a wedding in Brooklyn once he made me wear a napkin over my chest because he thought there was too much cleavage. The dress I wore at the embassy that night showed nothing.

That was another thing about Louie. He was a prude. Not in the bedroom, where he was a wonderful lover and far from shy, but in public he wanted me to look good without dressing like a hooker, which in those days could be the fashion with some of the wives we knew.

Now he was working himself up into a rage. He grabbed me by the shoulders and shook me, hard. "You danced too close to that fucking guy, you were coming on to him, laughing like that!"

I think the only reason it didn't get worse was because we had to meet the Jamesons for breakfast in the morning and it wouldn't look good if I showed up with bruises all over my face.

There was another party the next night. I told Louie I couldn't go. I was still feeling sick from lunch after Jameson took us to some restaurant on top of a hill. They served moose and other animals, which I couldn't eat. There were animal heads hanging on the wall and we sat next to a huge fireplace stuffed with burning trees. It made me feel woozy. Watching Fat Bob sucking on big slabs of moose didn't help.

"You have to go to the dinner," Louie said. "It's important for Bob because the host is the main business connection to the ambassador. He's the guy who has to okay the triticale deal."

"Let me stay in bed," I told him. I didn't want to go anyplace where trouble could be waiting.

At the house that night the first thing I noticed in the dining room was a large roasted animal on the table with some kind of yellow fruit in its mouth. The guests were tearing it apart with their hands and eating it. "It's a sheep," Fat Bob explained. "You have to eat one of the eyes. It's a special honor in Egypt."

"Maybe it is," I told him, "but we're not in Egypt, we're in Norway, and I would sooner hang myself than eat any kind of eyeballs."

A couple of half-naked Arab women took the floor and started belly-dancing, which was okay by me even if they didn't measure up to the Radio City Rockettes, and the music sounded as if it were being played backwards by an orchestra of drunks. But Louie and Fat Bob were having a good time, and I was about to say something to Louie when the host came up from behind and starts whispering in my ear. Would I do him the honor of joining him in his new Jacuzzi?

Not to start trouble, I told Louie I didn't feel good and wanted to go back to the hotel.

The four of us returned to New York a couple of days later. On the plane I said to Fat Bob Jameson, "So, Bob, how did we make out with the triticale deal?" and he goes, "Well, we'll be taking care of the details when we get home."

He and Louie met several times in New York afterwards.

I never asked him what happened with Jameson and he never mentioned it again. One day he said he had word from Benny Lima that he should break the connection with Fat Bob because he was not to be trusted. A dollar short and a day late, I thought. The Jamesons faded out. I never saw them again and never heard the word *triticale* again. All I know is that we spent $7,500 to go to Norway for five days for no good reason I could think of.

But he was in no mood to hear that his multimillion-dollar triticale deal had turned out to be a loser, and I certainly wasn't about to remind him.

As soon as we got home he left to go hunting in Pennsylvania. He said he wanted to be alone for a few days. He had to know what I was thinking, that he had spent money on something that didn't work out, and I think he was upset with himself because of it and probably figured if he stayed home there would be a fight over it.

Not from me there wouldn't. I was at the stage where I didn't want to fight anymore—not with him, anyway. I couldn't fight him, I couldn't leave him, and I couldn't stay with him. All I could do was do what he did: take everything one day at a time and hope for the best. Something would have to change. I wanted to be content with my children, hoping one day things would stop and the four of us would be happy.

At the back of my mind was the thought that if he got a conviction in the Dunn murders, he could go away for such a long time that part of my problem would be solved—I would be free of him and he could do nothing about it. All the fears I lived with would disappear and I would be alone. And at the same time I thought, Is that really what I want?

It would be lying to say yes. After all the abuse and everything that went with it in the years we'd been together, I still didn't know what I felt about him—it changed constantly from fear to anger to love, and then the cycle started all over again. I know I hid it from everyone. I really didn't have any true best friends.

I know at the best of times he loved me; he loved the kids

and they loved him. He could have walked out on us and he didn't. We'd seen other marriages fall apart and ours just kept going on. We had built a life for ourselves, the four of us, and maybe that was all we needed.

Or so I thought then, but I see now that I was lying to myself and had been lying to myself from the time we started going together. I wanted him to be what I thought he could be, not what he was. And I wanted the same thing for myself and for our family, but the truth is that everything I wanted was out of reach and would always be out of reach.

Over the years we would have everything that counts to be considered successful in America—money and property, and more than enough of both—but it would never change the fact that Louie was what he was because that's what and who he wanted to be. That so-called honor and respect that came with membership in the Mafia turned out to be as worthless for him as my dreams were for me.

CHAPTER 14

Cash Makes People Smile

For years, Louie told me not to get involved with his business and not to ask questions. At the same time, not only did he *make* me get involved, he would ask for advice—should he do such and such? Did I think this or that was a good idea? Did I see any problems? Sometimes he listened, most of the time he just did what he wanted, anyway.

What he could not do was keep his thoughts to himself. It was a standing joke with us. I used to think he had people in the room with him. I'd pass the bathroom door and he'd be arguing with himself in the mirror, taking both sides while he worked out something that was on his mind. You could hear him in the shower, singing a Dean Martin number and making gunshot noises. "Everybody loves somebody—*katchow!*—sometime, everybody loves—*pchoo! pchoo!*"

Once, driving home from a weekend in Pennsylvania, with Deena and Louis in the backseat, Louie started talking to the steering wheel about a meeting coming up that night at Paul Castellano's house. The two kids were asleep, but even if they'd been awake I don't think it would have made much difference.

"Frankie will vote to clip the kid," he said. "Neil will want to give him a pass because he owes the kid's uncle a favor. Tommy won't say nothing unless Paul says something, and Paul won't say nothing until the rest of us puts in their two cents. And Tommy will go along with whatever Paul says."

None of this made any sense to me.

"Louie," I said, "what is this clipping business?"

"Nothing," he says. "Frankie D has this friend and his kid's been having a hard time. He's broke, can't get girls. Frankie thinks we should buy him a couple of outfits, maybe send him to New York for a fancy haircut."

"Why can't his own father pay for it?"

"He's away for a few years."

"So for this they have a meeting?"

"We have a lot of business to discuss. I can't talk about it."

So I shut up and we drove a few more miles before he started up again. Nothing made sense to me. That's what Louie wanted.

"The best thing is to wait and see what Benny and John think. I should wait for them. If Paul says, 'Louie, where are you on this,' and John hasn't said where he is yet, I'll say if the kid's a rat like they say and if Neil owes the kid's uncle a favor, maybe we should pay back the favor some other way. Since when do we give rats a pass?"

I asked Louie, "Is this the same kid?" and he said, "I just explained to you about questions. No, it's not the same kid, it's a rat punk kid."

Mafia, I used to say if the word came up on TV. To me it was still a joke word, it's something they made up. Mafia Schmafia, I said. Louie never laughed. What do you know, Lynda, you're Jewish. You can get me in a lot of trouble the way you act. Keep it to yourself.

From Louie I learned that no talking to anyone about anything was the number-one rule in his life, but he broke the rule all the time, even when he was telling me that people who talk too much are digging their graves and don't know it. Poor, trusting Louie! Looking back, I understand how ironic it was that when his time came he saw everything except the warnings his enemies wrote on the wall.

He had been locked up in Riker's Island again, I forget why—like I've forgotten and don't want to remember a lot of what happened in those years—but not long after he got out he met someone called Bobo at a lounge that was a wiseguy hangout on Neck Road in Sheepshead Bay. Bobo was an expert on making money in the wholesale car business by buying and selling at auctions, and he told Louie how it worked. When Louie explained the ins and outs I got really excited. This was no racket, it was a legitimate proposition and it was something we could do together. Louie could take care of the technical side of the business, the engines and electrical systems. My main job would be the buying and selling, which was something I happened to be pretty good at.

The company name we put down on our business license application was Milito Cars Inc., but just before we were supposed to go in front of the licensing board we found out we had to be fingerprinted, which ruled out Louie because of his record. The guy on the board said this was no problem. The smart thing to do, he told Louie, is keep your name out of it and put your wife on the license, which we did. We called the new company L&M Motors.

We started small. In fact, the first car we sold was Louie's 1972 Caddy, which was 100 percent legit except maybe for the wheels and the seats. With the cash from this we started placing sale cars in gas stations around Brooklyn. Building on that, we were working the auctions seven days a week before long, handling maybe thirty to fifty cars a week and making a profit on everything we moved. Louie began calling himself an automobile wholesaler. We covered all the biggest auctions in Jersey and Pennsylvania.

Finally we had something where there was no need for stealing. No more swag, no more worrying about Louie getting pinched. I could even run part of the business from home when I wasn't at the auctions, and if I had to be out of the house we could depend on Inez to look after Deena and Louis.

I thought I had gone to heaven. The money was coming in and everything was going well, and then I caught Louie clocking back the miles on the odometers.

I didn't get mad, I tried to reason with him. I had just bought a black Corvette with a stick shift at the Bordentown auction in Jersey and made a thousand honest dollars on the resale at an auction in Mannheim in Pennsylvania. Louie was not impressed. He said the Corvette is a onetime thing, luck, a fluke, and, according to him, everybody knows you always get top dollar at Mannheim. Taking home two or three thousand dollars a week wasn't enough for him, he had to make more, and his solution was to roll back the miles.

I told him we didn't need to do this. Why run the risk of bringing another felony situation on himself? We had enough problems to deal with because at the time he had an old burglar-tools case pending from a pinch in New Jersey, on top of which I found out he had been doing paperwork on swag cars again.

But you might as well talk to concrete. Louie was made the way he was. Like he was always telling me, long after I get tired of hearing it, a leopard can't change its spots. I'm not rolling back the miles on *all* the cars, he said, only about 99 percent.

He didn't even try to hide it, he did it in the open, on the auction lot. A couple of minutes to get the screws out from behind the dashboard, take off the guard plate, turn the numbers back, and put the thing back together with Krazy Glue.

People we knew in the Bronx were getting heavy time for clocking. He wasn't worried. "Nah, not gonna happen," he

said, "and even if it does, it's white-collar crime. My first arrest for odometers. It's nothing."

The car auction business lasted on and off for maybe five
years. The "off" part came when we got the bad news from
Louie's attorneys that they'd run out of options on holding
back the trial for the murder of the Dunn brothers. Now
there was a court date for all four of them, Louie, Sammy,
Allie Boy, and Larry Martieri.

The trial lasted two weeks. Sammy Gravano was severed
right away—don't ask me how, I don't know what happened. One minute he's sitting at the defense table with
Louie and the other two, the next minute they put a hold on
the case against him and Sammy spends the rest of the trial
sitting with the spectators.

Louie was held in custody from day one because the DA
says he is an organized-crime figure who will take off to
avoid prosecution. Nothing Gus Newman says makes the
judge change his mind on this. He told Louie, "Mr. Milito,
you better have someone bring you a toothbrush."

"Why did they cut Sammy loose?" I asked Louie. "He's
free, you're in here. Don't you think there's something
wrong with this picture?"

"Lynda, leave it alone, this whole thing is a joke. There is
no case."

I had my doubts. If the DA goes to all this trouble, they
must have something. Three men taken out of their homes in
the middle of the night, terrifying their wives and children,
shaming the families in front of the neighbors. I was starting
to wonder if I'd been wrong to believe Louie when he told
me he was innocent. Somebody murdered the Dunn brothers, and from what I already knew about Louie and Allie
Boy and Larry Martieri, why not them?

The lawyers told me to be in court every day, not to wear
anything flashy, but to dress casually and sit where the jury

could see me. The courtroom was full from start to finish, so I had to make a reservation for a place. Louie's father came with me if he could get away from work, but mostly I went alone and took a seat on the other side of the room from Sammy Gravano. I didn't want anyone, particularly the jury, mixing me up with him in their minds.

Louie's mood went up and down. Sometimes when he called the house he'd be sweating bullets. One day he says they don't have a case, the next he figures he's looking at life. I could only tell him that everything would be okay, that if he didn't kill anyone there's nothing to worry about.

Michael Hardy was the state's only witness. Everything about him, from the swagger in his walk to the sneer on his face and the clothes he wore—black leather vest, black turtleneck, and black pants—made it clear he thought too much about himself. There was no mistaking this. Before he sat down he looked across the courtroom at Larry Martieri and ran a finger across his throat. We all saw it. I glanced over at Sammy. He was trying not to laugh.

Hardy explained how he met Dominick Scialo and Larry Martieri at a pizzeria in Coney Island. Dominick wanted to kill one of the Dunn brothers, who owed him money. According to Hardy, Larry Martieri advised Dominick to get in touch with Louie, Sammy, and Allie Boy.

I remembered Dominick Scialo from the neighborhood, but not by his first name. We all knew him as Mimi. I met him a couple of times and then he disappeared. The police found his body long before the Dunn brothers trial began.

Attorney Jack Evseroff listened to Hardy and told the jury he could describe him in three words. "He's a liar."

Jack brought out the owner of the pizzeria where Hardy said he met Larry Martieri, and the pizza guy swore on oath it had been twenty years since Martieri was in the place. Next came an ex-con who said Hardy told him in prison he would get Larry, whatever it took.

Point by point, Jack checked off everything he'd found out about this creep, and none of it was good. Michael

Hardy was a combination of serial killer and one-man crime wave. At twelve, he was caught shaking down another kid at the point of a knife. He had stolen 840 cars, pulled 250 stick-ups, and committed numerous murders, including the inmate he killed in prison in Mexico, and had been convicted of kidnapping. The kidnap victim testified. He said Hardy had bounced him off the walls of a room, beaten him with sticks, and shoved a gun up his ass.

Louie brought this man into our house—and with our children present. If he could do that, what else could he do, and what about all the other men who came to Arlene Street? What did he know about them that he didn't tell me?

Towards the end of the trial, the prosecutors came into the courtroom with a large box of tapes. We have all the defendants admitting the murders on tape, they said.

What the hell is this? I thought. Nobody said anything about tapes before. I looked at Louie, who had this stunned expression on his face. The lawyers were making so much noise, yelling across the courtroom that the judge called a recess while they listened to the tapes.

I was standing in the phone booth in the hall, calling Louie's mother, who was looking after Deena and Louis, when Sammy Gravano came along the corridor, looking pleased with himself. He stopped outside the phone booth. He was staring at me through the glass and tucking his shirt in his pants. He didn't even turn around, he just looked at me with this twisted smirk on his face. I hung up the phone.

"Hey, Lynda," he said, "did you see that box of tapes?"

I said, "Yeah, I saw them. Tell me, Sammy, are you on those tapes? Is Louie on those tapes?"

And he said, "Maybe."

As if it didn't matter to him one way or another.

I wished I could have thrown up in his face, he must have known what he was doing.

Louie called the minute I got home.

He sounded as if he didn't have a care in the world.

I didn't know what to think anymore.

"You lied to me about those murders," I told him. "They've got you on tape."

"What are you talking about?"

"You better get with your friend Sammy. If it's true about the tapes, you can do me and the kids a favor. When they let you out, don't come home."

I could hardly believe I was talking to him like this, it just came out of me.

Fifteen minutes later he was back on the line. He said he just spoke to Sammy and Sammy denied he said anything to me about the tapes.

"Lynda, I swear to God I'm not on them. You have to believe me!"

And that's how it turned out after everybody heard the tapes. I don't know who was on them or what the DA's office hoped to accomplish by pulling such a stunt, but Louie and nobody we knew was on the tapes.

Gus Newman did the closing. He didn't miss a trick. Recounting Hardy's testimony, he shook his head and raised an eyebrow. Lo and behold, he would say, every time we turn around there's a new can of worms staring us in the face.

The jury spent five hours deliberating and returned with not guilty on all counts.

That trial cost us nearly $90,000, including $38,000 paid out to a bail bonding company that went broke and took our money with it. It was all cash. None of which was borrowed.

Everyone loves cash, Louie used to say. It makes them smile.

CHAPTER 15

Fat Farm, with Bars

For the rest of the seventies, it was back to the old routine, a mixture of working every day of the week at the car auctions for me and for Louie—when he wasn't in prison.

Gradually I learned more about engines to the point where I could usually tell by the sound of the motor what needed fixing. Usually I didn't do the work myself because we had hired a couple of young guys to help out with the cars, one for the account books and a mechanic to look after that side of the business. My focus was still on buying and selling. Louie's friends in the business used to complain to him that I was shutting them out of the market.

Louie kept different hours from most people. He'd be out all night until around three, come home, and sleep until noon, then show up at the auction lot to see how much money we made that day.

The two guys we hired were teenagers from Brooklyn who so far as I know never committed a criminal act in their lives. One took care of the accounting and his cousin was our mechanic. I will call them Brian and Tommy. Their real names don't matter.

One winter day, the three of us were at an auction in Jersey and I was freezing both feet off after walking in slushy ice water all morning. We had a car on the block, and while I waited for it to move I went and stuck my feet in the toilet bowl, which was the closest thing we had to a defroster. Otherwise, it had been a great day. When Louie finally showed up I told him we took in a gross of $50,000 in checks.

I gave the checks to Brian so they could be entered in the book. Usually he did this at the lot but it had been a long day and when Tommy said he was ready to call it quits, he and Brian drove back to Staten Island.

There was nothing unusual about Brian taking the checks with him. It had happened several times before when we'd worked late. I would have trusted the kid with my life. He came from a decent family, his father was a fireman. They were good people, and his mother had always been grateful to us for hiring Brian and getting him away from the drinkers and dope smokers he'd been hanging out with. She told me once that if it hadn't been for Louie and me, her son would probably have been dead. Brian's only problem was he had never stopped drinking—he was basically a teenage alcoholic.

Even so, I wasn't worried about him taking the checks home that day. He would show up in the morning, as usual, and hand them over for banking. I thought about calling him to make sure he got home all right, but Louie didn't want to hang around, he wanted us to go out for a steak dinner at his favorite restaurant in Jersey.

When we called Brian's house a couple of hours later and his mother said he hadn't come home from work yet, we started to get anxious and it wasn't long before Louie was pacing up and down the kitchen, working himself up into one of his black fits.

"Fifty thousand bucks! What are you thinking? The kid's a drunk! I got people waiting for some of this money! What am I supposed to tell them? Sorry, my wife gave it to a drunk?"

I called Brian's mother again. She hadn't heard from him and didn't know where he was. Now *she* was worried.

Louie couldn't decide whether he should go and look for him or stay home in case Brian called. He was so mad he could hardly talk. He was up and dressed as soon as it got light, and going out the door with a tire iron. I grabbed at it, I pulled so hard it sprained my wrist getting it away from him. But he let go.

I was begging him, "Please don't hurt him!"

"I'll do what I have to do," he said, and left the house.

They came back a couple of hours later. Louie found Brian asleep in a bar where he'd spent the night. The kid was still half-drunk. Evidently he rolled his car somewhere near Midland Beach on Staten Island and left it there. Louie drove him to the site and found the checks and titles inside the wreck.

Brian was a lucky young man. Louie gave him a new name—Birdbrain.

I had a couple of minutes alone with Brian after Louie went back to bed that morning. In a few hours it would be time to start work again. "Listen," I told him, "when you screw up, I get stuck in the middle between you and Louie. So don't do this to me anymore. It's not a good idea."

I don't think either he or Tommy knew about Louie's connections, or if they knew they didn't talk to us about it. Telling Brian how close he came to getting hurt or even killed would be saying too much, so I said nothing about that. But I was pleased with myself because for once Louie took my advice and gave someone a pass. It wasn't something he made a habit of.

It's easy enough to see now that with Louie I was always trying to think what I wanted to believe—that if he stayed out of trouble, we could still make a good living and be like any other family, and even if we didn't get to be millionaires we could make enough from the car business to give Deena and Louis the education Louie and I didn't have. I was determined to put them both through private school and college.

Of course nothing changed. At the auction lots he was still clocking the cars—rolling back the miles on the odometers.

White-collar crime, he kept saying. White-collar, Lynda. It's nothing. Don't worry about it.

Nothing? I thought. Not when your name ends with an A E I O U, it's not nothing.

We were at an auction one afternoon with eighteen cars about to go on the block. That was my job, getting up close to the auctioneer and waiting for a bid I could live with. I used to give the auctioneer a little kick in the leg and a ten-dollar tip when I heard the right price. That day Louie and I were taking a coffee break in the office when he said, "Cops! Tell the boys to get the cars off the lot!"

Then he pushed me out of the back door.

There was no way Tommy, Brian, and I could move the cars before they got seized—they had already shut the place down and put troopers on the exits. Nobody was going anywhere except Louie, who they took away in handcuffs. Somebody must've ratted him out about the odometers.

They gave him six months' state time in Jersey, and eventually he would get three years' federal for the same thing. While he was doing the state time we heard from our attorney that the IRS had been in touch, asking questions about Louie's finances. From what the attorney said, it sounded like they already knew most of the answers.

While he served his time I carried on with the car business, but not in Jersey, because we had now been banned from the state. Instead I took Brian and Tommy to Southern Auto Auctions in Connecticut, which was small potatoes, as we were moving only three or four cars a week, just enough to make a living and cover legal expenses.

Louie called from the prison most nights. We all talked to

him. We were about to hang up one night when he said, "Do me a favor. You have to stay out of Jersey for the next couple of weeks. Don't be driving on any major highways over here. Especially not with the kids."

I asked him why and he said it's because they were giving him one of those pointy sticks and a bag and putting him to work picking up litter by the side of the roads.

Deena kept asking me, Where's Daddy? I told her he was at a fat farm and coming home when he lost a few more pounds. It was as good an answer as any. Louie was always going on diets—he was a man who loved to eat.

CHAPTER 16

Sammy Gravano, Animal Lover

I think about Debbie Gravano now and then and wonder how she and her kids are getting by. Like us, she and Sammy had a son and daughter, Karen and Gerard. They were about a year or two younger than Deena and Louis. All four children would eventually go to the same private school, the Staten Island Academy. Debbie drove them there and back. She would call me at seven every morning to remind me to have Deena and Louis ready for pickup at seven-fifteen. I'd usually been up late working the car auctions, so I would beg her for another fifteen minutes, and at seven-thirty on the dot she'd be at the front door.

Karen became a good friend of Deena's as they grew up, but not Gerard and Louis, who had their own circles. In my opinion, Gerard was always a nice kid, he got along with Louis even though he was always withdrawn. If you knew how his father brought him up, or didn't bring him up, and always wanted to change him, you would understand why.

He had his own friends and Louis had his. Debra used to pick up Louis when it would snow and take the two boys sleigh-riding by her house. I trusted Debbie; she cared about Louis like her own son. Karen even looked up to Deena.

The boy had always wanted to be a fireman. Sammy said this was a job for losers—his idea of a great career was professional boxing. Sammy even forced Gerard to take boxing lessons at a gym because he said this would toughen him up. I read in a newspaper article back in the eighties that the owner felt bad for Gerard. From the look of the kid as he grew older, I figure his father probably fed him on the same steroids Sammy took to make himself bigger. Just about everything that scumbag ever did was to make himself look bigger.

I'm an animal lover and I heard from Louie that Sammy bought a rottweiler that was trained as an attack dog. Unlike our Doberman, Lady, who would carry her leash in her mouth when you walked her and who was about as savage as a butterfly, Rocky, Sammy's dog, would rip your face if you got close enough.

Louie came home one day and said, "You hear what happened to Rocky? Gerard was out in the backyard and the dog bit him. Sammy got his gun out of the car and shot him. Killed him in front of the kids."

Isn't that nice? I thought. Why would he train the dog to attack if the dog is going to be with the kids? He should have put the gun to his own head.

Not that Louie was any better when it came to setting examples. A guy in the neighborhood sold some M80 firecrackers to Louis and a couple of his friends. Firecrackers? They were more like sticks of dynamite. One of them went off in a boy's face and almost blinded him. When Louis came running home and told his father what had happened, Louie and a friend went to the guy's house. The friend stood guard at the door while Louie beat the man senseless with a baseball bat. Louis and his friends were out in the street, watching.

So I could imagine how Debra must have been feeling after Sammy shot the dog. I've had dogs all my life—even now it makes me shudder to think that anyone could be so cruel as to hurt a defenseless animal. Deb would have felt the same way.

To this day I think of Debbie as a good and kind person—she was one of the most accommodating people I ever knew, always asking if she could do anything to help out. She took the kids skating, she took them to the movies, to eat out, and in the winters, when it snowed, they all went sledding in the park.

We had much in common. We both took a lot of shit from our husbands and didn't have whatever it takes to get out from it. We talked just about every day, but not about that. And for all the talking between us over the years we never once talked about the life, about the people we knew in it or about what Sammy and Louie did when they were together. We knew better than to talk about certain things.

Anytime there was some kind of function like a wedding or a party, it was always the two of us, Debbie and me, sitting at the same table with other friends, gossiping about this and that. About our kids, mostly, and about clothes and houses and whose marriages were in trouble or which of our friends was expecting or had just had a baby.

Louie came home one day and said that a man called Carmine Galante had just been whacked at a restaurant over in Bushwick. The *Daily News* had a front-page picture of the scene the next day. The old man had a cigar in his dead mouth. Louie said, "Carmine was a stool pigeon. A fucking rat. He had it coming." I didn't say anything. This was one of those occasions where saying nothing was the unspoken rule. Louie never once said to me, Don't talk to Debra about this or that. Whether Sammy said the same thing to Deb I don't know, and I never asked her if Sammy told her as much about his business as Louie told me about his, or whether Sammy asked her for advice, like Louie did. Silence was the understood golden rule.

These were subjects we knew better than to mention in any way, shape, or form. Debra and I didn't even talk about what happened to her own brother, Nicky Scibetta, who disappeared years earlier.

I didn't know him well, but we saw him at their house once or twice and here and there, and for an out-and-out gay guy who didn't try to hide it, he seemed harmless enough. Nicky's problem was he made things difficult for himself by mouthing off to people and starting fights he couldn't win.

After he disappeared they found body parts around Brooklyn. A hand or a piece of an arm, I forget which. The Scibetta family just about fell apart, his mother in particular. She was destroyed by his death. People thought she would go mad from grief, and perhaps she did, because she never got herself back together afterwards.

Her son's murder was a mystery. For a while, anyway. Everybody wondered who would do such a thing and why.

The only person not wondering about it was Sammy Gravano, who had Nicky killed. Sammy made no secret about this. It was in his book. Why was Nicky killed? Well, if you disregard the weasel words Sammy used in his book to justify himself, he had Nicky killed for two reasons. Number one, Nicky was gay and Sammy thought having a gay brother-in-law made him look bad, and number two, by killing Nicky it would show the Gambino bosses Sammy had the guts to be a made man.

So here's a man who let his own wife's brother be killed and kept it a secret from her for ten years—and even when Debra found out about it, she still stayed with him.

I used to wonder if maybe Louie was involved in Nicky's murder, if he helped Sammy or even did it himself. Louie didn't like talking about Nicky Scibetta. And I didn't push it. He would have said, It's none of your business. Why are you asking so many questions? And the right answer would not be, Because I'm your wife and I have a right to know what you're doing. These are not things you bring up with him if you don't want to get your teeth knocked out. But I would learn many years later that Louie *was* involved. Not just him, but another guy in his crew, a young man called Stymie D'Angelo, and Stymie I'd known for years. If you can believe Sammy, it was Louie and Stymie who cut up Nicky's body.

That's what I remember from 1979, and I wished I could forget it and just about everything else from the time Louie had come into my life fifteen years earlier. I didn't have any illusions left about him. No dreams, no fantasies, and no hopes that anything would change for the better. There was no peace in my heart. Our life was mainly about tension and fear. For me it was a pretend life. Pretending everything was okay when it was anything but. Pretending to like people I couldn't stand to be around. Pretending that if I kept smiling I could hold the family together. Pretending I could handle whatever came along.

There was nothing to be done about Louie and his activities; he would do what he wanted for the rest of his life and take whatever chances he felt like taking. It had always been like that and it would never change. But I still wanted something more, and towards the end of that year I decided that one way to get it was to find a business—a legitimate business—where I could earn a good living and not have to depend on him. About the only skill I had was selling. I seemed to have a natural talent for it, and since it couldn't be in cars anymore, it had to be in something else, something that brought in a solid return with low overheads. The answer was obvious: real estate. I would do whatever it took to make it in the real estate business.

I applied for a New York State license, which meant sitting for an exam, and this scared the hell out of me—I had a problem reading anything longer than a couple of lines. Now I would have to read books and questions and write down the answers. Preparing for this turned out to be much harder than I expected. My mind was all over the place. Forget about concentrating on the questions and coming up with the right answers—I couldn't understand the words on the page. It took me three months hitting the books day and night before it started making sense.

When I thought I knew it all, I took the exam and failed. I had to wait a month before they would let me take it again, and again they failed me, so I went back to the books and passed on the third attempt.

To make the kind of money we needed, I decided that starting out on a peanut payroll with a big real estate corporation was the wrong way to go. The big time could wait until I knew my way around the business. I wanted to be with a small company, take no salary, and work on commissions only, and I knew just the place. It was a storefront real estate office at the bottom of Todt Hill that was owned by a woman called Mimi Neuhaus. She and her secretary, Marie, and a couple of salespeople were the entire staff. This was perfect for me, because I prefer working with women, and they both made me feel very welcome.

Mimi was busy investing in apartment buildings herself, so I was left to handle most of the business that came over the phone. It was just the experience I needed.

I sold the first house a week later but the deal didn't go through because the central agent held out for too much. Then I sold a semi-attached for $76,500 to a buyer who wanted an adjustable-rate mortgage. It's the small things you sometimes remember. I remember this deal because we called the client the guy in the white socks and because he had a talent for making educated guesses about the mortgage market. He bought at 17 percent, and a year later it was down to 11 percent.

All of this was exciting to me. It made me proud to feel that I was in charge of my life again, at least a big part of it.

I was making money honestly, learning a new profession, and loving every minute of it, and I felt certain I could be a success in the business if I didn't mind working day and night, which is what it takes. In the first year I made $40,000 in commissions and improved every year afterwards. When I finally had to give up real estate after ten years, I had broken a lot of records in sales and won quite a few awards.

Louie complained that I was working too much. "You'd pay more attention to me if I was a four-bedroom colonial," he said.

I told him this was true but only if he was priced under market value.

The Gravanos bought a house on Staten Island soon after we bought ours. Theirs was on Lamberts Lane, and it was kind of small and semi-detached. Sammy didn't like having close neighbors. Now he had eyes for Todt Hill, the most exclusive part of Staten Island, known to the locals as Mafiaville because Paul Castellano had a huge white mansion at the top of the hill.

Louie called the office one day. "Find a house for Sammy on Todt Hill," he said.

I told him I wasn't doing Sammy any favors. I'd find a house for him but I would want the full commission.

Debra and I drove all over the Todt Hill area until we found one on Beebe Street. The owner wanted $395,000. We closed at $375,000, half cash, half mortgage. They put the deeds in Debra's and her father's names.

Two years after they bought the place, Debbie told me her kids didn't like living there. They missed their friends from the old neighborhood.

I could understand that. Todt Hill had many advantages: it was exclusive and expensive, but it wasn't the kind of area that encouraged children to play outside. Debra was also worried about Gerard's grades at the Staten Island Academy. He wasn't doing so well and neither was his sister, Karen.

It was Debbie who found their next house, on Lamberts Lane in Staten Island, and she asked me to close the deal.

They never spent a night in the place. Sammy knocked it down and built a mansion on the same site. People called it Sammy's Shrine to Sammy.

Louie was amused. This was after Sammy screwed with the Plaza Suite and the house farm, so Louie didn't care how much I made. (The Plaza Suite Disco was one of the largest and most popular discos in Brooklyn. Louie had a piece of it.) He said, "Go ahead, do what you gotta do. People have to pay for your services. I don't expect for you to have to do it for nothing."

III

1980-1988

CHAPTER 17

Tough Guys Fall

In the car business we made enough money to buy three one-story commercial buildings on an acre and a half in Staten Island. They were cement block buildings rented out as body shops and for other automotive services. One of them burned down. I don't know how it happened or if it was deliberate or an accident, but I know the damage came to around a thousand bucks. The insurance people paid out $300,000, which was divided between two insurance adjusters and Louie, who took his hundred grand in cash and put it in a briefcase he kept in his mother's attic.

That was the money he used to start out in the shylocking business, which for those who don't know how shylocking works is basically lending cash at high interest to degenerate gamblers and people who for some reason can't use banks. In the life, these are called vig loans, which is the word for interest. Louie's vig was 6 percent. A guy who borrowed a thousand made payments of sixty bucks every week. If he paid off the thousand in one lump the week after he took out the loan—and nobody ever did, as far as I remember—all he would have to give Louie was a thousand and sixty dollars. But since the customers were mostly no-hopers who had to scramble for dollars to throw away on the next horse, the next fight, the next football or baseball game, or whatever, they mostly paid the minimum and never ever got close to paying off the whole thousand.

For friends, Louie made exceptions. A regular customer could go on paying off his vig loan for years, for the rest of his life if he was unlucky. Friends got a pass. Louie charged them 33.3 percent interest on the condition they would pay off the loan in a certain time frame, so if a friend borrowed a thousand, the most he would have to pay back was $1,330.

It was my idea for Louie to go into shylocking. He was already taking a nice percentage from a guy who worked for him on the waterfront, running numbers based on attendance at different racetracks around the country. Numbers, like shylocking, was a way of making safe, easy money, and I thought that if Louie stayed smart he could keep out of trouble with the police. Shylocks take risks with their own money, which means they don't have to make big turn-ins to the bosses, like they do when they're working other kinds of scores. Louie could keep what he made and, more important in my mind, he would also be less involved with Sammy Gravano. I guess I was still hoping that with shylocking, Louie could make the break. But like everything involving Sammy, I was wrong. They couldn't get enough of each other.

The rumors are that shylocks bust your legs, crack your head, or kill you for nonpayment. But Louie was convinced by me that sometimes you can't take blood out of stone and sometimes something is better than nothing. Louie then created a system whereas the borrower could knock down the loan and eventually pay it off. I used to tell Louie all the time, Use your brain, not your fist. He actually listened. He used to tell our kids, Listen to your mother. She's a witch, she's never wrong.

Tommy Bilotti was Paul Castellano's bodyguard, chauffeur, and gofer. Tommy talked in four-letter words and could hardly get to the end of a sentence without falling over himself. Paul was an intelligent and well-read man with fine taste in food, clothes, and music. Why he picked Tommy for his sidekick was something nobody ever figured out. But the two of them were so close. Although he was tough, he was a very loyal captain to Paul Castellano.

Paul gave the impression that he was an important and successful businessmen, which he was—in construction, meat packing, and supermarkets. Except for police departments across America and just about every federal law enforcement agency, nobody would have guessed that this man was the head of the country's largest crime family.

Tommy worshiped Paul. He would have given his life for him, and in the end that's exactly what he did, except he didn't so much give it as they took it away from him.

I told Louie that if he wanted to succeed in the shylock game, he should forget about copying Tommy's method. It could only come back on him. "You should be like Joey Mann," I said, "he doesn't go around breaking people's legs when they can't pay. Have compassion, first try other angles."

I have to figure that Louie took this advice, because shylocking was one business we talked about a lot, so if anyone had been falling behind on their payments he would have said something, and he never did. And, like me, he respected the way Joey Mann ran his business.

Joey Maniscalco—Joey Mann—we had known since Bensonhurst. Joey was a shylock and a captain with the Colombos. While the rest of that outfit sat around doing nothing after Joe Colombo died, Joey was making a pile of money putting his money on the street. He was what you call a full-time earner.

I had always loved everything about this guy, I don't know why. Every time we saw each other we started laughing, like there was a private joke between us. All he had to say was, "What are you doing, Lyn?" and something in his voice and his face made me crack up. I was crazy about him as a friend, nothing more.

Joey and Louie were good friends, too. Louie called him Ed Norton and Joey called Louie Ralph Kramden on account of the fact we were all big fans of *The Honeymooners*. It doesn't sound so funny now, I guess, but when Louie used to dance around the floor like Jackie Gleason and say in his Ralph Kramden voice, "To the moon, Alice," even I couldn't help laughing.

Ah, Joey! He reminded me of the young Sinatra. Skinny as a stick, always trying to gain weight. Big smile. He started losing his hair when he was about twenty-five and put in a few rows of hair plugs, which did him no good. He married a hairdresser called Marie. They were crazy about each other but they couldn't live together. Or she couldn't live with him. Joey was in a panic. We asked them to come with us on our honeymoon to see if this could put them back together, but Marie didn't want to hear about it. Eventually she got a divorce.

Joey then married a wonderful girl called Lorraine. They had a couple of little boys she dressed in coordinated outfits, and they bought a broadside ranch on a double lot in Great Kills, Staten Island, with a ramp down to the garage and steps up to the front door.

People thought of Joey as an eccentric. He was always immaculately dressed, without a wrinkle in his clothes, and he never drove anything but a white Cadillac. People might laugh at this, but he was also a modest and humble man. Sure, he didn't have any scruples when it came to business. In the life you don't go far with scruples.

Joey collected butterflies. They came from dealers all over the world. He kept the live ones in glass tanks in his den in the basement. When they died, he put them in frames and hung them all over the house.

Of all the people I knew from before, I wish I could speak to Joey Mann one more time. But it's not likely to happen. He became one of Sammy Gravano's victims. Sammy didn't kill him, but when he rolled over for the FBI, Joey was among those who got pulled in. Last I heard he was doing life. I don't suppose that seeing him again would make the two of us laugh like we did in the old days, but I would sure like to find out.

Louie made a lot of money shylocking. He took my advice: he never laid a finger on his customers and didn't have a bad loan in his shylock book. The business lasted close to ten years, and in that time he must have moved around $10 million through that book.

So, what with his money coming in and the commissions I was making in real estate, you could say we were making a fortune. Louie kept his in hundred-dollar bills in a pair of cowboy boots in the bedroom closet. Some weeks they would be stuffed to the top and other times he would start worrying because he was down to a boot and a half. Some of it he would eventually take out to Hofstra University on Long Island to pay for Deena's education.

I think of our house now as a place filled with money, and it was. But in the early eighties, if I had paid closer attention to what was going on outside the house, I might have realized that changes were taking place in the life that nobody could have imagined a few years earlier, because at this time many of the people we knew started dying, none of them naturally.

One of the first to go was Ralph Spero, the father of Tommy Spero, the guy who married Camille Colucci after Tommy had her previous husband murdered by Sammy Gravano. Next was Tommy's uncle, Shorty Spero. With his two main protectors gone, you didn't see too much of Tommy Spero afterwards.

We heard later it was Jerry Pappa who killed Shorty Spero. This was the same Jerry Pappa who hung around with Jimmy Emma when I was still at Lafayette High. After Jimmy was killed, Jerry hooked up with the Genovese people. Now it was his turn. They say he forgot to ask the bosses for permission before he killed Shorty. Jerry was sitting in a restaurant at 14th Avenue and 69th Street in Brooklyn when a man with a shotgun came up to his table, and blew his brains out.

"What about that?" I said to Louie. "Jerry Pappa shot. Tough guys fall."

"It's what happens when people get stupid," he goes. "Forget about it, it's none of your business."

As always, one killing led to another. One day in the spring of 1980, he told me he had to go to the funeral of a friend's son who died in a traffic accident. I hadn't heard anything about this, so I asked him, "Who's the friend?" Louie said it was a man named John Gotti, who lived in Queens.

He told me afterwards that Gotti cried and embraced him.

"You know what he said, Lynda? He said I was lucky I still had a son."

Not long after the funeral, the driver of the car that killed Gotti's son disappeared. There were stories in the newspapers wondering if John had anything to do with it. The name John Gotti was starting to appear all over the New York papers.

In the summer of the same year, Frank Amato was killed. Frank was married to Constance Castellano, Paul's daughter. She was a slim and very pretty blonde. Paul adored her. They say Frank died because he'd been cheating on her. That's rich—they say in the papers for years Paul was cheating on his own wife with their housekeeper under their own roof! Even so, Frankie had to go. His murder remained a mystery for years until it was reported that he was killed by Roy DeMeo, who cut up the body afterwards.

Roy I had known since the mid-seventies. He came to the house on Arlene Street a couple of times. The only way I can describe him is to say he was a very serious person. But he sure did talk a lot. He was known for it. Louie spoke of him as being a man's man, which in his language meant that Roy was a very hard guy, the type who was good at his work and didn't take any crap from the men in his crew.

"Crew?" I said at the time. "You mean like in construction?"

Now I knew better.

Roy and a friend of his, a guy named Hymie, used to show up at the auctions when we were car dealers. For years, Louie had been selling him swag cars with phony titles—fancy automobiles, Porsches and BMWs and Jags, which Roy shipped to Puerto Rico. According to the FBI, Roy DeMeo had killed at least forty and maybe as many as two hundred people who disappointed him.

By comparison, Louie was a lightweight when it came to numbers, but I figure he was doing his share in the early eighties. If what Sammy Gravano told the government is true—and of course I have to swallow very hard to believe anything he ever said—it was him, Louie, and Stymie D'Angelo who killed John Simone, an old Philadelphia wiseguy known as Johnny Keys. Sammy said they drove him to the woods in Staten Island and Louie shot him in the back of the head. This happened maybe a week after Labor Day, 1980, and it was all over the newspapers when they found the body, which was barefoot.

Louie was nervous for weeks afterwards. When we drove anywhere he was constantly checking the rearview mirror and making sudden turns. I did the same when I drove, and didn't know what I was looking for.

Sammy and Louie involved in the murder of Johnny Keys? Louie shooting a guy in the back of the head? Why not? But Stymie D'Angelo? Stymie and his wife, Karen, were two of the nicest people I knew. When I eventually saw Stymie's name in the FBI reports years afterwards, I still found it hard to believe Stymie could murder anyone. He was such a low-key sort, and what a gentleman.

Hindsight tells you everything except what you need to know when it counts most. If Louie had been paying attention or if I had known more than I did, instead of picking up scraps here and there that meant nothing when you put them all together, everything might have turned out different for us. The fact is, I don't think he knew any more than I did about how things were changing around us. And even if I had known what was coming—that Sammy would make a deal with John Gotti to move in and take over the Gambinos—you think he would have listened to me?

So far as Louie was concerned, Sammy was his partner and his best friend. Sammy would never turn on him. Frankly, I thought the same thing myself. Sometimes he had me fooled, but not for long. Maybe I didn't like the man and maybe Louie sometimes laughed at him when he wasn't there—he used to say Sammy Gravano was so short he had a Napoleon complex—but in those years, I always took it for granted that nothing would ever change for these two. One way or another they would always be together.

The Plaza Suite Disco opened in late 1981 and soon became one of the city's hottest and most popular nightspots on our side of the East River, with big-name acts appearing on special nights. Stretch limos lined up in the street outside, young people with and without connections to the management jammed the entrance, begging for admission, and others waited in lines that reached around the block. I don't think Brooklyn ever saw anything like it—not in my lifetime, anyway.

Louie was one of the owners, along with Sammy Gravano and one or two others, although, as I have said, who owned what and how much of it they owned were details known only to those who had a piece. In our life, secrecy about business partnerships was one of the many unspoken rules. The fact that Debra Gravano was listed on the property deed as the owner of the building meant nothing, except that it was to conceal the identity of the actual ownership.

Louie was involved with the place long before it opened. His part was to organize the electrical and construction work. After the opening he became a "host," one of several who welcomed customers and kept an eye out for trouble-makers on the weekends, when it was usually filled well beyond capacity.

I never went, partly because Louie was against it and also because at the age of thirty-five I had no interest in mixing with a crowd that was mostly younger than me. Deena, who was around fourteen when the place opened, pleaded with Louie to be allowed in. He refused. He told her he would have pictures of her posted at the Plaza Suite and in every club in Brooklyn and Staten Island, with a notice saying that she was a minor and that if she showed up he was to be called immediately.

Deena ignored this, and one night when Louie was off, Sammy saw her on the dance floor and told her she would have to leave. He also promised not to say anything to Louie, but I guess he couldn't resist the opportunity to play the rat, because a few nights later, while I was helping Louis with his homework, I heard Louie lecturing Deena about going places she shouldn't when she was underage. He was trying to be angry with her and failing completely. Where Deena was concerned he couldn't help himself; everything that was hard and vicious in him simply melted away—and she knew she had this hold over him. I didn't have it and neither did Louis— Louie used to say our son was too much like his mother, he was too Jewish—but Deena in his mind was every Italian father's ideal daughter. She was Daddy's little girl. She was his princess and she could do no wrong. Even his friends nick-named her the princess. I used to think Louie favored Deena but I guess he felt a boy should be raised rougher. I tried to shield Louis as much as I could. It was Louis who wore penny loafers and corduroy hats, and not pointed Capezios. It was Louis who wore Ralph Lauren shirts with the Polo emblem at the age of five. I was different, and wanted my children different: no black leather jackets.

We knew most of the Plaza Suite staff, among them Mike

DeBatt, whose father once owned a Bensonhurst bar called the Bus Stop. Sammy stole the place after Mike's father died from an illness. He told everyone he was doing this out of the kindness of his heart for the DeBatt family, because the old man owed him money, and by taking over the bar, Sammy was wiping out the debt.

Mike DeBatt was floating around Sammy, but Sammy wasn't letting him earn. So Louie took Mike DeBatt personally under his wing and put him on the front door as a bouncer at the Plaza Suite. He was also a natural sweetheart, this Mikey, a big, friendly kid—a huge kid, in fact, who played football in college and became pretty much a lost soul without his father around. But he certainly looked up to Louie—you could see that plainly enough when you saw them together.

Another friend of ours who worked the door with Mikey was young Vince Sabbatino, who was in no way connected but was close to Louie. Sammy hated him, like he hated many of Louie's friends—but with Vince it went a bit further. Sammy wanted him gone. For months he'd been telling Louie that Vince had been stealing cash from the Plaza Suite. Louie didn't buy it. He was naïve in many ways, especially in his judgments about people, but where his investments were concerned he didn't miss much. If Louie suspected that Vince had been stealing, he would have killed the kid himself.

I believe Sammy wanted him dead because Vince was too close to Louie, and for that reason alone threatened Sammy's relationship with Louie.

But killing Vince Sabbatino could be a problem for Sammy. Vince was a nephew of a Gambino, and his father was connected to one of the bosses by marriage.

I don't mind saying that when Louie told me about Sammy's complaints—and by now Louie was coming to me with information that he should have kept to himself—I thought for a moment that perhaps it wouldn't be such a bad thing if Sammy actually killed Vince, because he would almost certainly be killed himself. But of course I couldn't let that happen. Instead I stepped in for Vince and told Louie he should ignore Sammy's wishes and make it plain to Sammy that there was no evidence of theft, so Vince was not to be harmed.

There was another point to consider. The friendship between Sammy and Louie had cooled off lately, even though, or perhaps because, they were partners in the Plaza Suite. As usual in the life, when large amounts of cash were involved, greed, egos and intrigues among the numerous partners came into the picture. Some of those involved would pay a heavy price.

Knowing nothing about these developments then, I focused all my attention on the real estate business.

In 1982, I was in my third year with Mimi Neuhaus and learning a lot, quickly. Business was great. I bought a condo in Pompano Beach and started thinking about moving out of Arlene Street and buying a house on Todt Hill.

Both the children were still at the Staten Island Academy. Deena was a B/C student, but her teachers said she had outstanding verbal skills and could do better for herself if she spent less time socializing with her girlfriends.

Some mornings she was up at five, finishing her homework. She was a captain of the basketball team and a member of the softball team. Eventually she would be elected president of her graduating class, with a lot of help from her brother Louis, who ran around the school grounds pasting up her campaign posters.

Deena had inherited some of her father's dark good looks and was turning into a very pretty girl. She was polite, she carried herself well, dressed nicely, and was popular among the teachers and boys and girls. Only once did she bring any trouble home from the school, and that was when she and a friend, a doctor's daughter, went to Greenwich Village and bought a bottle of something called Rush, which kids then inhaled for kicks.

Deena told me they had been caught with it at the school.

She also said that the headmaster would like to talk to me in his office.

It was a short interview. I explained that Deena had confessed, that she was so worried she had been unable to sleep for the past few nights, which was the truth, and had given me her promise that it would never happen again. The headmaster said that as far as he was concerned, it was a closed case.

School was a problem for Louis, though, and it became a nightmare for him later on, after his father went to prison again. The boy had trouble memorizing his lessons. His grades were constantly in the C and D range. He was teased because he was chubby and had a cast in one eye. They called him four eyes. Children can be so mean. I told him four eyes are better than two. He smiled when I said that.

One boy, the son of a doctor, threatened to kill him. He told Louis he should come to school the next day ready to defend himself. Louis, who was then about nine, said nothing to me about this threat. A teacher sent him home that day when he was found carrying a knife.

He was asked to name the other boy but he refused. Louis was taught not to be a rat, but I knew who it was. I sent Deena to his house to tell the boy's parents—politely—that they should instruct their son to leave Louis alone before someone got hurt. I didn't tell Louie about this. Sending him to see them would have been a bad move—he wouldn't have been satisfied with words.

Money was pouring in from the Plaza Suite but not in Louie's direction. Sammy kept telling him his payoff would come later on, which was enough to make me smell a rat, but again it was something Louie didn't want to hear about. Something else was going on behind the scenes that I knew nothing about and only put together much later, after just about everyone involved in it was dead.

A man called Frank Fiala rented the place for a private

party that ended badly when his guests got out of control and almost wrecked the interior. Sammy was so enraged, he wanted to whack Fiala on the spot—and he would have done it if Fiala hadn't offered to buy the place for a million dollars cash, with another half million under the table. Or these were the numbers that eventually came out. What the true figures were, I never found out—and neither did Louie.

At that time he must have been confident that the Fiala deal was a major score in the making.

There were many rumors about Frank Fiala. It was said he had a couple of Rolls-Royces, a private jet, a helicopter, expensive homes around the world, and who knew what else, including the fact that in addition to being a successful and legitimate businessman, he was a major cocaine dealer and had a taste for kiddie porn. This alone would have condemned him in Louie's eyes—he thought that child pornography was totally repulsive.

My guess is that when he and Sammy realized how much Frank Fiala was worth, they decided to accept his offer for the Plaza Suite, take his money, kill him, and keep everything. First they made the deal and took the money—how much exactly and where it went, who can say, but I could name one or two possibilities if I thought they were dead by now.

Fiala's time came early on a Sunday morning when the place was still crowded. Mikey DeBatt was at the door. A car pulled up with two passengers and double-parked outside. When Fiala arrived with his group, someone gave Mikey a signal to close the doors to stop anyone from leaving. Two men in ski masks stepped out of the double-parked car.

The *New York Times* reported on June 28, 1982, that Frank Fiala was found dead on the street after being shot in each eye and once in the mouth by a man wearing a ski mask. The next day it was reported that he was shot five times in the face. The *Times* also said that Fiala had just paid $300,000 for the Plaza Suite plus another $300,000 under the table.

Ten years later, when Sammy Gravano gave himself up to the federal government, he told them that the two men with the ski masks were Louie Milito and Stymie D'Angelo. Louie did all the shooting, he said. There are reasons why I think that for once, he was telling the truth.

Right after Frank Fiala was murdered, Louie said that even if the man went to hell he would be blind and could never again get off on kiddie porn. Perhaps he said this after reading the papers, I don't know. But a couple of days after Fiala was killed I was putting away some handkerchiefs in the top bureau drawer and I found a revolver, two ski masks, a fake mustache with a bottle of glue, and a pair of gold-rimmed glasses.

"What's this all about?" I asked Louie when he came home.

"It belongs to Sammy. It's got nothing to do with me."

"Did you kill that guy outside the Plaza Suite?"

"What's wrong with you? You think I could do something like that?"

He was starting to get steamed. I knew that if I pressed it he would knock me down, so I let it go. I didn't believe him, but I wasn't about to tell him so. I had made excuses for him over the killing of young Billy Stagg mostly because I knew how much he liked Billy's company, I made excuses so far as Mickey the Mutt's murder was concerned. All I had was a hunch that Louie did it. Everything else—his involvement in the killing of Nicky Scibetta and that old mob guy from Philly, Johnny Keys, the biker shooting when he was with Sammy, and who knows how many other murders and how far back they went—all of that came out years later.

But I didn't have a doubt in my mind about who killed Frank Fiala, and Louie didn't give me much cause to think it was anyone but him. He just about threw the fact in my face.

Everything I had seen in the bureau drawer was gone the same day.

The paperwork for the Plaza Suite deal, along with the money Frank Fiala paid for the place, was put in escrow in the office safe of Sammy's attorney and accountant. His name is unimportant. Louie used him when we set up the Mildeel Realty Corporation to handle the purchase of the three commercial buildings we bought in Staten Island. These were listed under the name of one of our friends, Nicky Mormando, who was known as Cowboy. Louie put the deeds in Cowboy's name because he was the only person we knew who filed an income tax return every year.

The attorney's office caught fire and was completely destroyed, along with the safe and its contents. As usual, I warned Louie that Sammy had everything to gain by this convenient fire while we had everything to lose, and as usual, Louie told me to stop disrespecting Sammy, that the fire was an accident and didn't matter because we could get new copies of the paperwork.

When I asked him about the money he said it had been taken care of and to shut up. End of conversation.

For his end of the Plaza Suite, Louie ended up getting nothing unless you count his share of a restaurant in Brooklyn and the piece of a horse farm Sammy bought in New Jersey, both of which turned out to be worthless.

I found out about the place in Brooklyn when he asked me what I would choose as my favorite dish if he took me to the fanciest restaurant in town. I told him stuffed artichokes.

Next thing I knew, we're pulling up outside the Golden Gate Restaurant on Knapp Street in Sheepshead Bay. The building was notorious—not as a restaurant, but from its previous function as one of those short-stay hotels where couples checked in for a couple of hours and paid up front. It was quite well known.

So I was not very impressed when Louie told me he owned a chunk of the place. The décor was what some people call Mafia glitz. Gold and silver mirrors all around the room and green and beige wall coverings. Jade green upholstered banquettes and two diagonal tablecloths on each table, a green one underneath and a white one on top. This was typical Sammy Gravano style, tacky beyond belief. All it needed was a couple of disco girls in cages.

Young Mikey DeBatt was at the door, escorting customers to the tables. As far as I could tell, most of them were wiseguys we knew from all over New York.

The chef came to our table with a plate of stuffed artichokes. Not bad, not great.

"Why are we here?" I asked Louie.

"We own it," he said. "Me and Sammy and Stymie."

"That's nice. Since when do you three know anything about running a restaurant?"

"You know your trouble, Lynda? You're a very smart woman but you don't have vision. You need to stop criticizing. Look at the crowd here. This place will be a winner."

There was no point in reminding him that this particular crowd was probably eating and drinking for free in return for old favors. Louie always saw what he wanted to see, no more, no less.

The Golden Gate closed without even getting its name in the phone book. Louie never saw a dime out of the place.

The horse farm turned out to be even worse.

For months, Sammy had been talking about property he bought in New Jersey. I didn't know Louie was a partner in the deal, not then, but I found out one holiday weekend when Sammy invited us to a barbecue. I didn't want to go, I had some real estate paperwork to catch up on, and the thought of being around Sammy made me feel ill. And angry, because it was clear to me that Louie got the shaft in the Plaza Suite deal and I wasn't sure I could trust myself to keep my mouth shut in Sammy's company, knowing Louie was used. But the kids wanted to go—Uncle Sammy! Uncle Sammy! Let's go see Uncle Sammy's new house in the country!—and Louie insisted on it, so I didn't have much choice.

It's not until we're in the car driving to the place that Louie tells me he and Sammy are partners in the farm. A year or so before this I wouldn't have dared to challenge him about anything, and on some matters I still didn't, but now my blood was boiling.

"Horse farm?" I said. "Who wants a horse farm? What happened to the money? We have tuition fees to pay and you're talking about a fucking horse farm? Did Sammy ask you if you wanted a horse farm?"

"Let's just look at it," he says. "Maybe it's better than you think."

Stymie D'Angelo and his wife, Karen, were there, with Mike DeBatt and his wife, Dawn, some other men from Louie's and Sammy's crews, with their families, and of course Debra Gravano and their two kids, Karen and Gerard.

The horse farm needed lot of work, to say the least. This was obvious the minute we pulled up. The buildings were falling down, the place looked as though it hadn't been lived in or used for years. It was filthy. Louie was watching me.

"You like it?" he said.

"Like it? What's to like! Look at it! I can't believe you allowed Sammy to put your money into this. What do you know about horses? We have bills to pay. We need money for the kids' tuition."

I just went off at him and for once he didn't say a word. I think he was starting to see what I saw, finally.

Our host was at the barbecue grill in a cloud of greasy smoke. I could only hope that he would fall face first in the fire and burn up. I didn't trust myself to speak to him so I went inside and found a chair, where I stayed until we left.

Sammy came in and said, "Lynda, let me show you our barn."

I told him I had sprained an ankle walking in my high heels on the rocks in his so-called driveway. What I thought was this: He could stick his barn up his ass. He manipulated his partner; he did something Louie would never do to him.

Louie brought me a plate of food and went back outside

to join the crowd. I didn't say a word. He knew I was mad.
We left as soon as the children finished eating.

When we got home I told him I was disappointed in him.
I wasn't scared of him now, I was just angry and I didn't
mind telling him why.

"You got screwed on this deal, that's what happened here.
Your own partner took your money and put it where he
wanted it. You like that? You really like that? Did he ask
your permission to do that? Did you tell him it was okay to
do this?"

Louie was always telling people when we were in the car
business and after I started in real estate that he was a kept
man. I heard him tell his friends that when his wife answered back she was usually right. He used to tell Deena
and Louis, "Listen to your mother, she's a witch and a very
smart witch."

He was just sitting there, saying nothing.

I think Sammy understood when we drove away that day,
he was going to have a problem with me. And I didn't have
a doubt that he would do whatever it took to fix me before I
fixed him. As Sammy wrote in his book, *Underboss,* he and
Louie had a split of waves. All along he knew I was responsible for that. I was tired of Louie being used by Sammy and
Louie not seeing the obvious.

Except in jokes now and then, when he called him a crazy
Polack or something like that, I never heard Louie say a
word against Sammy, but after the Plaza Suite deal I got the
feeling that something must have happened between them.
Or maybe he'd been adding up the twos and twos himself
and coming up with fours.

Sometimes, when he came home from seeing Paul Castellano he would repeat things Paul said about Sammy that he
would never have told me before.

"Paul's got it in for Sammy. I don't know what to tell him.

I'm not sure what he's getting at. He keeps asking me questions I can't answer. Today it was, 'What the fuck is Sammy doing? Why is he keeping everything? Keep Sammy away from here, we can't trust him! Don't bring him to the house! How do we know he's not a fucking rat!'"

Louie said he always stood up to Paul for Sammy. But there was no question in my mind he was starting to have doubts of his own.

When he was home he no longer called Sammy nine times a day, and Sammy wasn't calling him so often either. I noticed this and said nothing. I was still the best of friends with Debbie Gravano, who continued picking up Deena and Louis for school and bringing them back to the house at the end of the day. If she knew something had gone wrong between Louie and Sammy, she didn't mention it. We carried on like we always did, talking about our kids, their schools, movies, TV, the new malls opening up out on Long Island—talking about nothing, really. I guess we both found comfort in it.

I wanted to ask Debra if Sammy ever said anything to her about the new laws the feds brought in against organized crime—the RICO act, they called it. Lately, Louie couldn't stop talking about it. He was deathly afraid of this RICO thing, whatever it was. You don't understand, Lynda, two guys could be discussing business over the phone or someplace and the feds can make a pinch under this new law.

I didn't know what RICO meant then, and as things turned out, Louie could have saved himself the worry, because he didn't live long enough to get pinched for it, but once he heard about it he started calling every attorney we knew to find out more.

But I didn't bring this up with Debra. You open one door and you might find yourself walking through another one, the wrong one, and that wasn't a risk we could afford to take. Over the next few years, there were more killings of people she knew, people I knew—the same people, friends of our husbands—and like me, she must have read about them in the papers or heard it on the TV news, but anyone listening to our conversation the next day would never have guessed it. We talked about nothing. It was safer.

Louie no longer used the phone at home so often, but would go out and make his calls. He started doing this after I noticed a beat-up old van parked on the opposite side of Arlene Street one Saturday. It was there when we woke up and it was still there four hours later. Louie brought it to my attention. I quickly said I was going over there, and he said to me, "Are you sure." I said, "Yes, I'm sure."

He was doubtful. "You sure you want to do that?"

I was mad. I told him I was sure.

There was a man in the front seat of the van. I knocked on the window. He rolled it down. There was another man in the back of the van, watching TV.

I said, "Excuse me, what are you doing?"

"Why, do you live around here?"

"Yes, and I don't like people parking in front of my house, if you don't mind."

He was very polite.

"In that case," he said, "we'll leave," and they drove away.

Louie panicked when I told him. He kept saying, "What are we gonna do? What do you think they're doing there?"

"Don't use the phone," I said. "They're watching you, they're listening to your conversations. Be very careful."

Louie and a lot of other people would have been safer just turning themselves in to the feds. Their friends sure didn't do them any favors. Now it was Roy DeMeo's time to go, serious Roy DeMeo, the man's man who took nothing from nobody and who for years had worked with Louie in the swag car business. Roy's turn came in 1983, when they found him in the trunk of his car. The police said he was roped up and frozen solid. They didn't find the bullet holes in his head until they thawed him out.

"Another tough guy falls," I said to Louie.

He was watching TV. Didn't say a word.

Roy DeMeo had been to the house twice when I was there, maybe more often when I was out. He had the same look as a lot of Louie's friends—they didn't avoid your eyes but you got the impression it would be a mistake to look at them for too long. I guess some people might have said the same thing about Louie. I still thought he was the most handsome man alive, but maybe if he didn't know you and you caught his eye at a bad moment, you could find yourself in a lot of trouble. The main difference between him and Roy DeMeo was that Roy looked as if he had too many bad moments. He behaved like a gentleman when he stopped by the house, he was always very polite, and, like I said, he was fond of talking, but at the same time there was something about the way he carried himself that made me uncomfortable. He was one of those people who, when they looked at you, gave you the impression they knew things about life that you would never know.

In their report, the feds said that in addition to killing maybe a couple of hundred people, Roy and his associates stole more cars than anyone in history and made a fortune shipping them out to the Middle East via the Caribbean. Louie must have been one of these "associates" and maybe he also worked with Roy on the killings—who knows? For a while there was a rumor that he had something to do with Roy's murder, but later on there was a report that Roy was killed by other people we knew—Nino Gaggi and his crew—which in some ways came as an even bigger shock to me than if Louie had been mixed up in it.

Last time I saw Nino was at his daughter Regina's wedding reception at a ballroom in the Plaza Hotel in Manhattan. Nino was dressed impeccably, as always. No stains on his tie, no wrinkles in his suit—he looked as if he'd just been polished—like he was about to open in Vegas. He had that show-biz look; in fact, I thought of Nino as Paul Anka's double but with lighter skin.

That day at the Plaza he was making a stop at all the tables and collecting fat envelopes for his daughter, which he handed over to one of the men walking with him. It was something you always saw on these occasions. I wasn't taking much notice. Only two things stand out in my mind about that wedding—a buffet table with an ice swan on it the size of our double front doors at Arlene Street, and the ballroom ceiling. There were windows up there and I thought I saw something or someone moving. I told Louie, who took a look himself and immediately went over to Nino.

Next thing you know, everyone is looking up at the ceiling. Nino is going red in the face and yelling for someone to get the manager. It turned out there was a small room overlooking the ballroom and the FBI were up there, taping the reception. Nino took his lawyer with him, along with Louie and John Bontate, and found their way up to the room. The FBI agents refused to leave. They said the Plaza Hotel was a public place and a listed building or some such bullshit, and this being the case, they were entitled to stay.

"These people are ruining the biggest day of my daughter's life," Nino complained to the manager when he finally showed up.

The manager must have figured this was a no-win deal. For him basically it was a choice between getting on the wrong side of the U.S. government and irritating a lot of people who anyone in his right mind can see without looking twice are nothing but well-dressed thugs with a lot of influence. He was not happy with the situation.

"I'm sorry, Mr. Gaggi, the room is a public facility. In matters like this we have to obey the law."

It was probably the first time Nino or anyone else in the

room ever heard that expression used in conversation, and I remember someone making a joke about it at the time, but as we moved through the eighties it was getting harder and harder to find much to joke about. I felt things were starting to slip away from us.

CHAPTER 18

Moving Up to Todt Hill

We owned a condo in Florida at 777 Federal Highway in Pompano. It was the three sevens that got my attention, plus the fact that an old friend of ours from Bensonhurst lived close by and had a couple of kids who were good company for Deena and Louis whenever we went south for vacations. But what really caught my eye was the bathroom wallpaper, which had a pattern of automobiles all over it and which I saw as a good-luck sign because when we bought the place we were still in the car business.

By the eighties, the good luck had pretty much worn off and what with working at real estate and this and that, we were using the condo less and less. I decided to sell it to invest the money in something new.

Louie met a guy called Joe Polito, who was in the steel erection business in Cleveland and wanted to move to New York and open a new company. Louie could be a partner if he put some money into the deal. He had already lined up a few contracts for new construction.

Joe needed $60,000 to cover moving expenses and set up two offices, one in Corona, Queens, the other in a trailer across the street from the World Trade Center. According to Louie, if he came up with the money, Joe would get him into the Ironworkers Union as a supervisor, which meant a salary plus medical and pension benefits.

"What do you know about steel building?" I asked him.

One thing about Louie, when he applied himself to something he wanted to do badly enough, he didn't let anything get in the way of learning about it, and he was a fast learner.

Louie had a friend in Las Vegas, Jimmy DeNiro, who worked in steel construction. Jimmy explained the basics over the phone. Basically all you have to do, Louie told me, is read the blueprints, join the beams together with welding and nuts and bolts, and keep going until you get to the top.

Out of the $67,000 we got for the condo, Louie fronted Joe Polito with $60,000 to open the new company, Gem Steel. It was a shylock loan with three points a week vigorish. Part of this came back as Louie's salary and the rest in what we called gratuities—two new Cadillacs the first year, an Eldorado for him and a Seville for me.

By now we had moved from Arlene Street to a house on Todt Hill, just down the hill from Paul Castellano's mansion. The new place was big, around five thousand square feet. Louie loved the house—we all did, but to him it was the most beautiful house in the world, or would be once he'd finished putting in a new interior, building a wall around the front yard, and stocking the backyard pond with fish, ducks, and geese.

We bought two geese and named them Ralph and Alice, after the Kramdens. We also had two black ducks, and named them Ed and Trixie from *The Honeymooners,* and two white ducks called Tic and Tac. Whenever I came home they honked and kept on honking until I went out back to say hello. At the local supermarket once, I ran into a woman I'd seen on Todt Hill, although we had never spoken. She recognized me. "Oh," she said, "you're the people with the geese and the ducks."

If she only knew about "the people."

Louie did all the work on the house—even the interior, which was torn out and rebuilt by Louie's worker. But it was Louie who came home with a truckload of slate for the roof and mossy rocks a Pennsylvania farmer had given him. He used these to build the front garden wall, smoothing off the cement with a Popsicle stick, and when he finished the wall he planted a row of white azaleas in front.

Not long after we moved in he said he wanted a new table and I asked him what kind. "A godfather table," he said. "Glass top with high-backed chairs. It's for meetings. We need a bigger table for meetings."

The one we bought was twelve feet long without the extensions. It came with ten chairs and four matching armchairs. Pretty soon he was having two or three meetings a week, usually with the same men, sometimes with new faces, and they'd show up in a group of ten to twenty guys— Louie's crew, only he didn't call them a crew. When he referred to them it was always, "my men," or "my guys." And just like he never told me he even belonged with the Gambinos, he also didn't tell me that by this time he had made captain in the Gambino family.

It's wrong to judge a book by its cover, so they say, but none of the men who came to the house could have been mistaken for anything but wiseguys or wannabes, so I can't say it came as any great surprise a few years later when they began disappearing one by one, as if they had never existed.

I have no idea what they talked about at these meetings, although sometimes if I had to go into the room, a couple of them would be gossiping about somebody who wasn't there. Louie disapproved of gossip, it made him uncomfortable, and he would roll his eyes at me while they mouthed off like a bunch of yentes about how much they hated this one or that one.

The only thing that concerned me was the mess they made on our beautiful glass table, dropping cigarette and cigar ash all over the top and spreading crumbs from sweet, sticky Italian pastries. As soon as they left I used to throw a bottle of Windex and a roll of paper towels at Louie and tell him to start polishing.

"What are you laughing at?" I asked him once.

"You don't want to know," he said, and kept on polishing.

The thing is, I did want to know. Maybe if he had told me more at the time, between us we could have connected the dots, but he told me only what he wanted to tell me, and my guess now is that he didn't know enough himself about what was happening under his nose.

I believe the two years he spent working on that house were the happiest of his life. Planning the work, bringing in the materials, and putting them in place—every new project was an exciting adventure to him, whether it was inside or out. And he wasn't just skilled at the work; he took pains to get everything the way he wanted it. The azaleas he planted bloomed like clockwork on Mother's Day. Unless someone pulled them up I guess they must still be there, and I hope they are, giving pleasure to passersby, though it's funny to think how surprised those people might be if they knew who planted them.

Apart from the house and shylocking, Gem Steel was now his whole life. Five days a week he was up at five-thirty, out of the house an hour later, and on the site by seven-thirty. The cash was rolling in again and rolling out just as fast. Where and how he got the money I had no idea and didn't ask, though sometimes I got a hint of the how.

"What's on the other side of that wall?" he asked me once when he was dropping me off at my office at Schlott Realty, on Highland Boulevard. There were several companies in the same building.

"Staten Island Furriers," I told him.

"Is that a fact. And where does that ladder go that's in the hallway?"

"To the roof," I said. "Louie, what are you thinking about? If you're thinking what I think you are, you can forget it."

"My men have to eat," he said.

"Look," I told him. "I work here. My last name is Milito. Who do you think they'll suspect if someone breaks into the fur guy's place? Don't you think the cops will come straight to me with a whole bunch of questions? What happens if they hook me up with one of those lie-detector machines? This is not the right score for you and your guys, it's too close to home."

"Ah, forget about it. I was just curious."

We started spending weekends at Atlantic City with Joe Polito, his partner in Gem Steel. Joe was a high roller at the craps and blackjack tables and he sometimes won so much money, the casino gave him two armed guards as escorts. Louie played baccarat. He preferred it because it was quick and because they played with twenty-dollar bills. I never did understand the rules of the game, and to tell the truth, I didn't care. All I know is that the casino people treated us like royalty, and apart from what Louie lost at baccarat, which was never much, they picked up the tab from the time we left the house until we got home.

Joe Polito had an attitude and got into a habit of mouthing off at wiseguys, so Louie had to keep defending him, even though Joe was in no way a mob guy himself. In the first year of Gem Steel, Louie was constantly having to go to sit-downs, mostly to stop Sammy from killing Joe.

There was a third partner at Gem Steel, or if he wasn't a partner, he had some kind of job at the company. Mario Mastromarino, who Louie said he had known since he was a kid. Louie chose him as second godfather to our son, Louis. That's where I first met Mario, at the confirmation, when Louis was ten. I didn't like being around him, not because he reminded me of a gorilla, which he did, but because he walked out on his wife and five children and moved in with another woman, Eleanor, who had money of her own and lived in a big house in Dyker Heights. They eventually married.

Eleanor sometimes put him down in public by calling him Marian and talking to him and about him in a high-pitched, whiny voice. If I'd done that to Louie he would have punched me. Mario pretended not to notice.

There was another reason I didn't feel good about Mario Mastromarino. While he certainly was no made man in the sense that he belonged to a crime family—no made man who let himself be insulted in public by his girlfriend would last twenty-four hours—Louie insisted that I show Mario respect at all times, just like he still insisted that I show respect to Sammy, even though Sammy was no longer his closest partner.

Respect Paul Castellano, okay. And Neil Dellacroce, who was like Paul's number two, no problem. I had a lot of respect for men like Paul and Neil and many others, not because Louie said I should respect them, but because they were men who had some dignity and manners, who had the same old-fashioned values Louie had—and if this sounds hard to swallow, considering their willingness to order the murder of anybody who got in the way of family business, I can only say that most of the guys they killed were stone-cold killers themselves.

The way I saw it, with Mario it was different. To me, he was just one of those guys who liked to hang out with people in the life. Maybe it made him feel important when they sent him out for sandwiches. I thought he was nothing more than a glorified gofer for Louie, and probably he knew the way I felt about him, because when the time came to settle old grievances, Mario would put the knife in and twisted it, hard.

That time was getting closer. The first sign of trouble came in late 1984.

We went down to Miami for my niece's wedding, which happened to be on the day of our own eighteenth anniversary. In fact, a bellboy had just delivered eighteen roses Louie had him bring up to our room at the Fontainebleau. The phone rang. It was Michael Rosen, one of Louie's attorneys, calling from New York. For almost five years Michael had been trying to make a deal with federal prosecutors that would keep Louie out of jail for tax evasion and for turning back the odometers when we were car dealers.

The government claimed that income tax returns filed in 1978 and 1979 were short by $1.6 million, numbers which stunned me, because we didn't make that kind of money in the car business. The $50,000 we made the day Brian got drunk and totaled the car was a freak event; it wasn't an everyday thing.

The reality was that Louie's punishment was a payback for everything else he got away with, and we both knew it.

We always figured that Mike Rosen could work things out with the government. I thought of him as a good friend and a miracle maker who could make problems disappear. But this was one problem even Mike couldn't solve. The best he could do was get an agreement from Doug Grover, the federal assistant DA, that if Louie copped a plea he wouldn't have to go to trial. So Louie pleaded guilty to the tax evasion pinch, and he did that mainly for my sake, because he knew another trial would have finished me off. I wanted him to plead not guilty, because a jury just might rule in his favor. Not too many people like the IRS—besides, the figures weren't what they said.

Mike called us in Miami that day in 1984 to say there would be no miracle this time. The feds wanted Louie to turn himself in immediately and start a three-year sentence at the federal prison at Allenwood, Pennsylvania. If he didn't show up he could consider himself a fugitive from federal justice.

Now we both had a problem, because it was my signature he forged on the income tax returns for 1978 and 1979 and sent to the IRS after I told him I wouldn't sign it. I refused because I knew they were fraudulent—not on the scale the feds claimed, that's for sure, but still way out of line with the true numbers.

What was I supposed to do? Turn him in to the IRS? And if I did, how would I explain this to him and hope to keep breathing? The truth is, I could no more rat on Louie than I could on anyone else—it went against everything I was taught. This is what I thought I should do: Handle the problems as they come and do the best I could with what I have. Always stand by Louie, right or wrong.

We flew out of Miami on the first flight back to New York.

The holidays were coming up. On the flight back I asked him, "What do we tell Deena and Louis? What about Thanksgiving? Christmas? What about next year and the year after that? What do we tell the kids?"

He didn't have any answers.

I didn't tell him how I felt. That if he went to prison again I didn't know if I could stand it one more time. Remembering those visits to Riker's Island, the disgrace and disgust I felt, and how I had promised myself never to go through such an experience again—to me it seemed that we were stuck in the same place, back in time, not moving forward, but falling backwards. It wasn't just the fact of him going away—in some ways it was a relief knowing I wouldn't have to watch my mouth, and of course if he wasn't there he couldn't hit me—but not knowing what would happen next or what he would do next and how nothing in our lives was certain or free from fear, this made me feel helpless. And more and more hopeless.

How could he have not seen, with all the killings of people we knew, that the walls around his world were closing in on him—or did he think he could escape the worst if he was in prison? My children were hurting and I could not stand to watch this. I felt I was in a house that had a curse on it. Those walls were closing in on all four of us.

CHAPTER 19

Burying the Needle

His old friend Vito came to the house in a stretch limo early the next morning. Louie had already packed what they told him to bring—three T-shirts, three pairs of underwear, money for the prison commissary, a robe, and a pair of rubber thongs. It was cold that day. I didn't want to get out of bed when he left the house, but at the last minute, as they pulled out of the drive, I watched from the window, and I thought, There goes my life.

Deena and Louis were still asleep. Deena was then at Hofstra University and had exams coming up. We decided not to wake her, figuring she would be so upset she wouldn't be able to concentrate on her books.

For a while I told the kids their father was away on a long hunting trip.

Deena didn't buy it.

"Over Thanksgiving? He never misses holidays! How come he's not calling? You know Daddy—he always calls!"

After three weeks I told them the truth. Their reactions were completely different from what I expected. Louis was devastated. Deena, once the shock wore off, didn't seem so bothered. Maybe it was because her social life at Hofstra and with her friends at home helped her put it at the back of her mind. Having a father in prison even seemed to be a social asset, which is not very surprising, since some of her friends had fathers who had either been inside or were already there. It gave them something in common, they didn't feel alone. Maybe they could even comfort each other.

I love my daughter, but I have to say that she was like any popular, pretty teenager—what she cared about mainly was her friends. Back then, image was everything. The right clothes, the right music, the right friends, the right car. I could understand that, I'd been there myself, but I was terrified that she would kill herself, the way she drove. I opened the glove compartment of her car once and it was stuffed with traffic tickets, nearly all of them for speeding. She acted like it was nothing.

Or maybe she was just pretending she didn't care. Whatever the reason, it wasn't something she wanted to talk to me about. As the months passed, it was difficult for us to talk about anything without getting into a fight.

All three of us drove to Allenwood the weekend after I told the kids what had happened to their father. The visit didn't go well. Louie was uncomfortable. He told the kids to go out in the children's playground and leave us alone while we discussed business. Money, as usual. Vito helped out with the collections. Mario was also supposed to give me a weekly payment of $1,700, part of which came out of the book and part from Gem Steel.

If Louie had any interest in the children, he kept it to himself during that visit. I wanted to tell Louie I was trying to get Louis to play soccer, which would be a good game for him, but he didn't ask one question about Louis or Deena, and I didn't tell him what was on my mind: that I felt I was losing control of Deena, and that Louis was spending hours alone in his room, watching TV and hardly talking. He became almost a recluse.

There are prisons much worse than Allenwood, which didn't even look much like a prison. It was in the country, with deer running through the woods and coming up to the fence to be fed. It had a library, with magazines. When Louie wasn't working out with weights, he was in the library, copying ideas for the house out of *Architectural Digest*.

A couple of days after he got there he ran into an old friend and neighbor, Tony Padrone, who was doing time for a heist at JFK, and Tony introduced Louie around and helped him settle in. Eventually, he would even make money at Allenwood. He met Paulie Lombardi, who owned the biggest car dealership in the tri-state area and had also been locked up for income tax evasion. Paulie needed a $6 million renovation at his plant in New Jersey. Louie got a percentage for arranging the steel work through Joe Polito at Gem Steel.

While Deena's friends seemed to think it was okay that her father was in prison—or at least didn't think it was that big a deal—for Louis it didn't go so well, not with the snotty boys at the Staten Island Academy. Some days he came home crying, begging me not to make him go back to school the next day. There were boys chasing him around the yard, yelling at him, calling him Jailbird.

"Look," I told him, "your father is in Allenwood for not paying income tax. It's not like he killed the president. They gave him three years, which means he'll be out in two, probably in time for your thirteenth birthday."

I gave him a picture of myself to put in his school briefcase and told him that whenever there was a problem at school he should go somewhere and look at the picture. It would remind him that his mother loved him and wouldn't let anyone hurt him. "Ignore the bad names," I said, "the names are just words, they don't mean anything."

I was boiling mad with Louie. He was destroying our family, that's how I saw it. You can say, Well, he destroyed other families, too, what's so special about his own? And of course I understand that and can't deny the truth of it, but I didn't know then what I have learned since, and all I worried about at the time was how Louie's absence from home, his being locked up again, was his own fault, not ours, but it was his family who had to pay for it. Louis especially.

At this point Louis needed his father more than the rest of us did. For most of the day I could stay busy with real estate, dealing with business problems that usually had solutions. There were no solutions to our problems at home, but at least when I was working I could pretend they didn't exist. And Deena was old enough to face up to the world. She had the drive and the energy to live her life the way she wanted, like any girl her age, on top of which, she had the kind of personality that made her popular wherever she went.

But for her brother it was nothing but torture, and I blamed Louie for this. The boy was going through hell and there was nothing I could do for him except let him know I was on his side.

For a long time after Louie went to prison I thought about killing myself, and I knew I could do it. The other option, staying alive, didn't make sense. Staying alive meant uncertainty, fear, and danger, and no way out from it. Nothing to hope for, ever, nothing to look forward to. I wanted to stop thinking and worrying, never feeling safe, always being scared—scared of him when he was there, and scared when he wasn't. I was starting to hate him. If I killed myself I wouldn't have to worry anymore, I wouldn't have to go to bed and lie awake all night.

And I couldn't kill myself because Deena and Louis would be left with nobody to take care of them, no one to teach them right from wrong. But the time would come soon enough when even that responsibility was too much for me to handle.

During the first eight months he was at Allenwood I called all the attorneys I could find. I called government prosecutors and people in the Bureau of Prisons—anyone who might be able to lead me to someone who could get his sentence reduced. And every day Louie called the house collect to curse at me for not making it happen. His true violence came out in his words and in a tone of voice that left me shaking after we hung up.

"What the fuck are you doing to get me out of here? After everything I've done for you! You wanna wind up in a trunk? Is that what you want?"

Everything he was doing for me? By this he meant the $1,700 Mario was supposed to bring to the house every week. Some weeks Mario showed up with half, sometimes it was less. I made the mistake once of complaining about this to Louie, which set him off again.

"You're disrespecting Mario! What did I tell you? You don't ever disrespect Mario!"

I had more respect for a rabid skunk than I did for this miserable creep, but I had to pretend otherwise.

And Sammy Gravano was back in the picture again. I figured Louie was probably calling him from Allenwood, and Mario must have told Sammy I'd been bitching to him about the short payments, which was true enough, because even with my income from real estate, the bills were coming in faster than I could pay them.

Sammy put the knife in because that's what he does best and because he hoped it would poison Louie against me. That was another mistake—reminding Louie what Paul Castellano said about Sammy and saying that I agreed with every word.

"I don't wanna hear that! You show respect to Sammy! And shut up about Mario—he's doing the best he can!"

Most times Louie called he hung up on me, and every time he called back I felt I had to apologize for upsetting him and pretended that it was my fault, hoping by saying that, it would put him in a better mood. I told him I was sorry for whatever I said before and for still not having any good news from the lawyers—as if I were in some way responsible for him being locked up. The lawyers could do nothing to help him get out, he was guilty, he got pinched, and now he was paying for it. But maybe something else was eating at him, maybe he figured that his world was turning inside out while he was away, and it was, judging by everything that happened when he was in Allenwood, so there was not much he could do to keep his place in it except hope that he would stand with the survivors when it was all over.

Visiting hours at Allenwood on Sundays were from nine to six. Deena usually had plans on weekends, so Louis went with me, not always, just now and again. We made a little game out of it, driving the three hours it took from Todt Hill to the prison. Our name for the car was the World Famous Silver Bullet. Louis would be in the backseat looking over my shoulder and staring at the dashboard to make sure I didn't go too slowly, and if I did, he would shout out, "Bury the needle, Ma! Bury the needle!" And I'd have to drive so fast the speedometer needle would go off the clock.

He couldn't wait to see his father, and he always hoped this visit would be better than the one before, because nearly every time we went, Louie would come out into the visiting room and tell Louis to go outside and play on the swings because he needed to talk to me.

Sometimes I would find myself crying on the drive there and back and not knowing why. I thought I was too angry to cry. One minute I would be feeling okay, all things considered, trying to occupy my mind with work or something safe and ordinary, and the tears would come—they just sat there and then they overflowed.

If Louis was with me, he would usually fall asleep when we started for home. We never played "bury the needle" on the drive back.

It was work that helped me stay sane. Work was safe. It had rules and routines. Sometimes things might not pan out the way you expected, but mostly it was just a question of taking on a problem and solving it, which for me meant finding a house someone wanted to sell and finding someone who wanted to live in the house. In real estate I found that I had a natural gift not just for selling but also for negotiation.

My golden rule was never to sell anybody a house I wouldn't want to live in myself. For some reason this theory fascinated one of the real estate lawyers I worked with, and he gave me the impression that this wasn't the only thing that intrigued him. Friends in the business noticed this and commented on it.

This was the last thing I wanted. For years Louie had been telling me I should have been with a Jewish lawyer instead of him, and here comes a Jewish lawyer, Ken—which is not his real name—whose professional advice I needed and valued, but nothing else.

Whenever I went to Ken's office I was always in a hurry to leave, or pretended I was. I'd tell him I couldn't stay, there were papers to sign, I had to see a client. Or I needed to be home for when the kids got back. And he would say, Slow down! Stay and have some coffee. Don't you like me?

The problem was the opposite. I was beginning to feel attracted to him, not in a sexual way—I think by this time I was completely turned off by the idea of sex—but to his easygoing manner and his legal talent. At one time he was handling at least fifty of my property deals, so there was always a lot of business to discuss between us.

Any thought of romance was out of the question. Impossible. If Louie heard even the faintest rumor, he would kill us both when he came home or arrange for someone else to do it before he got back.

Ken was everything Louie used to be but no longer was. Relaxed, straightforward, and considerate. He was just a regular and completely normal man, and because of this and his lack of anger and his openness, he was like no man I'd been around in almost twenty years. And because he was friendly and went out of his way to help others without asking or expecting something in return, people liked him. So did I. He was someone I felt I could trust.

We started having lunches together, talking, mostly about business, at places where I could be pretty certain I would be unrecognized. It was an innocent friendship but I wasn't about to run the risk of one of Louie's friends seeing me with a stranger and jumping to the wrong conclusion.

To be out with a man who liked my company, who didn't curse or yell or threaten, was such a new experience that when Louie called the house, his yelling and rage had no effect. I would listen to him, apologize for not having good news about lawyers, promise to show more respect to Mario and Sammy, then I'd hang up and go meet Ken for a closing or a lunch.

I didn't tell him about Louie, who he was and what he did, or that he was in prison. He knew I had a husband and two children—and that was all he knew, and I was glad he didn't ask too many questions. If he'd known the answers he might have left, and I couldn't stand the thought of losing contact with the one person in my life who made me feel sane.

A woman friend in the real estate business once asked me if there was something going on between Ken and me, and I said, "What are you, crazy? He's just a good friend who helps keep my deals together."

On Sundays I still went to Allenwood, sometimes with the children and sometimes alone, and I'd have the car radio on both ways, burying the needle and singing along with the music.

It was Louie's anger that led me to lose hope in him—in us, really, since it was harder and harder to think we had a future together. All the abuse—physical, mental, and emotional—had turned me off, worn me out. That and the fear of what might come next. I felt sorry for him and didn't dare admit it. Perhaps I wanted to love him but couldn't, not anymore, and I didn't dare tell him that, either.

It's easy to see that now, but if anyone had asked me then how I felt about Louie I would have been stuck for an answer.

He had chosen to do things he knew would never allow him to live at peace with himself, but he did them anyway because it was expected of him—demanded of him—and because he had taken an oath that gave him no choice. And I think when he was in Allenwood he had reached the point where he could no longer live with himself. I don't know what he thought when he went back to prison that last time but I believe he knew he was being forced into a corner, and maybe he was losing the will or the strength to fight his way out.

He said once, a few years before Allenwood, that the only time he felt good was when he left the city and went hunting. For a few days, he could forget about the world. Then he would start for home again, and as soon as he reached a certain exit on the New York Thruway, everything came flooding back. His brain would start working over-time and in a split second he would be just as tense as he was when he left. There were meetings he couldn't miss, places he must be at certain times, money to be picked up and passed on, and who knew what else. Maybe there was someone who had to be killed, an old friend who trusted him, who would never suspect that the last face he saw before dying was Louie Milito's. Driving back into the city, Louie told me, he could feel himself turning back into a monster.

CHAPTER 20

No Longer Bulletproof

The shylock business went on without Louie and he still had a guy running numbers for him on the Brooklyn waterfront. Vito collected the shylock money and Mario Mastromarino helped with the clients. When somebody needed a loan he would arrange it with Louie over the phone, and if the loan was more than Mario had available, Louie would call me to say I should take the cash out of the cowboy boots. Since it was a sure bet the prison phones were tapped, we made these arrangements so that nobody listening could understand what we were talking about. Deena and I kept the book up-to-date when the money was dropped off.

Everything was written down in a loose-leaf black book, which was about five by seven inches. As payments came in, the boots in the bedroom closet began filling up again, but not for long, because there was a steady demand for new loans and money would suddenly get tight. At one point Ken had to advance me a $2,500 commission so I could pay tuition fees for Deena and Louis. He also gave her a summer vacation job in his office.

I was grateful for this, but as the months passed and Louie's release date came closer I began to worry. It wouldn't make any difference to him that my friendship with Ken was based mainly on business—to Louie the idea that I spent any time alone in the company of another man was unforgivable. And how would Louie be after all this time? Would I still feel afraid? Was his mental state worse than what it was when he went in?

I wondered if I should tell Ken about Louie. I could say to him, You don't understand what can happen, you don't begin to understand. Staten Island is small. A lot of Louie's friends live here. What do you think Sammy Gravano would do? Don't you think he'd tell Louie the first chance he got?

I couldn't bring myself to tell him.

It wasn't just Sammy I had to worry about. Louie's parents had moved from Bensonhurst to Arlene Street, our old neighborhood, and I had been really happy to have them so close, but now I was terrified that his mother would somehow hear I'd been seen with another man. In her mind there was no such thing as an innocent friendship between a man and a married woman.

The relationship with Louie's mother had gone right down the toilet. She told me to my face that she blamed me for everything that happened to Louie. It was my fault he was in prison again. "You're too greedy," she said, "You spend too much. You let Deena and Louis have anything they want. You don't give Louie any choice but to go out and steal just to keep you happy."

She hated me and I guess that Louie's father must have felt the same way, because after that conversation I didn't hear from them again. Louie was furious when I told him— they have no right to put you on the pay-me-no-mind list, was how he put it. So now he was at war with the rest of his family.

He had also lost his brother, Bobby. Long before Louie started his sentence at Allenwood, Bobby told him he wanted no further contact with him because of his lifestyle.

Louie couldn't believe it.

"Bobby says he's disgusted with me, that I am a disgrace to the family and as far as he's concerned he doesn't consider me his brother anymore. He doesn't ever want to hear from me again."

To this I said, Bobby didn't have any objections when your parents lived with us for two years. He didn't complain when we gave them the $5,000 they needed to close the deal on their own house and he didn't complain when we paid another $5,000 so they could fly out and spend all that time with him in California.

If I had been a man I would have gone to California and kicked Bobby up the ass for treating his brother like that, and I wanted to say this to Louie, but this was not what he wanted to hear. Being disowned by his own brother was like being stabbed in the heart. It was something I could not forgive.

But in one way his mother was right about the money. We always did spend a lot, especially on the kids, and most of all on Deena, who would throw a fit if she heard no when she wanted to hear yes. For a while I was tougher with her than Louie was—he was incapable of saying no, but now that he was away, I couldn't deal with it alone. I didn't want to. If buying new clothes and running around with her friends all night every night gave her some happiness when everything else was falling apart, maybe she was entitled. I know she missed her father more than she let on to me.

Louie would call from Allenwood and listen to my complaints. You have to be firm with her—let her know you're the boss, he said. This from a father who was like putty in his daughter's hands. I would try to make her stay home more and she would either run out of the house or go to her room and turn up the music. With Deena I felt like I was walking on eggshells.

The one piece of good news I heard in 1985 was that Sammy finally got indicted for screwing the government out of taxes on the money they claimed he made on the Plaza Suite deal. They pinched him for conspiracy and income tax evasion, which meant that he could be looking at twenty years plus a fine of half a million dollars. He tried to beat the charges by giving $300,000 to the feds, but they told him he was more than a few dollars short and a year too late.

They also arrested Eddie Garafola, Sammy's sleazebag brother-in-law, a man who people used to say was so slimy his socks wouldn't stay up with garters. Even Louie, who could find a good word for just about everyone he met, couldn't take to Eddie. Sammy used him for years as a gofer and personal doormat. How he escaped being killed a hundred times, I don't know. And now it turned out in court, according to the prosecutor, that Sammy gave Eddie $40,000 for his end in the Plaza Suite!

The trial was a joke. Sammy's accountant told the court it was all his fault, not Sammy's. He said it was his idea to delay the payment to the IRS, not Sammy's, and if the judge was looking for someone to blame, he was the one who deserved it, not Sammy.

The defense attorney was Gerald Shargel, who would soon become famous as one of John Gotti's lawyers. He worked himself up into a sweat and asked the jury what they would do in Sammy's place—take their accountant's advice or ignore it? In no time flat they came back with a verdict to acquit, and Sammy and Eddie Garafola walked out free.

I was so mad when I heard this on the news I screamed at the TV.

Stymie D'Angelo was killed right around this time.

The version Sammy put out is that Stymie was shot by a

coked-up Colombo guy after they had words in Tali's, which was a bar-restaurant in Bensonhurst. Sammy bragged about how he rushed to the hospital when he heard. He found Stymie DOA with a head full of bullets. He says he was so choked up over this he couldn't think straight. You bet he was. Sammy and Stymie had been partners in Tali's. Now Sammy had it all to himself. He must have been laughing himself sick on the way back from seeing his ex-partner at the hospital.

A few weeks before Christmas of 1985, Neil Dellacroce died after a long illness. Louie didn't mention it when he called from Allenwood that night but I'm sure he was shaken up by the news. In the Gambinos, Neil was next to Paul Castellano and, like Louie, Neil had old-fashioned ideas when it came to dealing in drugs and porn. Louie said Paul felt the same way but I'm not sure I believe that now, knowing how much Paul loved money. So far as I know he was never too fussy about where it came from.

With Neil dead and some of the other old-timers, like Benny Lima and John Bontate, either in the same condition or on the way there, and with Louie, who stayed loyal to Paul, in prison, Paul would have been wondering who he could promote in Neil's place. At this time he was jammed up with a federal case after he got indicted along with four other New York bosses by Rudy Giuliani, who was then the U.S. attorney general in New York State. The feds said all five were the heads of the New York Cosa Nostra, with Paul at the top. They set his bail at $4 million. Paul came up with the money after one night in jail.

He didn't know it but he had a bigger problem on his hands than finding someone to take Neil's place and worrying about the federal government. A couple of weeks before Christmas 1985, Tommy Bilotti drove Paul to Sparks, a steak restaurant in midtown Manhattan. They parked outside and were getting out of the car when three or four men ran out of the crowd on the sidewalk and shot both of them dead.

The papers gave a lot more details about the murders, and

a long time later, so did the FBI, based on what Sammy told them. For all anyone knows, some of this or even all of it was true. When it happened I didn't take much notice.

But I was shocked to hear about Tommy. They could have let him live. Without Paul he was a nobody. Killing Paul was part of business. He stood in the way of the money.

Years afterwards, Sammy took all the credit for arranging the murders and said that he and John Gotti were parked down the block from the restaurant, ready to help out if anything went wrong. At this time Sammy was so full of himself he couldn't think straight. He was also full of steroids and anything else he could do that would make him feel bigger and help his self-esteem.

Their problem—Sammy's and John's—was that they had reached the point where they believed their own hype, that they were criminal masterminds who had figured out all the angles. They figured out nothing. The truth is, John and Sammy didn't begin to measure up to Paul Castellano—not when it came to intelligence, anyway. These two were a couple of pumped-up street dogs who thought they were starring in a true-life gangster movie. Maybe they were both so high on dope most of the time, they didn't have a clue what they were doing.

By getting rid of Paul and the people around him they only destroyed themselves.

Louie called from Allenwood the night Paul and Tommy were killed.

"I'm going to ask you a question," he says. "Try to understand what I'm saying. Is it true?"

"It's true."

He went real quiet. Didn't say a word. In his world, taking Paul Castellano down was like taking down the president of the United States. Now he had to figure out who did it and why and how it would affect his own situation.

I went to see him at the prison just before Christmas, and there was Sammy's signature in the visitors' register from the previous week. He must have gone out there right after the killings. I felt sick, and I let Louie have it the minute he came out to the visiting room.

"What are you doing, talking to Sammy? You know they're looking at you all the time. You know they've got cameras and microphones everywhere. You want to stay in here the rest of your life?"

To this he says, "Sammy never came in, he stayed outside in the car. It was Vito who came in to see me."

"What do you think, I'm stupid? You think I don't know what Sammy's signature looks like? Don't tell me he didn't come in. How could you jeopardize yourself like this, knowing what can happen if the FBI finds out what's going on?"

He didn't answer. Christmas was close and maybe he was thinking the same thing as me, that this year it would be different for the four of us. In the old days we went over to his family's house. His cousin Sonny dressed up as Santa Claus, we had a tree, everyone got presents. I tried to make that a family tradition.

"I'll be out for next Christmas," he said. "We'll go away somewhere, the whole family."

I waited for him to say something about Paul and Tommy. He didn't even mention their names. I was bursting to tell him what I thought—what I was certain in my gut—that Sammy was mixed up in it somehow. And he must have been thinking along the same lines.

"This thing is gonna cause problems," he said. "It doesn't look so good for Sammy, huh, Lynda?"

By this I figured he was telling me he knew what had happened. I thought, Screw Sammy, and at the back of my mind was another thought, that if Louie had been on the streets when they whacked Paul and Tommy, he would also have died, because there was no way in a million years he would agree to kill Paul Castellano.

It didn't look good for anybody. It seemed to me that all of these men had been fooling the world with their secret oaths and all that crap about honor and respect. Most of all, they were fooling themselves—Louie was proof of that. He believed in it. But these guys were never anything but thieves and killers. Where does honor come into that?

Unless somebody we knew got his name in the papers, usually from being found dead someplace, I never paid much attention to TV talk or newspaper stories about the Mafia. For one thing, Louie didn't like hearing that word in the house, even when it was used as a joke. We were watching the TV news once and some reporter started jabbering about how his inside sources in "the mob" had tipped him off about a struggle for power shaking up the New York "crime families" and the "Mafia hierarchy."

"Mafia schmafia," I said to Louie.

"What do you know?" he said. "You're Jewish."

What I knew I kept to myself. When Louis or Deena asked me if their father was part of organized crime I used to say the government invented the expression to cover up their own crimes. Watergate was organized crime. Trading weapons for drugs with foreign governments was organized crime, and so was giving money and guns to dictators around the world. To my mind, price-fixing in the New York diamond trade was organized crime, but because most of the traders were Hasidic Jews and our government didn't want to upset the Israelis, they ignored it.

People like Louie did a lot of damage, no question, but mostly they did it to themselves, not to ordinary Americans, people who worked their whole lives to put something aside for their old age and then lost everything when these corporate types looted the companies, wrecking the lives of tens of thousands of people who trusted them. Maybe I missed it, but I don't recall hearing that even the Mafia did as much damage to so many innocent people as these big-time executives did.

But in one way they had a lot in common—Louie's people and the crooks in suits. They all followed the same rule. Give a favor, take a favor. You tell me when your company's about to drop dead, we'll split the swag before anyone else finds out, plus we get to go home with a half-billion-dollar bonus when we quit.

These people should not be locked up, they should be shot. For what those CEO types did, the government should tie one of those yellow plastic crime-scene tapes around the entire United States of America. The only difference between them and organized crime is they took more money from more people in a shorter time than all the Mafia crime families combined took in the past fifty years.

Which is another thing they have in common. Just like in the Mafia, it was all about the money.

These so-called experts on "the mob" never seemed to understand this, which is one reason I didn't pay attention to what they wrote in the papers. What, they called up some wiseguy boss and he tells them the what and the where and the who? The reporters made it up! They had no choice— they didn't know anything! Even the cops didn't know much, and they were the ones running around doing the pinches and picking up the bodies in the streets! They would hold a press conference and the FBI would say, Well, this family is having a war with that family, and it looks to us like they found a rat, because we just fished Wiseguy X out of the East River with his lips stapled together.

The Mafia is only about money, earning—always was, still is, always will be for as long as it lasts. Everything else aside from money means nothing. Men got killed because the people who wanted them gone figured they could make more with them dead. A rat or a dial-a-matic—someone who calls the police because he's in a jam and wants protection—they don't kill him just because of that, it's because he's a threat to the bottom line. The guy is no longer needed, he's standing in the way of the money. He's redundant, so he gets laid off permanently and loses his life along with his gratuities and pension. It's business, it's nothing personal.

And even when it seems it's personal, like with Sammy Gravano killing Joe Colucci so that Tommy Spero can marry Joe's wife, underneath everything else was the fact that Joe was also seen as a renegade, a loose-cannon type who—too bad for him—happened to be less important for the Gambino bottom line than Tommy Spero and his wiseguy father and wiseguy uncle.

It's the American way. It's all about the money. It's also about a man's head between his legs.

The life was biting all of us in the ass, one way or another. Early on in the summer of 1986, I started getting headaches that turned into migraines. I took some Excedrin. It didn't help. I was smoking too much, I still wasn't sleeping through the night, and one night I found myself doubled up on the bedroom floor with an agonizing pain in the stomach. I was trying to call out to Louis but all I could do was whisper.

When he came into the room to see why I wasn't up yet I told him to call my friend Teresa and ask her to stop by the house on her way to work, but by the time she arrived Louis had already dialed 911 for an ambulance.

At the hospital a doctor said I had a hole in my stomach from the ulcer they'd treated years before. He wanted to operate immediately. I asked him to let me have some painkillers instead. I could go to bed for a couple of days and everything would be okay. "You have two choices," the doctor said, "surgery or death." All I remember after this was lying on the operating table and watching the lights go out.

"You're lucky you're alive," the doctor said afterwards.

"You think so?" I said.

CHAPTER
21

I Know About Frankie

Four months after they murdered Paul and Tommy,
Frank DeCicco was blown to bits when somebody put a
bomb in his car in Bensonhurst. The cops and the newspapers came up with their usual cockamamie theories about
who did it and why, but nobody except the people who put
the bomb in the car knew why, and they didn't give inter-
views. I still don't know who killed him or why.

Years afterwards, when Sammy rolled over for the feds, he
spun one of his fairy tales about how sad he was about losing
Frank. Sure. After Paul was killed, Frank became number two
in the Gambinos, after John Gotti. He must have been over fifty
when they killed him, so he was older than John and most of
the men around John. Maybe Sammy figured the number-two
slot should have gone to a younger man—himself, for instance—and that's how it worked out. If bringing Sammy close
to him was John's first mistake, putting Sammy in Frank's
place was the second biggest mistake John Gotti made.

Louie called from Allenwood the day that Frankie was killed.

I asked him if he had seen the papers.

"I know all about Frank," he said.

We never talked about it again.

Robert DiBernardo disappeared a couple of months after Frank went. Poor DiB—gone and never heard from again. Sammy told the FBI he called DiB over to his office and helped kill him.

The FBI said DiB got rich from kiddie porn, but from everything I knew about DiB, somebody sure got something wrong. I know how much Louie hated the kiddie-porn business and anyone connected to it. But it's no secret that the cops make up all kinds of stories when they want a suspect to look worse than he is, and maybe that's the way it was with what they said about DiB. It's just not the way it was in reality. DiB was already making his fortune from his Great Bear auto franchises all over the country—besides a few deals here and there. So what? I wouldn't mind betting there are millions more Americans watching porn than there are going to church on Sundays. But as far as I know, DiB had nothing to do with that other stuff, the kiddie porn.

Louie inviting a kiddie porn merchant to our house? Impossible. And DiB was in our home more than once, although the only time I was there at the same time, it was just him and Louie in the kitchen, talking about DiB's Great Bear franchise business.

Sammy said that after they killed DiB, they put him in a bag from a funeral parlor and took it away. He says he had no idea what happened to the body. My guess is that DiB and his new Mercedes ended up in one of those auto crushers at a wreck yard owned by a guy in Sammy's crew.

Louie was due home from Allenwood in the late summer or early fall of 1986, the release date changed according to who you asked, but it seemed pretty certain he'd be back by early October, maybe in time for the thirteenth birthday of our son, Louis. I was dreading it.

The two years he was away made many differences in the way I thought about him and about our marriage. He was a lot tougher, a lot harder when he came out. From spending time with Ken, who had no connection with the life and wasn't always looking for ways to get something for nothing, I was starting to appreciate the feeling of not being scared day and night, at least not by Louie. That was one reason I felt I was changing and another reason was that I was becoming more and more successful in real estate.

I still hadn't told Ken about Louie's situation, just like I didn't tell him that Louie would be home before the end of the year. As usual, I was pretending to myself that if problems came up when Louie came out of Allenwood, I would handle them when they arrived. Once again I was stuffing everything I didn't want to deal with in that "file and forget" box in my head.

Let me tell you something. You can file it and you can try to forget it and you can try to convince yourself you're running away from reality, but everything I thought I was getting away from came back in the end, years later, and when it did, I still couldn't face it. All I wanted to do was run away from it again, and I did, I kept running, with the result that I made one stupid mistake after another, trusting people when I should have known better, making decisions that only made everything worse for me and my children, and all the time telling myself it would all work out in the end.

The only consolation was that I couldn't seem to put a foot wrong in my business. In five years I had somehow become one of the Staten Island stars in real estate, winning awards from the industry by selling millions of dollars' worth of property. I was paying taxes just like everyone else and starting to rack up annual commissions of around $80,000.

Why should I have to give up the independence that came with this success? Why go back to life with Louie and all its fears and uncertainties when I now had an option? I could think of no good reason except one, that he would sooner kill me than let me go.

All through the summer of that year he called from Allenwood just about every night, sometimes keeping me on the phone for two hours, screaming, cursing, and threatening. When he wasn't getting on my case over Deena and her speeding tickets, he was yelling and cursing at me because of Mario Mastromarino.

"When I tell you to do something, you do it! I don't wanna hear any more complaints about Mario! If he tells you to do something, you do it!"

I would shake when the phone rang, and the shaking didn't stop when we talked. At night I lay in bed, crying. I couldn't stop crying.

Louis used to say, "Don't answer the phone, Ma!"

Something was happening with Louie; he was losing it more and more often, and at the time I didn't understand why, but now I believe it was because old friends of his were going down and my guess is that he hadn't yet figured out who was behind all the murders. Or maybe he knew and was just waiting to come home from Allenwood and make his move. He had to know that with Paul Castellano and his underboss Neil Dellacroce gone, John Gotti was now running the Gambinos and Sammy had been jumped up to John's underboss. If he knew that much, how could he not know who the killers were? In the life, when the boss goes down you don't have to look far to find out who pulled the trigger and why. It's usually the guy who takes over the empty chair.

So what Louie knew or didn't know, I didn't have a clue.

Naturally, both the children were excited about their father coming home, my son especially, because if Louie was released on time, he could be home for Louis's birthday on October 28. That would take a big load off my mind.

For months Louis had been pestering me to let him use some of the money he'd saved from the envelopes our friends gave him at his confirmation two years earlier. He

wanted to buy one of those cross-country cars for his birthday. ATVs—all-terrain vehicles—that's what the kids called
them. They were all the rage that year.

I thought he should wait a while. I knew he could drive
one because his father put him on a 50cc mini-motorcycle
when he was five, against my wishes, and later on he taught
him how to ride a full-sized 250cc motorcycle. But that had
been out in open country, on our property in Pennsylvania,
and I wasn't about to let him drive on the streets around
Staten Island. In fact, I never wanted Louie to teach him how
to ride. I thought he was too young, I tried steering him more
into sports like hockey and soccer.

But Louis was like his father. When he got an idea in his
head, he wouldn't give up until he got what he wanted, and
his constant nagging began to wear me down.

"Ma, what about my ATV? It's my money! When are we
going to get one?"

"Absolutely not," I told him. "Wait and see what your father says when he comes home."

This was about the time his father pulled one of the dumbest stunts of his life. It started when he called the house from
prison one night.

"Put Deena on."

There was no hello. He didn't want to waste his time on
me. I told him she had gone out to see her friends, which
she had.

Our telephone sessions had been especially rough over
the previous couple of weeks. Face-to-face, when I saw him
at Allenwood, it wasn't so bad, but when he called the
house, the coldness and anger in his voice scared the hell out
of me. I didn't know who he was anymore.

When he asked for Deena I thought it was to give her a
lecture about staying out late. He knew she had been running ragged most of that summer. She wrecked two cars, an
Audi and an Eldorado, and she still had a glove compartment full of tickets for traffic violations. Deena parked when
she found a space. If there was a No Parking sign or a fire

hydrant, she ignored it. If the sign said Speed Limit 35, she went 75. Trying to make her change these habits was a waste of breath. She didn't care, and I didn't have the energy to make her care.

I was hoping that when Louie called that night he would read her the riot act. It didn't happen.

"I need her to do something for me," he told me. "I need her to get me some stuff. You have to bring it next time you come out here."

"Stuff? What's wrong with you? Don't you realize you can get her in trouble? Don't you realize you're in a federal prison and there are probably people listening to you right now?"

"Shut up! Tell your daughter to be by the phone tomorrow night."

"Louie, I don't know what you're doing here but you're making your own daughter an accomplice to something."

"Fuck you!"

Click. That's all I heard, so I went to tell Deena.

Deena was by the phone when her father called the next night. She was listening hard, making a list as he talked. Provolone. Pepperoni. Salamis. Pasta. Mozzarella. A bunch of other meats and cheeses. Chianti. A quart of J&B. Black hair dye.

He told her to buy everything at certain stores. She had to remove the labels and store names on the packaging. Everything had to be packed in a carton and dropped in a field near the prison. He gave her directions to the field, the time the box had to be left there, and the exact place to drop it off.

He didn't ask to speak to me.

"Dad wants you to take it out there when you go and see him on Sunday," she said. "You have to get Mario Mastromarino and Vince Sbarbaro to drive you. They'll drop off the box."

Great. If I did what he said there was a good chance the three of us would get pinched—me, Mario, and Vince—if I didn't take the package he would make me pay when he came home. Why he wanted this stuff I could only guess. Louie had never been the kind of man who tried to impress people—at least he wasn't before he went to Allenwood. To me, this was another sign of change in him.

It seemed to me that he must have shot his mouth off to his friends at the prison. Maybe he promised them a feast as his going-away present. But the black hair dye must have been for someone else—Louie had always been proud of his thick salt-and-pepper hair.

Deena did exactly what he told her and packed everything neatly into the box. Vince was at the wheel of Mario's black Cadillac when they picked me up early on Sunday morning for the drive to Allenwood—and all the way there I kept asking them why they wanted to get mixed up in this. Didn't they know they could get into serious trouble? Why didn't they tell Louie not to ask for these kinds of favors?

"You worry too much," Mario said. "Give him a break, Lynda, the guy's in prison."

We parked down the road from the field, behind some trees. I stayed in the car. Mario and Vince had no sooner put down the box than a half dozen police and unmarked cars drove onto the grass and uniformed cops and men in FBI jackets with shotguns jumped all over the both of them.

Any minute I expected them to drag me out of the car, but nothing happened. After a while I drove back to a country store gas station we passed on the way. Then I walked back to the prison to see Louie. They wouldn't let me in.

"Sorry, Mrs. Milito," the guard said, "your husband's getting no visitors today."

I left the car at the gas station and took a bus back to New York.

This disaster had two results: Mario and Vince got jammed up with federal charges because they were trespassing on federal land and carrying contraband for a federal inmate. Also aiding and abetting a criminal in a criminal act. In court, their attorney managed to have the charges reduced to misdemeanors and the judge gave them probation. They also had their names taken off Louie's visitor list.

Louie's punishment was an extra two months on his sentence. It sounds like nothing, but what happened as a direct result of this will haunt me for the rest of my life.

Louis started up again about buying the ATV for his birthday. His friend Ritchie's got one, other kids at school are riding around in these things and they're the same age as he is and he'll be left out of the picture if he didn't get one. It wasn't fair making him wait now that his father won't be home for his birthday—and so on and so forth.

He kept on at me in the house, he called me at the office, he left notes on the refrigerator. I told him I was against it but would ask his father and let him make the decision, and the next time Louie called I told him the same thing.

"Listen to me," he said. "You're making that kid into a mutt. You want him to be a mutt? Buy it and make him leave it in the garage. We can take it out after I get home."

Deena was all for it, telling me all his friends have it: "Ma, Daddy's in jail. Let him have it."

Louis started jumping up and down with excitement when I gave him the news. He spent the whole morning going through the Yellow Pages, calling dealers and drawing blanks until he finally found one who had an ATV in stock. The good news as far as I was concerned was that the dealer wouldn't sell it unless Louis showed the dealer a copy of his father's or my driver's license. I refused to let him use mine, hoping that this would force him, but that didn't stop him. It just delayed things, and when Louie called the house that night and told me his license was hidden in one of his drawers and I was to hand it over to Louis, I did what he told me to do.

The dealer checked out Louis on the controls, and when he was satisfied the boy understood how everything worked, the ATV was loaded onto a truck and brought home. We put it away in the garage.

Ten days before Louis's birthday I was in the office catch-

ing up on some calls. It was a Sunday. The police called to
say that Louis had been in an accident. They didn't know
whether he was dead or alive. They wanted me to meet them
at the site of the accident.

It was at an intersection. The wreck was still there, pushed
to one side, a heap of torn-up fiberglass and metal junk. It
looked as if somebody had dropped it off a building. There
was blood in the road and Louis's helmet on the sidewalk. I
picked it up and put my arms around it. One of the cops
came over and told me what had happened. A girl had driven
through a stop sign and smashed into the side of the ATV.
Louis had been taken to St. Vincent's Hospital in an ambulance. That was all he knew.

At the hospital, I was about to go to the emergency room
counter when I passed some people talking about a boy who
had just been killed on a motorcycle. My first thought was
to run outside and throw myself in front of a truck—anything to get away from this—but they must have been talking about somebody else, because when I asked for Louis at
the counter, the receptionist gave me his room number.

A doctor and some nurses stood around the bed. He was
unconscious. They had hooked him up to IV and blood
transfusion tubes.

I don't remember what the doctor said except that Louis
would survive, which was all I cared about. But he was very
seriously injured, and although the doctor thought some of
his injuries could be repaired by surgery, he didn't like the
look of his left leg, which had taken the force of the colli-
sion with the girl's car. I asked the doctor how bad it was,
and he said Louis was lucky he still had the leg. From what
he didn't tell me I got the feeling that even if my son sur-
vived, he would be crippled for the rest of his life.

CHAPTER 22

Maybe We'll Get a Miracle

In my mind Louie was directly responsible for the accident, so I blamed him and eventually hated him, and at the same time I hated myself and blamed myself since it happened while I was supposed to be in charge. I should have made the dealer keep the damned ATV until his father got back, or I could have put the keys someplace Louis couldn't find them. I didn't, and because I didn't, our son will be in pain for as long as he lives. Every time I see him now, fifteen years after the accident, the guilt and the anger I feel—about Louie, about myself—are like a knife stuck in my heart.

I called the prison that day and told them it was an emergency, our son had been in an accident and please to get Louie to call me. The phone rang a few minutes later.

"How bad is it?" he said.

"It's bad. He'll live but there's a problem with his left leg."

Louie said, "You let my kid get hurt, I'm gonna fucking kill you."

They let him come home for an overnight visit a few days later. Vito and Huck Carbonaro picked him up at Allenwood and drove him to the hospital. I was already there. Louie was standing in the waiting room with them and with Mario Mastromarino, who was patting Louie on the back. They were all laughing about something, even Louie, with that big laugh of his. You would have thought they were at a party.

He stopped laughing after he saw Louis. When he came to the house afterwards he wore dark glasses. I could see he had been crying. We were all crying, including Deena, who was very close to her little brother. There was no arguing or shouting between Louie and me that night. We didn't talk when we went to bed. We fell asleep holding on to each other. Huck and Vito picked him up in the morning for the drive back to prison.

At the hospital they put a cot next to my son's bed and let me stay there nights. I felt that I had destroyed his future, and I had. Louis always talked about being a plastic surgeon. If he never walked easily again it would be my fault. But blaming myself or his father—blaming the both of us—didn't make things any better. We did it between us, and there was and is no hiding from that. All I could do when Louis woke was tell him we loved him and would find the best doctors in the world to bring him back to the way he was before the accident.

One specialist told me that his leg might stand a better chance of healing if we let him wear a kind of flexible apparatus on his leg and join a physical therapy class with other children. This would help him walk and prevent his knee from stiffening up. It would need surgery—they would have to put a metal rod in his leg while the bones healed. Louis, who was in a body cast and in traction, begged me to do this. His father refused.

"Forget it! Mario spoke to his doctor and he thinks it's a

bad idea. He says we should let nature take its course. The kid's young. His bones will fix themselves."

I wanted to ask him: since when did Mario get to decide what's best for our son? And of course I didn't. Instead, I told Louie, "But the doctors I've spoken to say the breaks are too serious—they can't be fixed on their own. I'm going to tell them to go ahead with the operation."

"You'll do what I fucking tell you to do!"

When I told Louis this he said we should do it anyway. I had to tell him the truth, that if we did and something went wrong, his father would kill me.

Louie got out of Allenwood just before Christmas, 1986. I can't say I felt happy to see him back, in fact I don't remember feeling anything. Everything had changed for the both of us. If he was worried about what was happening in his life after Paul Castellano's murder and how John Gotti had moved up and taken Sammy with him as his *underboss,* he didn't talk about it—and how he dealt with this inside his head, he kept to himself. He had a whole new set of problems to think about now, and they were a lot closer to home.

By then Louis had come back from the hospital, wrapped in a body cast that reached from just above his ankles to his shoulders. It weighed 200 pounds. There were holes in the front and back for him to go to the toilet. We had to get a full-time nurse in to help turn him over and hold him over the bedpan. Because of the bedsores he had to be rolled over every half hour, day and night. He couldn't do anything for himself except help push with his arms when we turned him over. Even when he was dosed with painkillers he cried out—when he was awake and when he was asleep.

Louie ruled out the idea of surgery. Many years earlier, his sister had died on an operating table, and because of that there would be no operation. Louis would be kept under Mario's doctor, but I told Louie I didn't like this idea one bit.

"Mario's been with this doctor for twenty years," Louie said. "He trusts him, and I trust Mario's judgment. You can forget about surgery. Mario showed his doctor the X rays. The doctor says we have to let the leg mend on its own. The kid's not getting any operation or any pins in the leg. Lynda, I don't want to hear about this again."

I could see no end to this nightmare. The more I thought about it, the worse it got, so I tried not to think about it and of course it was impossible to stop thinking about it. Our house was like a funeral home. There was no life left in it.

Louie never took his dark glasses off when he was home. He sat upstairs on his own with Louis, waiting for him to wake so that he could talk to him.

"You should take some of the guys and go hunting," I told him. "You're not doing yourself or Louis any good sitting around here. Take a few days off and go to Pennsylvania."

Louie said, "You know what saved me from going nuts in Allenwood? They had whole families of deer running all over the place. The fawns ate out of my hand. Lynda, you can't believe how beautiful they are up close. I don't think I'll be going hunting anymore."

Good for the deer. They got a pass. I wasn't so lucky.

Soon after he came home we got into another fight, one of the worst, and this time it was about money.

Not long before Louie came out of Allenwood, Mario Mastromarino stopped by the house and said he needed $25,000, and could I get it for him by the next day. I took the money out of the briefcase in Louie's mother's attic, where Louie kept the cash he got from the insurance payout for our commercial buildings.

I must have figured Mario had already cleared this with Louie, and knowing what Louie's response would be if I questioned him about anything concerning Mario, I handed over the $25,000. Then I clean forgot about it. Louis's accident, Deena worrying me sick, the pressures of work, Louie coming home, the fights—it was like my mind became full up, it couldn't take any more in.

About a month after Louie came out of prison he went to his mother's house. I was up in the bedroom with Louis and the nurse when he came in.

"We have to talk," he said. "Downstairs."

I asked him if it could wait. We were about to turn Louis over.

"No."

I followed him down to the basement. As soon as the door closed he smashed me in the face with the back of his hand.

"Where's the fucking money?"

"What money?"

"The twenty-five thousand dollars I left by my mother. She says you were up there. What did you do with it?"

I told him I didn't know what he was talking about.

"Listen, you piece of shit—I got no time for this!"

He pulled me up off the floor with both his hands around my throat and threw me up against the washing machine.

"Where's my money? You better think fast, Lynda! You took twenty-five thousand dollars, I want it back! I don't get an answer soon, I'm gonna put you in the fucking ground!"

He was yelling so much I couldn't focus. I was trying to find an answer and there was nothing there. I'm thinking, What's he talking about? I didn't take any $25,000 out of the briefcase—and then I remembered.

"Mario got it! Call Mario, he'll tell you! I forgot to put it in the book."

Louie raced up the stairs and got Mario on the phone. He was just hanging up when I got there. He ran out of the house without another word.

Over the ringing in my ears I could hear Louis calling me to come back up to his room, but I didn't want him to see me. My face looked as though someone had hit it with a baseball bat. I told him I had to have a shower first and go out for some groceries.

Somebody once asked me if Louie apologized.

Louie apologize? I said. Are you kidding me or what?

Or maybe he did apologize in his own way, because after

that he never again raised his hand against me. I wish I had known it at the time, but of course I didn't—there was never a day when I didn't go back to the house terrified by the thought of another beating and wondering how it would work out this time, but from then on all the rage seemed to have drained out of him and I don't know what made it go away.

It was around this time, not long after Louie came back from Allenwood, that I met John Gotti for the first and only time. We had driven over to New York to eat in some place on Mulberry Street, and I don't think Louie planned on introducing. It happened when we parked outside a club near the restaurant. I guess it must have been John's club, and Louie left me in the car while he went inside to do some business. Five minutes later he's coming out with this very well dressed, distinguished-looking guy who I immediately recognize from the TV. What struck me was how much he and Louie looked alike— they even cocked their heads in the same way, kind of friendly, smiling, but sharp. The same kind of confidence, not cocky, just sure of himself. This John Gotti was one good-looking guy, not as handsome as Louie, I thought, but very impressive.

There wasn't much conversation. He came around to my side of the car, said he had heard a lot about me, and now he knew why. Louie was a lucky man, he said. Our family was lucky to have each other. End of meeting.

The thing with John was that he took dapper to a whole new level. Gotti wanted to be seen, to walk the walk, but Louie and his crew weren't like that. They didn't want to be. Castellano was never like that. The more Gotti dressed for the cameras, the more Louie scaled back. Louie didn't want to be noticed. After a while he stopped wearing those sharp suits. Instead, Louie wore cheap ten-dollar sneakers that he bought from the flea market. He stopped wearing designer suits and always put on sweatsuits. To Louie, this was a way to start drawing attention away from the family.

I've asked myself a million times since, Is it possible that Gotti, who seemed so genuine to me, so pleased to be with Louie and so naturally friendly to the both of us, was the one who ordered my husband to be killed? Gotti may have been a lot of things, but nobody will ever convince me that he was the one who initially wanted Louie dead.

In the months after Louie came out of Allenwood, I figure he was seeing Sammy and John and other Gambino men, and I guess he must have been doing business with them at night after working at Gem Steel five days a week, but where he went after work, what he did, and who he did it with was something he didn't discuss. If he was trying to work out in his mind how and where—or if—he fitted in with John and Sammy's new regime, he kept it to himself.

And I kept my thoughts to myself. One of the conditions of his early release was five years' probation. If they found him hanging out with the Gambinos they would just drag him back to Allenwood for the full five years of his probation. Maybe more. Reminding him of this would have about as much effect on Louie as trying to put out a forest fire with a damp Kleenex.

But there was no more shouting from him, no more threats, no violence. I used to watch him from an upstairs window, on his knees, feeding the ducks and geese in the pond in the backyard. He had to stop every couple of minutes, take off his dark glasses, and wipe his eyes.

On the weekends, he worked on the house, laying polished granite on the floors so that when you went in the front door the inside looked like a bank or a library. We built a thirty- by forty-foot extension for a new master bedroom with two queen-sized beds with custom-made black-and-white Formica headboards. Not so long ago I couldn't wait to install the new furniture and complete all the renovations. Now I didn't care if the house was ever finished.

Every day, I stopped off at the house from work to check

on Louis, hoping to see some improvement and never finding it.

Maybe they will learn how to do leg transplants, I thought. Maybe his bones will join back together. Maybe after he's rested up long enough . . . maybe we will get a miracle.

Every couple of weeks, the ambulance came to take him to the doctor's office—Mario's doctor, who didn't make house calls. All he did was charge a thousand dollars for every visit. I was beginning to hate this doctor almost as much as I hated Mario.

It took four paramedics to take Louis down the stairs on a stretcher and into the ambulance, and at every step he would cry out, "Ma, don't let them drop me—make sure I'm okay."

Six months of this was all I could take. When the ambulance came to the house to take Louis to see Mario's doctor I told the driver to take us to Manhattan instead, to the Hospital for Joint Diseases. He was admitted as an in-patient and given a dose of the painkiller Percocet. In almost no time he became addicted, so the nurses cut off the Percocet and wouldn't let him have anything but aspirin, which was about as much help for pain as a Band-Aid for a broken leg. He was screaming at me day and night.

"Ma! You gotta make them give me back my meds! Ma! You gotta do something! You're killing me! You don't care what happens! What kind of mother are you?"

That was another question I couldn't answer and didn't want to think about.

When they finally cut away his cast, one of the specialists told me that Louis didn't have any bone or muscle strength in either leg. "Your son has ghost bones," he said. "If we operate immediately there may be enough left to attach a rod to help support the leg. I can't promise that. But if we leave that cast on him it will only get worse."

I called Louie at Gem Steel and told him he should come to the hospital.

"Our son's bones have turned to mush," I said. "They think it may be too late for surgery."

He showed up twenty minutes later. I didn't trust myself to keep my thoughts to myself so I waited in the corridor while Louie talked to the specialist in his office. The doctor didn't look too happy when he came out afterwards. Louie had told him there would be no operation.

"Your husband is too strong for me," the doctor said. "You don't tell a man like that what to think."

What happened in the rest of 1987, the exact when and the how, I don't want to remember. Louie finally agreed to surgery for Louis. It was a mess. The operation to put the rod in his left leg took four hours instead of the two the specialist said it would take. But at least he was out of the body cast, which was some consolation, but not enough, because by then he had almost lost the use of his uninjured leg and now had pain in both legs.

Right after the operation, Louie told Mario Mastromarino to bring his doctor to the hospital for a meeting. I was there when they arrived. Louie took hold of the man by the neck.

"I'm going to wait and see what happens to my son," he said. "If it turns out he can't walk, you're dead. Get out of here."

Mario turned so white he looked like he was about to keel over.

"Listen to me," Louie told him. "You are going to know where that motherfucker is at all times. You will sleep, eat, and drink with him. You will never lose sight of him because one of these days you will be putting him in the trunk of a car. You understand me?"

Remembering this scene now makes me think that Louie had more than enough guilt to handle over the accident. I supposed he must have blamed himself for teaching Louis how to ride motorcycles out in Pennsylvania, and I'm sure he blamed me, too. But I believe he put most of it on himself. One thing's for sure. He didn't blame the dealer who sold the ATV, because that man would have been dead the day Louie first saw our son in the hospital.

I guess it must have been sometime in May I told Louie he had to move out of the house. What with Mario hanging around all the time, whispering with Louie in the living room and Louis upstairs screaming for painkillers, I thought I was going mad. One minute I could think and speak clearly, the next I couldn't finish a sentence. I'd start to say something and find myself yammering. I told Louie I needed time alone.

His response to this was to send airline tickets to my parents and brother Harvey in Florida and ask them to come up to New York and try to make me change my mind. They came, and I told them no. Harvey got the job of telling Louie he would have to move out.

He didn't even put up a fuss. Packed a few clothes and drove to Mario's big house in Dyker Heights and moved into the guest apartment.

Word obviously got around, because I ran into Debra Gravano at the Staten Island Mall one day, the first time we'd seen each other in quite a while. I have since come to the conclusion that Sammy must have told her to stay away from me, not that she dropped so much as a hint when we spoke that day.

"I wish I had the nerve to do what you did," she said. "I wish I could leave Sammy. Do you know we haven't had sex in nine months, Lynda?"

I didn't say this, but I figured she should think herself lucky not to have that shithead husband of hers crawling all over her.

Louie was back about a month later. I asked him to come back. I didn't tell him I couldn't sleep nights because I thought there were people creeping around and whispering, and I said nothing about Deena, who had been careful to come home at a reasonable hour when her father lived with us but was now staying out late with her friends again and refusing to pay attention to anything I said. With her father in the house again, it would be one less worry to think about.

One night not long after he moved back we were up in the bedroom with Louis when the TV news came on.

"Uncle Sammy!" Louis said. "Look, it's Uncle Sammy on the TV!"

It was him and John Gotti, only I didn't recognize him from the one time I met him. I guess I'd seen his picture in the papers and on the TV before this, but seeing him now on one of those fuzzy surveillance videos the cops use, his face didn't register with me. It was just Sammy and another man. They were standing on a street corner, with Sammy talking into the other man's ear. They were both laughing. I don't think they knew they were being filmed, or maybe they did know and didn't care.

"Who's the other guy?" I asked Louie.

"John Gotti."

Even standing still they seemed to swagger. They looked like people who were so important in their own minds, there wasn't enough time in the day for them to be important enough. I asked Louie to come outside the bedroom.

"Let's sell everything and leave. We can go to a warmer climate, which will be better for Louis anyway."

Louie said, "I can't. I can't leave my people. I can't leave Gem Steel. I can't leave Mario. Who is going to run the company? They can't do it without me." The only way out of the Mafia was if you had a heart attack. But Louie would never do that. When he told me that, I absolutely gave up. I didn't answer him, I didn't want to look at him. I was disgusted. Yeah, he was loyal to his friends. But not to his family.

I told him in that case we should just sell everything, take the kids, and leave. We could go to Europe or South America. We had some money, and we could get maybe a half million more from selling the house.

"Lynda, you know there's no getting out of this thing. I

can't walk away from it. Everything we have is right here. No way I could leave what I started."

Then he started going on about Gem Steel and the shylock book and the numbers and how we couldn't start selling up without people noticing—and I just went off at him because it seemed to me he was making excuses.

"You have to be careful about Sammy," I told him. "He's up to something."

"Me, be careful about Sammy? Hey, screw Sammy! Sammy needs to be careful about me."

He said this in the tone of voice I think of as typical Louie. There was no fear in it, no anger. It was just cold and confident, like a man who had figured out what his problems were and how he was going to deal with them.

He must have known he was alone, and he didn't care. And I think this is probably true because that night when we saw John and Sammy on the TV in Louis's bedroom, I believe he was blaming himself for what had happened to Louis—to all of us—and because of this he couldn't live with himself anymore. I'm certain he never stopped caring about his family, but from that day on, now that I look back, I think he gave up caring about himself.

CHAPTER 23

No Happy Hour at Tali's

They killed Nicky "Cowboy" Mormando later that year. It was Cowboy who we put on the deeds for our commercial properties on account of the fact he was legit and paid his income taxes just like regular people. Nicky had always been another fixture in the crowd—he wasn't a made man, that's for sure, he was harmless. He just happened to be one of the guys who grew up in the neighborhood and hung out with old friends after they got connected.

Sammy later told the FBI Nicky had to be killed because he got hooked on crack and couldn't be trusted, so he sent Huck Carbonaro and one of his other killers to pick Nicky up in a car and bring him over to Tali's Restaurant and Lounge in Bensonhurst. They shot him in the back of the head on the way.

With Nicky gone, Louie arranged with an attorney to have the deeds for our buildings backdated and put in Mario's name. He would be the custodian caretaker. I told him this was a bad idea. "You don't know what you're talking about," he said, "Mario would never cheat us."

Stymie D'Angelo was murdered in Tali's a couple of years before Cowboy, and at the end of 1987, young Mikey DeBatt was found dead behind the bar. In the papers it said he was shot several times. Mikey's wife, Dawn, was a friend of mine, in fact, at any social occasion with the Gambino people it was usually Dawn, Debra Gravano, Stymie's wife, Karen, and me who always made sure we sat together at the same table.

Dawn and Mikey DeBatt had a year-old daughter. The newspapers didn't mention that but they did say that Mikey owned Tali's. They also didn't mention his partner in the place, Sammy Gravano.

Oh, sure, Sammy told the feds a few years after this. I decided to have Mikey killed in Tali's to make it look like a robbery. It was too bad, I really liked Mikey.

We spent New Year's Eve 1987 in Atlantic City with Mario and his wife, Eleanor, Joe Polito, his wife, Eileen, Joe's two sons, and a couple I will call by other names, Lenny and Denise, because I have no wish to see any harm come to them. Lenny was someone Louie knew from years ago in Bay Ridge.

He later became a hack at Riker's Island, working on the psycho floor. In fact, it was a standing joke that Lenny was half-psycho himself after spending too many years wearing body armor while he was locked up with these head cases. He was still at the prison when Louie was an inmate—he helped people get messages to Louie through the hacks on Louie's floor and he did other favors, like giving him new clothes and telling the other hacks that Louie was his friend and to take care of him in any way they could.

After he got out, Louie hooked up with him again, and

Lenny became someone who was always there, one of his gofers—he would do errands and help collect stuff Louie needed while he was fixing up the house.

I wanted to include him and Denise at New Year's for one reason only, and that was because Sammy felt that Lenny was too close to Louie. This I picked up from remarks Louie had been making lately, about how Sammy was wondering out loud if they could trust Lenny. Sammy suspected he was a rat. Again I found myself adding up two and two and getting four. If Sammy Gravano was putting the word around about Lenny, I figured it could only mean Lenny was on his hit list.

I asked Louie, "Don't you think you owe this man something? Like his life? He's been your friend, he's done you many favors. Are you going to stand by and let them get away with this?"

Louie had no reply. I see now that he was in a bind—if he stood up for Lenny and Lenny turned out to be a rat, Louie would have to answer for it. And maybe he didn't worry about it, because that New Year's celebration we had in Atlantic City turned out to be one big party, and he and Lenny got on together just like always, cracking jokes like they didn't have a care in the world.

Sometime in February 1988, Louie came home around nine o'clock one night and said he had a problem. He had been in Sammy's house for a meeting and the FBI broke in with a search warrant and shotguns. Men jumped over the fences to get away. Louie stayed where he was.

I couldn't believe my ears.

"Meeting?" I asked him. "What are you doing in a meeting at Sammy's house? You know you're not supposed to associate with those people. Don't you understand you're on probation for five years? You have no business meeting with Sammy Gravano."

"I had to be there, they needed my vote."

I just about had to bite my tongue to keep from telling Louie what I thought of him. How could he take such chances?

His probation officer called him at work the next day and told him to report to her office immediately. In the past she had been kind to him, unlike some of the people in that office, and once again, even when she was very angry with him, she gave him another chance. But she also made it clear that if there was one more screwup she would have no choice but to send him back to Allenwood to serve the five years' probation.

It was while he was telling me about his visit to the probation office that I knew, once and for all, no ifs, ands, or buts, that this was it for me and Louie. There was no possible way forward. He could shoot me, strangle me, beat me to death—I didn't care. In fact, I wished he would kill me.

He knew it.

We were sitting at the kitchen table and out of nowhere he said, "I messed up your life, didn't I?"

"Somewhat."

"Yeah. I know."

"Not just my life. Look at what we did to Louis."

He started to cry. I couldn't look at him. After a while he asked me what I thought he should do. I told him he would have to leave. We were finished. There would be no moving back into the house.

"You can see Louis whenever you want," I said. "You could take him to see the ships at South Street."

"Yeah. He likes the ships. Lynda, are you sure about this?"

"I'm sure. It's no good."

He was gone the same night, back to Mario's.

On Valentine's Day of 1988, he came to the house and gave me a blue-and-silver balloon with a big red heart on it that said in the middle, I Love You. The balloon was still floating around the floor in the living room a few days later when he stopped by to spend some time with Louis. When he came back downstairs he said he had something to tell me.

"I know things about this world you don't know, and you don't want to know," he said. "It's a cold place, you have no idea how cold. But no matter what happens, you have to remember you're still my sweet girl. You know I love you. Always did, always will. Can't help it."

He wasn't asking me to take him back. We both knew it was all over.

CHAPTER 24

The Disappearance

Deena went out to dinner once or twice with her father later on that month, and once I met him for coffee over at the Holiday Inn. He looked so worn out I asked him if he was feeling okay. He said he had just realized that in another year we would have known each other for twenty-five years.

"That's a long time," he said. "That's what I've been thinking. It's a long time."

On March 8, he called the office that morning to say he was meeting Deena for dinner that night. Knowing him, he would be on the phone five times to make sure she remembered not to forget.

I called Louis, who had a phone by the bed. He still wasn't strong enough for school, so most days he stayed up in his room, watching TV.

"Did you speak to your father yet?"

"Yeah. We're going out Saturday."

Deena called the office. She got the message about dinner.

She's meeting Louie at Mario's house, but she might be late because there was something going on at school that she couldn't get out of. "When Daddy calls," she said, "tell him not to leave without me."

Louie had already gone when she arrived at Mario's and by the time she came home I was in bed. There had been no word from Louie.

I called Mario first thing in the morning. No reply. I called Gem Steel. Louie hadn't come in yet. He still wasn't there by nine. I called every hour throughout the day. Nobody had heard from him. I called Deena at Hofstra, I called Louis at the house. I tried Mario but there was still no answer. I began calling friends and people I didn't want to talk to. None of them could tell me anything.

Something wasn't right. Louie, who could never see a telephone without calling in? It was unheard of. I thought about calling Sammy but didn't want to give him the satisfaction. He would only say something like, "Gee, Lynda, what can I tell you? Relax, he'll be back."

When Deena came home the next morning I told her, "Come upstairs by your brother. Your father's missing. Nobody's heard from him. I have a bad feeling about this."

"Oh, Mom. You're always getting excited about nothing. Daddy's okay."

"You know what I think, Deena? Listen to me. I think your father's dead. I think Sammy killed him."

Right away she began yelling at me.

"Daddy's not dead! He's not dead! He's not dead! What's wrong with you? How can you say such a terrible thing? Uncle Sammy would never kill him! You're only saying that because you never liked Uncle Sammy! You always hated him!"

I told her I hoped she was right and I was wrong, but in any case I wanted her to come home immediately and stay home until we heard from her father.

We waited that morning, and I called Mario and told him I was going down to the One Two Two Precinct to report that

Louie was missing. Mario said, "Don't do anything until I hear from Sammy."

At first this didn't register. But then I'm thinking, Sammy? What does Sammy have to do with this? And I said to Mario, "If the man is missing, he's missing. If I have to, I will go to the FBI."

Mario said, "Don't go anywhere, I'll come over to the house."

By the time he arrived it was getting late. The three of us—Deena, Mario, and myself—went down to the One Two Two Precinct to report Louie missing. To the cops it was a big joke.

"Well, Mrs. Milito, if he moved out of the house a month ago, maybe he met somebody else. He's only been gone twenty-four hours. Best thing you can do is call us back in a few days if you don't hear from him. Have a nice day."

Deena and I took it in turns to call everyone we knew. His family, my family, his shylock customers, people he hung around with, people from the neighborhood. Nothing.

I had to drive over to the office to cancel appointments I'd made the previous week. I was in there for maybe an hour, and when I came out again my car had disappeared. It was a new Lincoln supplied by Gem Steel a few months ago. I'd locked it, which automatically set the alarm. There was no broken glass where it had been parked, so I knew it wasn't a break-in. Whoever took it had a key.

Right away, I'm thinking, Mario Mastromarino. He worked for Gem Steel, he knew where I parked. Either he took the car or he gave someone the keys.

This was when I knew without a doubt that something final had happened to Louie. He wasn't laid up in a coma in some hospital after a car wreck. If he'd been alive nobody would have dared touch the car. That was one reason I knew he was gone. There was another. It was impossible for him to go too long without hearing his children's voices once, twice, or five times a day. The fact he didn't call could mean only one thing. He was dead.

I didn't feel scared—nervous, sure, wondering how and when we would finally get the word he was gone. What I felt right then was intense anger, and when I'm angry it's just about impossible for me to get past it. The hard part is facing the people who make you angry and not letting your true feelings show.

I called Sammy's house. Debra answered. Yes, Sammy was home. I told her I had to see him right away. Deena drove me to the house.

Debra smiled when she saw me but I guess the look on my face must have told her this was no social call. I couldn't even bring myself to say hello.

Sammy was sitting at the living room table with a big cigar sticking out of his mouth. He wore one of his Hollywood silk jogging suits and he looked like he'd never had a worry in his life. Be humble, I told myself. Get what you want and get out.

"You know about Louie, don't you," I said.

I figured he could take that any way he liked.

"Yeah. I hear you can't get a hold of him. People have been calling. Where is he?"

He took his cigar out of his mouth and looked at the end. He was enjoying himself.

"Sammy, Louie always said if there's a problem we have to come to you."

"Lynda, you know how far back me and Louie go? Nobody goes back that far. Let me tell you, if I have to tear down buildings and lift up mountains, I will find Louie for you. I give you my word you will get him back."

I thought, Fuck you. He's dead and we both know it. Don't you go pissing on my leg and tell me it's raining.

"We're in a bind here, Sammy. What are we supposed to do? We have bills to pay, we have to eat. And somebody stole my car this morning."

"That nice new Lincoln? That's too bad. Fucking kids these days!"

He's shaking his head like he can't believe how wicked the world is.

"You hear about Mikey DeBatt?" he goes. "What a great kid! Something like that happens to him, you can't believe people would do such a terrible thing. We figure that must have been kids, too. Jumped him when he's closing up the bar. I feel sorry for Dawn. Got that little baby and she doesn't even have enough for a loaf of bread."

I told him I felt bad for Dawn, too, but right now we had problems of our own.

"Maybe, maybe not. Things will work out. Debra! Go down the basement and bring me up a package of five."

Debra came back with a bundle of notes in a wrapper marked $5,000. Sammy tossed it across the table and went back to work on his cigar.

"Quit worrying," he said. "Louie will show, I promise you."

I put the money in my purse.

"I have to ask you something, Sammy. Is it okay by you if I give Dawn a hundred dollars for a loaf of bread?"

"Don't worry about Dawn. You don't have to do nothing like that. Dawn will work things out for herself."

Debra came to the door with us when we left. She couldn't look at me. As we went out she whispered, "I'm so sorry for this. I'm praying for you and the children."

Five thousand dollars. That's what Sammy figured Louie and his family deserved.

Mario answered the phone when I called his house a couple of days later. I told him I wanted to know about Louie's shylock book and the cash.

"You don't want to be thinking about that," he said. "There is no shylock book. Louie told me. Louie put out a half-million-dollar loan and the guy left town. Forget about the shylock book." Louie was a rich man, this couldn't be true. He didn't owe anybody a cent. Everything he had belonged to his family, and already it looked like someone was taking it from us.

"Mario, what happened to Louie?"

"You tell me. I don't know. I haven't seen him."

"What about my car?"

"You want some advice from me, you better pay attention. You know what Sammy thinks? He thinks you need to move to Florida and spend some time with your parents and your brother."

I asked him if this was something we could take to the police and discuss with them.

"Listen to me. You have to think about moving away from here. You have to leave New York. You don't want to count on Sammy too much. He can be very treacherous. You don't know what he can do. He knows where your parents live, he knows where your brothers live."

Mario was scared to death. It was his voice that gave him away—it shook so much he could hardly get the words out. I wanted to tell him I had some advice for Sammy from Louie and me—that Sammy should go fuck himself. Instead I thanked him and hung up.

But to be on the safe side I told Deena and Louis about his warning. Louis I figured was safe enough at home but Deena I told to be extra careful when she was driving around and make sure nobody was following her. When I came home from work that day Louis was in his room with the Yellow Pages and a phone on the bed. He had been calling up companies that install alarm systems and electric gates and fences. I said that when I first figured out Louie was dead it didn't scare me—finding my son with the Yellow Pages terrified me.

I can't say I was ever a soft and mushy person with my kids, and while I wasn't hard on them—they could both run circles around me anytime they felt like it—I had certainly become harder and tougher in the years with Louie. But seeing my broken son doing what he could to protect the three of us was like a knife in my heart.

I had to take Sammy's threats seriously. I couldn't go to him and say, "Well, Sammy, Mario tells me you think we should sell the house and leave town." He would have laughed in my face. He would have promised me that no harm would come to us while he was around, and five minutes later he could be on the phone arranging for someone to throw a bomb into the house the same night. Back then there was no honor for wives and children. They were used for warning, and I would jeopardize my kids for no one.

I was lying in bed, listening to every sound inside and outside the house. If I heard a car I stopped breathing until it passed. Would they start shooting through the windows? Would Deena or Louis be killed coming out of the front door—and what would happen to them if I got murdered?

Except for my sister-in-law Sandi, who said we could go down to Florida and stay with her, nobody in my immediate family offered any help, not my parents or my brothers, and Louie's family acted like we didn't exist. Louie's mother made that clear when I called the house to tell her Louie was missing.

As always, she still referred to him as Bernie.

"You know your problem, Lynda?" she said. "You blamed Bernie for Louis's accident. He told me you did. How do you think that makes him feel? You should blame yourself. Now you're blaming his friends because you can't find Bernie. Well, you never liked his friends. All you ever did was find fault with everybody around him. Maybe he went somewhere to get away from you—and you know what? I don't blame him if he did."

She hung up on me.

In her mind, her son's wife and his two children were just as dead as he was.

Only she didn't believe Louie was really dead. Someone told me she never gave up on the idea that he was hiding out somewhere and would show up eventually. She wasn't the only one in denial. It took Deena and Louis a long time, too. With them all I could do was try to convince them that their father would never abandon them, because he loved them too much.

We never heard from the Milito family when Louie was killed, although years later Louis went to see Louie's father in St. Vincent's Hospital on Staten Island when he was dying of cancer. They talked about the days when they used to go fishing together. Apart from that, there was no further contact between us, and the last news I had of Louie's mother was that she went crazy and died not long afterwards. I often wondered if her strict Sicilian background made her prejudiced against her own grandchildren.

None of Louie's friends stayed in our lives—the other captains and bosses, the guys in his crew, the hangers on and the wannabes—they also disappeared, and I both can and can't understand that, even if I don't like it. I understand it because in the life, when someone in Louie's position gets taken down, it's like a loyalty test for the ones left behind. Will they be loyal to the one who got killed and get their revenge on the people who did it, or will they accept the fact and go back to business as normal? I can't understand it, because why would Louie's children be ignored, given his position? Well, there's no guessing. The writing was on the wall from the start.

Like they say, money talks and bullshit walks. Fear of getting killed yourself on account of talking to the wrong people, that's got something to do with it also.

I guess that's what happened with Louie's old friend Lenny, the prison hack from Riker's Island. He and Denise lived over by Marine Park, and I made a stop at their house just before I left New York. I didn't stay long. When he saw me, Lenny looked like somebody just told him he had twenty-four hours to live. He was scared stiff. He told me he met up with Mario somewhere and asked Mario, "Where's Louie, what happened to him?" And Mario replied, "You get back in your corner!"

We didn't hear word one from Louie's people—not then, anyway—but a couple of years later, when Sammy Gravano

was in witness protection, Joe Watts and Danny Marino flew
me into New York and put me up at the St. Regis for a long
weekend. Louie and me went back a long way with these
guys, they were senior men in the old Gambino setup, and I
went to New York for good reason. Joe and Danny wanted
to know everything I knew about Sammy murdering the old
lady on Bedford Avenue when he was out burglarizing with
Louie in the years of pulling scores for John Bontate.

I didn't have anything to give them apart from what Louie
told me, but I understand that Joe and Danny spent a couple
of million dollars trying to make a case against Sammy. I
guess they could afford it. Both of them were always impeccably dressed. Armani suits and dazzling white shirts
with long collar points. Joe was more flamboyant than
Danny—his neckties alone cost a couple thousand dollars.

My friend Ken, the real estate lawyer from Staten Island,
helped us to the best of his ability, which wasn't much, because he had his own financial problems. By then he knew
about Louie. He found out when Louie was still alive. From
the TV, newspaper stories, gossip, I don't know, but one day
he told me what he'd heard and asked if there was any truth
to it. I told him I didn't know what Louie did and I didn't care.
Of course I was kidding. By then I had a pretty good idea.

All through the last year of Louie's life, after he came out
of Allenwood, I saw Ken almost every day. Like always, it
was strictly business with him, but I still didn't want to take
the chance that someone might read something more into it. I
was grateful later for his friendship.

After Louie disappeared Ken stepped in to do what he
could. When I told him I planned on selling the house and
moving to Florida, he even offered to buy it, even though I
had already found a buyer for the place, a guy we knew in
the carting business, and was ready to close the deal with
him when Ken made his offer.

I tried talking him out of it. That house was up a steep hill and built in a gully between two smaller hills. When it rained, the water settled in a big pond adjoining the property and sometimes it flooded the area. Louie didn't realize this when he closed in the lower part of the house to build a basement, and the result was there were times when we had eight feet of water down there. It came up from the ground and under the walls, because it had nowhere else to go. Louie was still working on new drainage when he disappeared.

Ken said he wasn't bothered by any of this. He would buy the house and fix the drains, and I would have enough money left to move to Florida with Deena and Louis and buy a house down there, which we did in the summer of 1988.

The Todt Hill house was in my father's name and the asking price was $750,000. I told the carting guy our deal was off and Ken bought the place for $450,000 in as-is condition. The only problem was he couldn't pay the full amount right then, so my father took an unsecured note from him for $100,000. Big mistake, as things turned out.

Like Louie, I was always kind of superstitious. *Todt* is the German word for "death," and Todt Hill got its name from the old days when ice men drove their horses and wagons up the hill to collect ice from the local ponds. When the road was icy, the horses slipped back down the hill, sometimes destroying the wagons and killing the drivers. We lived on the Hill of Death.

I look back and I realize that in the end I got everything I dreamed about having when I was still living with my parents in Bensonhurst and longing for escape. I married a handsome man, we became wealthy, we had children, they went to private schools, we lived in a nice big house. So I got everything I always wanted. Some people might say I got everything I deserved. What do they know?

Epilogue

What you have read is not the whole story. I do not know the whole story. But I have tried to tell as much of it as I remember about what I saw, heard, and did before I met Louie and in the years we were together. I will do the same here, in what came afterwards, tell what happened as best I remember it. But the years after Louie's death were very troubled and difficult years. I learned that I am a manic depressive. The medicine and the therapy have helped me and continue to this day, and thank God for them.

This condition began before they killed Louie. I tried to hide it from myself, the people we knew, and most especially from Deena and Louis. For them I did my best to put on a front by trying to turn every negative into a positive, by encouraging them to do well in school, and to be kind to each other, as they were most of the time, but for me there was no escape from the realities in our new life, and the effort of trying to hide from it gradually wore me down.

Day and night, I was haunted by thoughts of Louie's last moments. This was one reality I could not hide from, and what made the situation worse was not knowing what happened. How did they kill him? Was it sudden? Did he expect it? Did he suffer? Where did it happen? What did they do with his body?

Not once did I find myself hoping that he was still alive—there was no doubt in my mind he was gone. I remembered what he said that day when John and Sammy were on the TV and I warned him to "watch out for Sammy." He said, "Sammy has to watch out for me." Even when the writing was in front of his face he refused to look at it—could not bring himself to believe it.

And Sammy took everything we had, just like he took everything from the families of his other victims. Not just the lives of the husband, father, brother, and son, but their possessions. My guess is that whatever Louie left with Mario got passed to Sammy, including both cars. One of Deena's friends saw him driving the Lincoln in Jersey a few days after it disappeared from outside the real estate office. She recognized it by the missing strip of chrome on one side.

I figure the total value of everything Sammy took from us was around $5 million.

Before leaving New York, I called Mario one more time. I told him there were things we had to discuss face-to-face that we couldn't talk about over the telephone. He showed up at the house around six in the evening. Deena must have been out because she wasn't there that night. It was just Louis, who was on crutches, and me and our dog, Lady Two.

I wasn't surprised that Mario brought his wife, Eleanor, with him. Italian men like Mario don't visit their friends' wives on their own. And I was glad she was there, because she and Louie had always gotten on well and I kind of hoped she would be on our side. Another delusion, as it turned out, but who knew at the time?

I said to Mario, "You were one of Louie's oldest friends. He counted on you to make sure his family was safe if anything happened to him. What do you think he would say if he could see us now? We have nothing. What happened to his money? The shylock book? The numbers? His piece of Gem Steel? Our buildings? The cars? All his belongings he took with him to your house? Where are they? What are we supposed to live on? How can I pay for Deena's education and for my son's medical treatment?"

"Well," he said, "for a start Deena can leave Hofstra and go to a city college. Louis will have to go to one of those welfare clinics."

With this, I lost it and started yelling. We were both yelling. Lady started growling and then barking at Mario.

Eleanor didn't say a word. She sat there like a statue. Louis was trying to calm down the dog, who looked as if she would jump on Mario at any moment. That's when he and Eleanor got up from the table and started walking out. I followed them all the way to the front door, screaming the same questions at him over and over again. He couldn't come up with a single answer.

That was the last time I spoke to Mario Mastromarino.

A couple of years later, I read a deposition he gave in a lawsuit against his doctor. Its answers made him look as if he had cared about Louis. In fact, it was mostly because of Mario's influence that my son never received the treatment he needed.

Deena and Louis went to Florida before me, in the early summer of 1988, and moved in with my sister-in-law Sandi and my brother Harvey. I had to stay behind, pack up the house, and sell it, arrange the move to Florida, and tie up the few loose ends in what was left of my real estate business. All of this took most of the summer to complete, and if it hadn't been for Sandi coaching me on how to pack up and arrange the move, it would have been impossible.

Harvey called me from his office one day. He had a question. When are you getting your kids out of here? In a panic I phoned Sandi at their home. "Oh, don't worry about him," she said, "Louis has got his days and nights mixed up, but apart from that, they're fine. Do what you have to do, everything's okay."

Alone in the house, I found I couldn't think clearly. I was being pulled this way and that by questions that kept piling up in my brain, to the point where I was so confused and scared that by the time I thought I had figured out an answer I couldn't remember what the question was. Maybe I didn't want to know the answers. On one of those nights when I was by myself in the house I swallowed half a bottle of pills, Halcyon, I think they were, hoping they would put me to sleep—for the night, forever, I didn't care, I just wanted to stop thinking—but at five in the morning I found myself waking up outside the front door of a friend's house in Staten Island. I don't want to use her name here. I don't know how I got there. She must have heard me, or maybe I screamed or rang the bell, and I don't remember her taking me inside, but she told me afterwards that she kept me awake until morning by talking to me and walking me around the room until she was sure she could trust me to be alone again.

I thought about Louie while I packed up the house. Knowing him, on the day he died he was probably still figuring out how to fix the basement drainage and finish a project he started in the garden. I wondered what he was thinking in the split second just before they killed him. I remembered the last time he came to the house that Valentine's Day. I was remembering too much and trying too hard not to think about it.

When my friend Ken picked me up at the house for the flight to Florida I didn't turn around for a last look. My thoughts were on Deena and Louis, and our new life away from New York.

Deena had ideas of her own. She turned twenty the month after Louie's murder and she wanted to get out of Florida as quickly as possible and go back to her old life, not with me, but with her friends on Staten Island and at Hofstra, where she would be graduating the following year. I didn't have the strength to resist. I told her, "You want to go back, be my guest, but be careful." She was gone soon after Labor Day that year. I went to her graduation in 1989. On the back of her cap she stuck white tape to make these words: THANKS MOM.

My brother Harvey wasted no time in pointing out that without Louie life would be different. When I first called to tell him Louie was missing and probably dead, he said, "That's too bad, Lynda. If he doesn't come back, I guess you can forget about the Lincolns and Cadillacs—you'd better get used to the idea of driving compact cars."

As for Lady Two, she would also have to go.

Harvey told me, "I don't want that dog in my house. You can't afford to keep a dog now, especially a sick dog. Find someone else to take it or get the vet to put it to sleep."

I didn't have the energy to look for a home for Lady. She had been with the family for years—how would she ever get used to someone new? And Harvey was right, she was getting weaker. Perhaps the best thing would be to take that beautiful, trusting animal to the vet and put her gently to sleep. So I did, and I have blamed my brother for it ever since, though nowhere near as much as I blame myself.

Harvey grew up in Bensonhurst. He had figured out long before that Louie was connected. I knew he bragged about his Mafia brother-in-law to his friends, which would have put him in the hospital or worse if Louie had found out. But Harvey was no worse than a lot of men outside the life—they like to get close to wiseguys, they think it gives them a status they don't have in their own lives, they eat the free meals and take anything else that's offered. When Louie was alive, Harvey laughed at all the jokes and acted like Louie was the greatest man he'd ever known. Now that he was dead, he couldn't stop kicking him.

In Florida he never missed an opportunity to remind me that Louie had screwed up his family's lives and left us with nothing. "After all the millions Louie made," he used to say, "you'd think he could have taken out insurance or something."

I didn't bother telling him that guys like Louie were superstitious about buying insurance—they thought it was a jinx.

It was Sandi who helped me stay alive after I moved to Florida. Such a personality she had! One of the most positive people I ever knew. And how she loved big parties, to be around people having a good time. Nobody stayed down for long in Sandi's company, she could snap you right out of it with a few words and her wonderful laugh. I adored her. I didn't feel that Harvey was my brother but I always thought of his wife as my sister. Next to my father, Sandi was my oldest and closest friend.

"Come on, Lynda," she used to say, "we have to get you back in circulation, see if we can't find you a good man." And the three of us, Sandi, her Chinese friend Chin, and I, would dress up and go out for the night at restaurants and clubs and have the time of our lives. As the only unmarried women, it was usually Chin and me who got the attention. Sandi was just happy to sit at the table and enjoy the parade.

I don't know if she realized she was dying. She was overweight and a heavy smoker. We all begged her to stop smoking and take better care of herself. I used to call Harvey to ask him to talk to her but she would just laugh at him, like she laughed at Chin and me, and shrug it off. "Where are we going tonight?" she would say. "We have to find someone for Lynda."

I have to say I didn't make much of an effort to break away from the old life after I left New York—not the life itself, of course, because there was no way I could be part of that without Louie. I just wanted to be around the people. I missed the city, I missed them and their jokes, and I missed the excitement. Kind of ironic, I can see that now, running away from all of that and finding how hard it was to leave it behind completely.

There are wiseguy hangouts all over south Florida—

restaurants and other places Louie and me went to in the old days—and at first when I moved down there I spent a lot of time in the same places and occasionally ran into people we used to know. We didn't talk about Louie or what happened to him. That would not have been a good idea. Some of them gave me their condolences, I thanked them, and we left it at that. And one or two let me know they were available, now that I was single again. Taking these offers any further wouldn't have been a good move, either, so I didn't.

I sat for the Florida real estate test, and it was like a rerun of the New York State test—I failed it twice and passed on the third attempt, with my father coaching me every weekend until I passed. I could have saved myself the effort. Four months in the business was all I could handle. I couldn't concentrate, I couldn't deal with the pressures of the job or with the suspicion that the people I worked for were anti-Semitic. Whether this was a symptom of my illness or my imagination, I didn't know, but it played on my mind every day I was there, so in the end I walked out.

I was losing control and didn't know what to do about it.

Someone told me about the Family Service Agency, which was funded by the United Way and offered therapy to those needing it. I made an appointment to see one of the counselors, Deborah Taylor, and showed up at the office with a bandaged wrist from another failed attempt to kill myself. Deborah recalled our first meeting years later.

"It was late in 1988," she said. "Lynda was pacing up and down and looking at the door as if she expected someone to burst through it. She had so much pent-up nervous energy she was almost flying around the room. She couldn't sit down, she refused to sit. She couldn't stop shaking. I made her tea and coffee to give her an excuse to sit. She was in a terrible state, worried sick about her daughter, her son, terrified that somebody would kill them or hurt them, and at the same time she felt guilty because of her son's accident and because she and her daughter couldn't talk without fighting.

"I didn't know what to make of it, because at that point I

didn't know what had happened to her and her family, and it was hard to take it all in when she finally told me. The clients we see are often victims of some kind of abuse, spousal or otherwise. But they're all in trouble. They all need help. Lynda was in big trouble, just like them, but she came from a world entirely different from anything I'd ever known at the agency.

"It was never boring, dealing with Lynda. She called me once to ask if I would speak to a man and explain to him that she wasn't crazy. But she was, she was well on her way to being very ill.

"She didn't have anyone to turn to except to her father. I got the impression that he was the only positive aspect in her life. She depended on him absolutely. She said she was estranged from her mother and three brothers. And she had terrible problems with her son and daughter. They seemed to think their father had left a lot of money and their mother was hiding it. They'd been accustomed to living well and now it was different, so they blamed her for not giving them what she didn't have.

"The bigger problem was that Lynda didn't know how to relate to her new self. She didn't know how to act, she couldn't express herself. She would start off with an idea and lose her train of thought, and by the time she found it again, she had forgotten where she started. She came to see me off and on for about three years. Her condition fluctuated from session to session. Then she changed her insurance program and was given a new therapist, another woman, a practicing psychologist. The psychiatrist Lynda saw after the new therapist diagnosed her mental illness as bipolar disorder."

I remember that meeting with Deborah Taylor. I really depended on her, even calling her at home. She was there for me. Always. She once told me, "Lynda, after one of your visits, I go home smiling."

I said to her, "Should I give you a check, or should you give me a check?" She laughed. I went to the car and the

next day realized what she meant. Debra was saying that I
was the only one of her patients who took this therapy seriously. She knew that all of her training, all of her schooling,
was going to something that was good. She was right on a
lot of counts. All I wanted to do was run out of the room.

The lithium the doctor prescribed wasn't helping. I checked
myself into Coral Springs Psychiatric Hospital and stayed
there for ten days. Sandi often came to visit. My brother
Harvey goes and tells the psychiatrist that my mental illness
was imaginary.

"The only thing wrong with you," he told me, "is that
you're afraid of the future."

I didn't know which scared me most, the past, present, or
future, but Harvey's attitude didn't help me feel better about
anything. He became just like my mother.

I got a call from one of our friends, it must have been
around late 1991 or early the next year. "Lynda, guess what?
Sammy just rolled! He rolled on John, he rolled on everybody! The feds put him in witness protection!"

I called Laura Ward, one of the prosecutors I knew in New
York. She was a nice lady. I asked her if it was true that
Sammy rolled. She sighed. Lynda, you know I can't tell you
about that.

But without saying anything more, she had told me all I
needed to know, and now the whole world would know what
I had always believed—that Sammy was a born rat.

Laura and an FBI agent, George Gabriel, came to Florida
before this to take a statement for the upcoming trial of John
Gotti. The meeting did not go well at first.

"What have you done for my family except make our life
hell?" I asked them. "Why should I tell you anything? Find
out what they did to my husband! Find out where they
buried him! I have nothing to tell you! You're feeding
Sammy Gravano, the scum of the earth, and you expect me

to sit still for questions? You've been my enemy most of my life and now you want information, like suddenly we're best friends?"

"If there's anything we can do to help you, please call us," the FBI agent said.

Then I realized they were only doing their jobs, and when they got up to leave and put out their hands to shake mine I could not refuse their gesture or ignore the kindness in their voices. In fact I even arranged a dinner date for Laura Ward with an attorney friend before she flew back to New York. And I still consider George Gabriel a friend.

When Sammy rolled and made his confession he told the FBI about the night Louie was killed. He said it was no sudden thing. Sammy said that he planned it and that John Gotti gave him the go-ahead. At his 1992 trial, John was on tape saying he was involved in Louie's murder, but in response to Sammy's constant pestering. Personally, I don't believe John had much to do with it. My view is that Sammy manipulated him into it, but with John dead I don't suppose we will ever know how much he was involved.

The story goes that Louie was shot in a club in Bensonhurst, around seven o'clock in the evening of March 8, 1988, the night he and Deena were supposed to meet for dinner. He was putting sugar in his espresso when a guy called John Carneglia put a bullet in the back of his head and another under his chin. A doctor once told me he would have felt nothing.

An old friend of ours told me, "That's Sammy's MO, Lynda. One in the back of the head and one under the chin. From everything I've been hearing, it was Sammy who killed Louie."

According to Sammy's account, Huck Carbonaro helped clean up the place afterwards. I don't want to believe that's true. Years ago, when we still lived on Arlene Street, Huck sent Louie a leather belt he made in prison with a note saying how much he respected Louie and how grateful he was to him for past favors. Louie showed me the note. It said something like, I think of you every day. See you soon, old friend.

"Look at this," Louie said, "out of all the guys Huck knows, he thought of me. Don't you think that's nice?"

This is what I think: Sammy pulled the trigger that night. Maybe Huck was there, maybe not, but nobody will ever convince me that Sammy didn't kill Louie, personally. He resented Louie, he was jealous of him, he was scared of him, and he had probably wanted him dead for years. He told the feds it was John Gotti's idea. I don't believe that, I will never believe that. Sammy was using John as an excuse, just like he used him as an excuse to kill everyone else we knew.

There is no doubt in my mind that Sammy pushed John Gotti to the top of the Gambinos because he figured John would take all the heat and leave him as boss. But somewhere along the line he must have realized he fucked up, and I think that time came after he killed Louie, because from what I was told, when Sammy and John were in the Manhattan holding tank, John was overheard on a telephone call, saying; "That son of a bitch killed Louie Milito for no good reason!"

From this, Sammy had to know he stood a good chance of being killed while he was still in prison, because right after this he made his deal with the feds for immunity from prosecution for the murders he admitted. And they let him walk in exchange for John.

One more reason I don't think John Gotti gave permission for Louie to be killed. My daughter, Deena, had to go and testify at his trial. She was already living in New York and I guess they figured it would cost less to have Deena at the trial than it would cost to fly me up from Florida.

Before she went I asked her, "Do me a favor. When you're on the stand I want you to keep staring at John. Tell me if he looks you in the eye, because if he does I will know he told Sammy to kill your father. It would show me that he did, and didn't give a shit if you knew. If he doesn't look at you, it means he had nothing to do with it, that's how I see it."

Afterwards, Deena told me that all the questions came from the prosecution—the Gotti lawyers let her leave the stand without asking one, and I believe this was because John told them not to ask any.

I asked her, "Did you stare at him like I said? Did he look back at you?"

She told me the questions from the prosecution—Did she love her father? Did she miss him?—upset her so much, she couldn't stop crying. She was almost hysterical.

She was trying to focus on John Gotti, and every time she looked over at him he was staring at the floor.

I understand that both John Carneglia and Huck Carbonaro are in prison for other crimes. I don't know John Carneglia but I knew Huck, and I would ask him the following: Please tell me and Louie's children the truth about that night. Who pulled the trigger? Who removed the body? What did they do with it? I want to know. It is my right to know.

❖   ❖   ❖

The situation with Ken, my real estate lawyer friend, did not turn out well. When I sold him the Todt Hill house, my father carried a $100,000 note for the place and now Ken had stopped making payments and the banks were foreclosing on some apartments he owned in Florida. This was news to me since he never told me he had property down there. Dad sued. It was too late, Ken had declared bankruptcy. My father was so pissed off, he sued him for unethical conduct and had him disbarred from practicing law.

I met other men in Florida. My mother thought it would be a good idea if I got married. "Lynda, you don't have any security. How will you look after Louis? Who will look after you when you get older? How are you going to live?"

When I met George, I thought he might be the answer to my prayers. He was maybe four years younger than me, he came from a French Canadian family in Maine, and had a legitimate career as an international consultant for a digital information corporation, so he had seen something of the world. I was impressed by the fact that he had several degrees and was, because of that, the most educated man I'd ever known. He also seemed kind and thoughtful, and I was overdue for some kindness. I fell for him.

It fizzled out after a few years. His kindness turned to condescension. In company he began referring to me as a know-it-all—the Captain, as he put it. Ask the Captain, he used to say, she knows everything. His prejudices began to show. "I just love Boca Raton," he said once. "If they didn't have so many Jews here, it would be perfect."

I had begun working in Fort Lauderdale for an executive head-hunting company and was beginning to get back on my feet. I enjoyed the work—I seemed to have a talent for putting the right people in the right jobs and had been fairly successful. Then George got laid off by his company. He opened a multilevel marketing company and begged me to steer some of my company's clients to him—which I did, stupidly and out of misplaced loyalty—because I wanted to help him, but when my company found out, they fired me.

I was falling into an old pattern, doing the wrong thing for a man for the wrong reasons and trying to convince myself it was the right thing to do.

The end came with George when Louis and two friends borrowed my car without asking. George called the police to report it had been stolen. You don't ever do that, I told him. I might have left the old life behind but I still had certain beliefs. Calling the cops on my son was unforgivable. I was furious with him. And with the two other kids, because it turned out that they had broken into another car just before meeting Louis and had left some of the stolen goods in my car. These included a business card holder with the owner's name and telephone number on the cards. Not only did George call the man, he also gave him my son's name and told him where he went to school.

Louis was in the classroom the next day when two detectives came in and hauled him off to the principal's office. Nothing came of it because it was clear to the cops that Louis knew nothing about the theft, but that didn't matter to me. I was living with a stool pigeon. That's what mattered. I couldn't stay with a rat.

Alone again, I began going out occasionally for a meal, usually at a place where they had music and dancing, which always made me feel good. I didn't mind walking in on my own. Being around people who enjoyed the same pleasures that I appreciated gave me a new sense of belonging. That's how I met Nick.

There was a crowd of people on the floor that night and I was standing alone at the edge, eyes shut, lost to the world and happy to be there, when a man's voice said, "Who are you and where do you come from?" I saw a darkly attractive man staring at me. He was older me than me, more than seventeen years older, which was another reason I was attracted to him. In my mind, as always, older men meant security. But what first caught my attention that night, apart from the man's easygoing manner and confidence, were his snakeskin shoes.

I was in the middle of answering him when he came up with another question, and what made him do this I don't know— maybe it was the way I was dressed or my New York accent— because his next question just about took my breath away.

"Do you know any Mafia people?"

If he had asked me that somewhere else, in a supermarket or a drugstore, I wouldn't have bothered with an answer, but as it happened we were in a five-star restaurant that had a certain reputation as a wiseguy hangout, and although I'd never been there with Louie, it was a name you sometimes heard among our friends. And I felt safe there, because by this time Sammy Gravano had disappeared into the witness protection program after spilling his guts to the federal government.

The man asked the question again: "Do you know any Mafia people?"

"If you want to call it that," I said.

We danced. He was pretty good. We talked. I told him about Louie. The name meant nothing to him. What he wanted to know were the details. Once I was satisfied that he wasn't a cop, I didn't hold anything back. If he had a thing about the Mafia, I had plenty to say and he couldn't hear enough. More important to me, he was a legitimate businessman in the construction industry in New Jersey— and no, he wasn't Italian and he wasn't connected. He was an Arab.

So I liked Nick from the start. We began dating. He was easy to be with—so easy that within the first year of meeting him he flew me to New Jersey and we moved into a house in Teaneck. He also gave me a job running his office.

It didn't take long before this new fantasy fell apart. I don't know a word of Arabic except one, *Yehuda,* which means "Jew," so when Nick introduced me to his Arab friends as *Yehuda,* thinking I didn't know what it meant, I knew I had taken yet another wrong turn. I also made the mistake of asking my mother for her opinion. She said I should stay with him and she reminded me that I wasn't getting any younger. In her eyes, Nick was an honest and successful businessman, he would take care of Louis and me. What she also meant was, I don't want your father supporting you any longer.

Nick and I got married.

I really believed he was the knight on a white horse. That's how stupid you can get when you want to believe something so badly, you ignore anything that tells you you've got it all wrong—again.

His only interest in me was in my past. The life. He couldn't leave the subject alone. What was it *really* like? What kind of man was Sammy Gravano? How many people did Louie kill? Did I know John Gotti? Was it true that Mafia hitmen rubbed garlic on their bullets? Did I ever see Louie do that? Was *The Godfather* true to life?

If Nick and I were together today, he'd harass me about

how similar my life is to life on *The Sopranos*. But I would have to tell the truth. Sometimes I watch *The Sopranos* and I laugh out loud. I laugh at the unrealistic stuff like Tony's size, when really no one in the family would get that big. Everyone was always smooth and dressed to the nines. Mostly I laugh and shake my head at how similar my family's life was to the Sopranos'. First of all, I'm not new to the movies. Louie and his friends were obsessed with *The Godfather*. Second, Louie and I were portrayed by *The Sopranos* actors Michael Imperioli and Katherine Narducci in the 1988 movie *Witness to the Mob*. For that movie, a producer, who my gut tells me ended up involved with *The Sopranos* somehow, interviewed me over the phone for three hours. I told him about *everything*. Our likes and dislikes, family dynamics and habits. Now, I see uncanny similarities between my family's life and the Sopranos' family life. Carmella Soprano speaks her mind just like I did, in a way women just didn't do back then; both Louie and Tony have two children, an older girl and a younger boy; I had to "buy" Deena into Hofstra just the way Carmella had to with Meadow and Columbia. The kids even look alike! Deena and Meadow both play the same sport and are called the same nickname by their fathers. Our houses were each on a hill, and even Louie and Tony eat the same way! Louie would eat from the refrigerator just the way Tony does. The Soprano household is very similar to ours. I just laugh and shake my head because it takes me way back. To what seems like another lifetime.

When Nick introduced me to his friends it was, "This is my wife, she was married to a hitman in the New York mob who got murdered. Lynda, tell them about Louie."

I hated it. I hated the looks on his friends' faces, the men fascinated and looking me up and down as if I were some kind of prize they wouldn't mind having for themselves. Them I could at least talk to and joke with, but most of the wives made it very clear we had nothing in common after hello. I was way out of my depth in that company.

Within a month of starting work for my new husband, it

was clear that while he may have been honest in business, he was a long way from success. The biggest entries in the company books were payables. There were very few receivables. That wasn't all. When his ex-wife sued for unpaid alimony, the cops arrested him and put him in jail for a week until we could find an attorney to get him out. It was like being back with Louie again but on lesser charges.

I left Jersey and went back to Florida to file for divorce on grounds of abandonment. Nick showed up soon afterwards and said he would do whatever it took to get us back together. He came with me to meet with one of the psychologists I began seeing after Deborah Taylor. I thought that Nick, who held similar views to my brother when it came to the subject of mental illness, might learn something. Fat chance. In the psychologist's office he was his usual impatient self.

I called her afterwards to ask what she thought of him. She said, "If you stay with that man, don't come back to me."

The choice was simple. I had no intention of losing my therapist.

I've been with the same man now for four years: Ivan Jay Levine. We've had our ups and downs, that's for sure. I've called the police on him many times and once had him arrested for battery. The court issued a restraining order.

Whatever else our life is, it's never boring. We split up, we get back together, some days we can't do anything except scream at each other, and when it all gets too much for me, I go back to my own place for a few days of peace and quiet. It worries him that I have somewhere else to live, because he knows I could leave him at any time. When I'm at my place, he calls constantly.

I turn my cell phone off so he can't call, then I call him a dozen times a day.

I love him, I don't trust him, I can't stand him, and I can't live without him. Is he with me because he thinks he will get something out of me, maybe money from this book, or is he with me because he loves me? The truth is, I don't know how I feel about him and I don't really know how he feels about me. Maybe he doesn't know how to love, and I don't, either. Maybe we have both lost the ability to love anyone and maybe with our family backgrounds we never really learned, because nobody ever taught us.

He cooks me wonderful meals, he puts the milk in my coffee, maxes out his credit cards buying me expensive gifts, he follows me around the house talking to me, he drives me crazy. There are days when I wish I had never met him and days when I don't know how I got along without him. We have stayed together in spite of my anger, confusion, and depressions. In the space of one day I see him as my best friend and my worst enemy—or maybe I am my own worst enemy, maybe that's the real problem. We are seeing a psychologist together. So far I have no idea if it's helping us.

We stayed together through my father's final illness, but at the hospital he would pretend he was asleep, and my father would say, "Lynda, he's tired. Why don't you go home?" This upset me because I felt that he was doing it deliberately, partly because he knew what my father would say, but mostly because it was his way of controlling me, of letting me know he was in charge.

He is a compulsive controller. He has to have his own way. You cannot argue with him, he is overwhelming. He will not shut up. Sometimes I feel like I'm trying to run up a down escalator.

For thirteen years, I had a little dog called K.C. I bought her as company for Louis when he had to stay alone in the house, and after Louis went back to New York she became my closest companion. When she died of old age, I thought I would go crazy with grief. My boyfriend stayed with me through this, too, even though I was impossible and inconsolable and would probably have handled everything better if I could have been alone.

I have left him many times. We have abused each other
and certainly we have hated each other. Yet here we are, together, and I can't say why, except that at the best of times
he can be gentle and comforting. At his worst, he is domi-
neering and obnoxious.

I suppose we could both do better with other people—
that's what I've told him a hundred times. Then the anger
wears off and the next thing I know, we're back together. My
energy is drained and I am tired.

He knows everything there is to know about me. It doesn't
bother him. He has no connection with Louie's world or
any part of that life. Perhaps he wishes he did, because I
think he's impressed by it, as many men are, but he's not
curious about it. He doesn't question me closely about my
life with Louie. He tries hard to build success for himself.
He is one of those people who never gives up, and I ad-
mire his persistence and his willingness to put up with my
moods and mental state. But I have questions: Is he with
me for love or money? Am I being used? I think about
this.

He has helped me through some of the worst times of my
life and has often stood up for me, stood by me, protecting
me against anyone who would hurt me. He protects me
against everybody except himself.

When he asked me if I would ever marry him, I told him
no, but that even if we did, I would never change my name
to his and would always remain Lynda Milito.

Knowing his background, I feel sorry for him. You don't
spend all those years in therapy and not learn something
about what makes people act the way they do. Like me, he's
another survivor. He comes from a family that fought and
bickered from morning to night. Anger seems to run through
his entire family. We were once in a restaurant when two of
his relatives, a husband and wife, started arguing about hav-

ing a baby—she wanted one, he didn't, and she burst into tears and started arguing in front of everyone.

So I cannot be around his family too long. When any of them comes to town, I move back into my place and wait until they leave. He knows how I feel. Perhaps the main thing we have in common is that we both come from families where they all argue a lot.

Perhaps what it comes down to is that we are perfect for each other.

People say the truth will set you free. Sometimes. With some truths, when you hear them you wish you didn't hear. Learning about Louie's last night alive was like seeing it happening in front of my face. Knowing that Sammy had gotten away with the nineteen murders he admitted to, and who knows how many more he didn't talk about, sent me into a depression that got progressively worse over the next ten years.

One of my therapists was interviewed for this book in December 2001.

"Lynda is mentally ill," she told Reg Potterton. "Whether it's bipolar disorder or something else, it's difficult to say. The labels for mental disease aren't always important. She has a very traumatic history, there's no doubt about that. When she came to me in 1995, she was extremely disturbed. She had seen two psychiatrists but was still very troubled. My view is that psychiatrists do not always take trauma history into account. They can prescribe medicine, which they did for Lynda, and she definitely needs it, but as a psychologist I take a more pragmatic view. What's the problem and how can we solve it?

"As I got to know her, I understood that she was attracted to powerful men, or men she believed were powerful. It's natural. Women are drawn to men with power and money and men are drawn to beauty. It's the way of the world. Her problem was that she thought she could pet the rattlesnake and not get bitten. She's always wanted to change the rattlesnake into a fluffy bunny. It doesn't work.

"What I saw was a very frightened woman who tended to

pull away from reality into fantasy. If you put too much
pressure on Lynda, she begins to crumble."

Well, I don't see it as crumbling. I didn't crumble after
they strapped me into a stretcher and took me in an ambulance to Englewood Psychiatric Hospital in New Jersey. Or
after being admitted twice to the Pavilion Hospital in West
Palm Beach. I didn't crumble when my sister-in-law Sandi
died, though I cried for months because I couldn't stand the
idea of not having her in my life anymore. How much do
you have to take before you crumble?

I sometimes think the best thing I can do is put myself
into a mental hospital and never come out. But that's on the
worst days. I wish I could say I enjoy life most of the time,
but that's not true. It's a day-to-day thing, you're always
hoping that something good will happen. My pleasures are
pretty simple. I like walking for miles on the beach or working on the sculptures and collages that started a hundred
years ago with the paint-by-numbers kit that Louie bought
for me when we lived on Brigham Street.

There's no pleasant way of putting this, so I may as well
put it the only way I know how. As a family, we are a mess.
The bottom line is, one way or another, we've all been
driven crazy and we can't seem to do anything to change it.
Blame, guilt, shame—they're all part of this. Shoulda
woulda coulda, didn't. Sometimes I wonder how life would
have turned out for my children if Louie had stayed alive
and I had died. He often said that he wouldn't know what to
do with himself if I died before him.

I look in the mirror today, at the age of fifty-five, and that
dark-haired teenager at Terry Lee's almost forty years ago
now has a platinum blonde ponytail. Filled out a little here
and there, but not much, and it's all in the right places and
firm enough so that I can still wear a bikini to the beach
without having to worry if I look like a deflated balloon. The
interior may be a mess—the gall bladder went in an operation in the nineties—but the outside seems to have a life of
its own.

Over the last years of his life, with my mother long since dead, Dad was moved from one of his children's houses to another, from Harvey to Arthur, from their houses to mine and back again, until in the end he was too feeble to travel alone and the illness that eventually killed him was too far gone to cure. Then we found a rehab hospital where they told us he would get the medical attention he needed. But he steadily got weaker, and the worse he got, the more my own mental state deteriorated.

My father had his faults; he didn't stand up for me against my mother when I needed his support. He was weak when I wanted him to be strong. But he was my best and my longest-lasting friend, and if there is goodness in me, it comes from him. For all his troubles, he was always positive, hoping for the best at the worst of times, and that's something else he passed on to me.

I like to remember Dad when Deena was little and the two of us would dance for him until he couldn't stop smiling— and he would dance for us, too, doing his old soft-shoe routines while Deena clapped and laughed out loud from sheer happiness.

Dad was the last remaining connection to my brothers, who, one by one, acted like they didn't want anything to do with me and my children, just like Louie Milito's brothers disowned him and cut us out of their lives. None of them speaks to me and I don't speak to them.

So we are no longer part of the Lustig family or the Milito family. But we still have the name. I'll always be a Milito. Louis also, but not Deena, who at the age of thirty-four is married with two children and thinking about moving out of state. My relationship with her goes up and down, depending on who says what and how the other one takes it. Like I said, walking on eggshells.

It is true that in trying to put my life back together I have yet to control the anger I feel towards certain people. This includes certain friends I had in Brooklyn who refused to return two matching wicker chairs I lent them.

They told me they had got used to them. I told them to get
unused to them. After I'd been calling for six months they
said they had given the chairs away. So I asked my
boyfriend to see what he could do, and they came back
with, How would you like to get your legs broken with a
baseball bat.

Eventually, I got an old Brooklyn friend to make the call.
He told them he was coming to their house to pick up the
chairs and was in no mood to listen to any excuses. They returned the chairs, with a message—tell Lynda to go fuck
herself.

I understand that this sounds like a trivial reason for
anger, but there was more to it than furniture—it reminded
me that people will treat you like dirt when they think they
can get away with it. Louie's absence gave them the courage
to say things they would never have dared to say when he
was alive. I saw another example of this when "friends"
came down to Florida and one of them started mouthing off
about Louie's murder.

"Nobody gets killed for no reason," he said, "they must
have killed him for something."

I asked him, "Where do you get the nerve to talk about
things you know nothing about?"

"Lynda," he said, laughing in my face, "why don't you go
pop a few more pills."

That's how it is when some people think you're too weak
to fight back. They do what they can to make you feel worse.
I know my son Louis felt this a long time ago, when his father was still in Allenwood. There was one particular kid at
his school who gave him no peace but chased Louis around,
yelling, "Hey, jailbird!"

"Invite this boy to the house," I told Louis.

When he got there, Louie's slippers were outside the bathroom door and the shower was running. I made sure the boy
saw this. I was calling out, "Louie, do you need another
towel? What's taking you so long? Louis has a friend here
from school!"

You never saw a boy look more surprised than he was when he left the house.

Yes, I am angry and I know it. This is how I am. I can be kind and I can be very cruel to those who ignore the golden rule, that you should not do to others what you would not want them to do to you. Louie used to say people should not mistake his kindness for weakness. What I say is this: Nobody is going to fuck with me and get away with it. That's what my life has taught me and I don't care who knows it. I have had it.

Every day I pray that somebody will tell me Louie's body has been found. Why can't they give him the respect he gave them and let his family have at least that small consolation?

Some years ago, Louis called me in Florida and said, "Ma, they think they know where Dad's buried. They're digging up the parking lot at the Staten Island hospital."

I asked him, "What's Deena doing, is she with you? Put Deena on the phone."

And he said, "She's not home, she's been camped out at the parking lot since they started digging three days ago."

They found nothing is what they found.

If this was a movie, it would be me and Deena and Louis against the world. But it's not a movie, it's only life. There are times when I think they hate me almost as much as they hate themselves and their ruined lives. Mostly, when we try to talk to each other we end up screaming.

Some people look back at their lives and wonder how and why it turned out the way it did. I don't wonder about mine. They say that life is what you make it. I'm sorry, but to me that's not how it works. Life is what happens to you and how you deal with it. If I had felt better about myself when I was a little girl, what happened with Selma in her bedroom all those years ago might have turned out different. I would have been confident enough and trusted my mother enough, knowing that she would stand up for me as any loving mother would, to tell her the truth instead of keeping it inside. I would have told her about the rape and she would have stood by me then as well.

If she had cared enough, she would have known or at least guessed that something had happened to me and she would have done everything in her power to let me know that she cared enough to do something about it—to at least report the guy to the cops to keep him from doing the same thing to some other confused and miserable girl. She would have seen that I was everything but happy, at home and at school, and she would have done something about that, too—shown an interest when I was at school instead of acting as if it didn't matter. As if I didn't matter.

From my mother I learned that nothing much mattered except money and respecting people who had it, looking down on those who didn't have it. Her brother, my uncle Sam Dostis, had it. Even my father made a few dollars eventually, enough for him and Mom to retire to a condo in Florida, anyway, and each of my three brothers did okay in the end. Me, too, once I got into real estate, but for some reason this didn't impress her so much. Knowing what she must have known about Louie after we'd been married twenty years, she probably figured that any success I had in life came from being married to him.

As for Louie, if I had grown up with just a little bit of self-respect instead of thinking I was pretty much worthless and longing to be different and better than I was, like I did, would I still have been dumb enough to run off with that kind of man? Would I have married him, and stayed married to him, had two children with him, stayed with him after he became hooked up with the Gambinos, after I knew about his violence, saw it, felt it, and was terrified of it?

And I think about the positive side of his strength, how it gave him confidence and how he never doubted himself or wanted to be anything except who and what he became.

I see now that Louie's confidence had a power of its own

that carried me along with it, because he made me feel
stronger and he made me think for the first time in my life
that a man loved me for all the things I didn't have, who
loved me for who I was, the way I was. Louie gave me the
confidence to believe that I could be better. The strength I
got from him helped me hold on after he was gone. It helps
me now.

It wasn't just the strength, it was also the happiness the
four of us shared, even in small, everyday things, and I remember that just as clearly as I remember the worst of my
life, the fear, and Louie's violence. But in our house, nobody
was left out or made to feel unwanted. The children had to be
at the table for dinner every night at six. No excuses. And no
phone calls for Deena, the social butterfly, while we ate.
Louie made a point of asking the kids about school that day.
Did they take any tests? How did they make out? How were
they doing at sports? And he would pay real close attention
to the answers and come back with more questions if he
wasn't satisfied.

In those years, my dream was that they would both go to
college. Deena would be a lawyer and Louis a doctor. He
said he wanted to be a plastic surgeon. Oh, sure, Louie used
to tell him. The day you become a doctor is the day I go out
and get drunk.

For me, this was happiness, this was normal, and that's
how I wanted our life to be, normal. And of course it was
anything but, and I always knew it.

At the time of this writing, Deena will soon be thirty-five.
She and her husband have two daughters of their own. They
live in Staten Island, and so does Louis. He will be thirty on
his next birthday. He lives alone. My hope is that the three
of us will find peace in our minds and in the relationship between us, and there are times when this seems close and
times when it seems impossible.

Louis has told me more times than I care to remember,
"Ma, you don't know what it's like growing up like this,
being like this, without a father."

Some days I feel like I'm making progress with him and Deena and in my own life, and sometimes, when I feel as if everything is slipping out of control again, I stay at home or I go to the beach, and wait for the day to end.

In the three years since I began working on this book and for the first time examining my life and trying to understand it, I won't pretend I've enjoyed it. To be honest, most of the time it's been a nightmare, and there were many, many times when I wanted to give up on it, not think about it, hide from it. And sometimes I did, for months on end, until I felt I could face it again.

There were countless times I wished I'd never met Reg Potterton, my collaborator on this book, times I wished he was out of my life so he could stop with his questions. The pain of reliving things I thought I had forgotten about—that I tried to forget about—made me hate him. It sent me back to the doctor for more medication and therapy, it made it impossible to sleep, and many times it turned me into a screaming basket case. No way I would have gotten involved if I had known in the beginning it would be like this.

But I thought it would help me and so did my doctors. "Let it all go, Lynda," they said, "don't let the past keep eating at you, bring it out in the open, get it all written down and move on." And that's what I'm trying to do with this book. Move on. The question is, where to?

One thing I am sure of. There is some kind of strength deep inside me that nobody—not my mother, not Louie Milito, not Sammy Gravano, or anyone who ever hurt me—has been able to destroy. So wherever I do go, I'll still have that. Maybe it's all I've got that's worth having.

In my dreams I see myself walking and laughing with my father. There will be dancing.

Acknowledgments

Special thanks to my children, Deena and Louis, for being strong.

In memoriam Sandi Lustig, my sister-in-law. You were like a sister to me. Guess what? Who cares if Harvey saw the molding on the car you burned tuff? It served him right.

K.C., my Yorkshire terrier, 1988–2001. You gave me strength; knowing you needed me kept me going. I love you, Kay; now you can watch over Dee-Dee.

I'd like to give special thanks to Dr. Gerald Ruth, Dr. Serge Thys, Dr. F. Leigh Phillips III, Dr. Thomas Roth, Dr. Laurence Levine, Marcia Leder, and Debbie Taylor. I'd also like to thank Maryann at Raspberries Salon; Susie and Peter at European Touch; Carrie Noris and Irma Landi at the Consignment Exchange.

Clyde Taylor, V.P., Curtis Brown Literary Agency. I had a dream and you believed in me. Thank you, Clyde, for allowing my dream to come true.

Many thanks to Maureen Walters and her assistants, Joanna Durso and Cameron McClure at Curtis Brown, for helping me complete what I started; I'll never forget how you were there for me.

Ron Martin (Polo Club). Thanks for tolerating me, and thanks for your support.

Ivan Levine (Jay). Well, Jay, this is it. I am proud of your perseverance. I guess it came from a life of struggle, too.

Last but not least, Kelli Martin, my editor—Kelli, sometimes silence is golden. You believed in me and took me by the hand and helped me up. This was a tough one but, thanks to you, it's complete.

I must thank you all. You are the best parts of my life.

Thank you, God, I did it.